RUBY

Ruby Walsh was born in County Kildare in May 1979. Amongst numerous other racing triumphs, he has won the Aintree Grand National twice, on Papillon and Hedge-hunter, and the Cheltenham Gold Cup twice, on Kauto Star.

Malachy Clerkin is a sports journalist and author in Dublin. Formerly the Chief Sportswriter of the now-closed *Sunday Tribune*, he now writes predominantly for the *Irish Times*. He has covered just about every sporting event, from the Olympic Games and World Cups in football and rugby to the Cheltenham Festival. This is his second book.

RUBY

The Autobiography

RUBY WALSH

WITH MALACHY CLERKIN

An Orion paperback

First published in Great Britain in 2010
by Orion
This paperback edition published in 2012
by Orion Books Ltd,
Orion House, 5 Upper St Martin's Lane,
London WC2H 9EA

An Hachette UK company

1 3 5 7 9 10 8 6 4 2

A CIP catalogue record for this book is available
from the British Library.

ISBN 978-1-4091-2112-1

Typeset by Input Data Services Ltd, Bridgwater, Somerset

Printed and bound by CPI Group (UK) Ltd, Croydon, CR0 4YY

The Orion Publishing Group's policy is to use papers that
are natural, renewable and recyclable products and
made from wood grown in sustainable forests. The logging
and manufacturing processes are expected to conform to
the environmental regulations of the country of origin.

www.orionbooks.co.uk

CONTENTS

LIST OF ILLUSTRATIONS

Azertyuiop in the Arkle, 2003 (Pat Healy)

Kevin O'Ryan, Gillian and Ruby on Derby Day, 2003 (Pat Healy)

Ruby on Florida Pearl and James Nash on Royal Alphabet (Author's collection)

Ruby, his mother and father at Cheltenham in 2004 (Pat Healy)

Ruby and his father at the 2005 Irish Grand National (Racingfotos.com)

Hedgehunter winning the 2005 Grand National (Pat Healy)

Patrick Mullins greets Hedgehunter at Aintree, 2005 (Pat Healy)

Moscow Flyer in the 2006 Champion Chase (Caroline Norris)

Ruby after winning his third Kerry National on Bothar Na, 2006 (Pat Healy)

Ruby ten days before Cheltenham, 2006 (Caroline Norris)

Wedding day, 2006 (Karl Mcdonagh)

Kauto Star winning the King George VI Chase, 2006 (Bill Selwyn)

Kauto Star winning the Gold Cup, 2007 (Racingfotos.com)

Ruby and A.P. McCoy at the Arkle in 2007 (Caroline Norris)

Ruby and David Casey at Punchestown (Caroline Norris)

Master Minded wins Champion Chase in 2008 (Racingfotos.com)

Ruby, Paul Nicholls and Clive Smith in 2008 (Pat Healy))

Andreas gives Ruby 200th winner of the 2008–09 season (Racingfotos.com)

Winning the Irish Champion Hurdle on Brave Inca in 2008 (Pat Healy)

Posing for the Injured Jockeys' Fund Calendar, 2008 (Caroline Norris)

Kauto Star winning his fourth King George in 2009 (Racingfotos.com)

Neptune Collonges winning the Irish Hennessy in 2009 (Pat Healy)

Denman's second Hennessy win in 2009 (Racingfotos.com)

Gillian in the winners' enclosure at the Gold Cup in 2009 (Racingfotos.com)

Paul Nicholls, Clive Smith and Ruby at the Gold Cup in 2009 (Caroline Norris)

Twist Magic winning the 2009 Tingle Creek (Racingfotos.com)

Seven winners at Cheltenham, 2009

    Quevega (Racingfotos.com)

    Mikael D'Haguenet (Pat Healy)

    Cooldine (Racingfotos.com)

ACKNOWLEDGEMENTS

I thought writing a book would be quite a simple task but in fact it was a lot more difficult than I anticipated. Therefore I would like to thank all those people who helped me to recount stories, verify facts and recall tales I had forgotten. Putting all of my thoughts and ideas into print was no mean feat so I would really like to thank Malachy Clerkin who somehow managed to complete the task and Noeline Mcgrath for her assistance in transcribing hours of tape. A book of course needs a publisher and I would like to thank Susan Lamb, Alan Samson and Lucinda McNeile of Orion Publishing for all their help; and to Jonathan Harris for all his energy. Also Pat Healy and Caroline Norris for finding so many pictures which help greatly to tell my story.

In order for me to have lived the life I have, a huge amount of people have helped me along the way for which I am most grateful. A very special thanks to my Mam and Dad, Jennifer and Katie my sisters, and Ted my brother for everything they have done for me. My life revolves around horses, as you will read, and my thanks go to all the owners and trainers who have given me a chance, but in particular to Willie Mullins and Paul Nicholls for the opportunities they have given me to ride great horses and live the life I dreamed of.

And finally, but most importantly, Gillian, Isabelle and Elsa. Gillian has been my best friend since I was twenty, my wife since the summer of 2006 and is the mother of our two daughters. She has been by my side for all the great days I have had but more importantly for me at my bedside in several hospitals. She has helped me to recover from countless injuries, listened to me complain for years, put up with my mood swings when things have gone wrong and yet has always been happy to do it. I would like to thank her so much for all her help and friendship. My biggest hero.

Ruby Walsh
February 2011

CHAPTER 1

The original Ruby

I guess I should start with the name. It comes from my grandfather, who was also christened Rupert Edward Walsh. He was born two days after the feast of St Rupert, on 29 March 1917, and Rupert was shortened to Ruby over time. I was named after him, but the only person in my whole life who has ever called me Rupert was a teacher, Miss Hannah Foley (RIP), who used it every time she caught me talking in class. To everyone else, it has always been Ruby.

Ruby Walsh Senior was my father's father. He was the youngest of a family of nine kids who grew up in Kildorrery, a little village on a hill halfway along the road between Mitchelstown and Mallow in north County Cork. He was born in the family pub called The Corner House which is still there. It's real racing country around there – the next parish over to the west is Doneraile, the finishing point for the first ever steeplechase back in the 1750s.

Horses were always in the family. The family business was buying and selling all sorts of horses, from troopers to point-to-pointers. A few of my grand-uncles emigrated to America in the 1920s and 1930s and went on to make names for themselves in racing over there. Mickey Walsh – known as M.G. – trained horses for nearly fifty years but his heyday was in the 1950s and 1960s. By 1964, he had become only the third steeplechase trainer in the USA to earn over $1millon in prize money and was champion trainer on three separate occasions.

He made it into the American Horse Racing Hall of Fame in 1997, where he was joined in 2005 by his nephew Tommy, my father's first cousin. Tommy was a jockey, the son of Jim, another grand-uncle. He rode the winner of the American Grand National five years in a row and six years out of seven in the 1960s, and is still in the top ten in the all time list of steeplechase winners ridden over there.

Ruby didn't follow his brothers to America for a long time. On top of trading a few horses, he ran a pub in Fermoy with his elder brother Ted from 1946. They also held the local hackney licence, and one of the clients was a young Vincent O'Brien, who in time would become the greatest racehorse trainer ever and the first master of Ballydoyle. Ted was seven years older than Ruby and they became very close after their mother and father both died on the same weekend when Ruby was just seventeen. There is an old story in our family of how, when they were digging the grave for my great-grandfather in Fermoy, the side collapsed, causing the gravedigger to declare that this was very bad luck. My great-grandmother died the next day and they were buried side by side. Ted took Ruby under his wing after that and they were inseparable for the rest of their lives.

My grandmother, Helen Walsh (née Buggy) from Gowran in County Kilkenny, was the daughter of a blacksmith and her brother Martin shod the Grand National winner Nicholas Silver in 1961. With Ruby she had a son, giving birth in the pub in Fermoy in 1950. They named him Ted: my father.

They went to join my grand-uncles in the States for a while in the 1950s but came home quick enough, and moved to Chapelizod in Dublin to train horses in the Phoenix Park. They only stayed in the city for a short time, though, and by the summer of 1960, they had moved down to Kill in County Kildare where Mam and Dad live to this day. When I was growing up, we lived on the Naas side of the yard and my grandparents lived on the Dublin side.

I was very close to my grandfather right up until his death in 1991. I remember him as a really kind, quiet man. When I was a small boy, he used to make thick toast for me that he would butter before he toasted it and then again afterwards. It was simply gorgeous, the softest toast I ever ate.

He and my grand-uncle Ted trained and traded horses all their lives. They are so expensive to keep and maintain that all you could do to keep the yard turning over was sell them. He went to sales and fairs all over the place, turning horses into money. Buy for £1000, sell for £1500. Buy for £2000, train to win a race or two and maybe sell to England for £6000. It's a tough life but an enjoyable life too, and it was the only life he knew.

Dad grew up with horses, with all the ups and downs they bring. He tells the story of when he was a boy and himself and a friend, Eddie O'Connor, watched the film *Ben Hur*. They loved the bit in the big chariot race, where the horses jump clear over a broken carriage with the chariot intact and with Charlton Heston still on board. The two boys obviously thought this could be done in real life.

So they went out into the yard and got the pony, harnessed it up to a long pallet and climbed aboard. Out into the field, and they pointed this pony at a gate and drove him on at it, trying to get him to jump it with them trailing behind on the pallet. The pony managed it, more or less, but the pallet flipped over and the two boys went flying.

If that had been the end of it, the story would have been bad enough. But there was more. The pony took off like a shot, still strapped to the pallet, and every bump and hollow in the field made the pallet bounce up and hit the pony on its arse, which only made it go faster. He came tearing into the field at the back of the house where my grandfather had two horses – one that was no good and cost half-nothing, and another that he'd dug deep for at the Derby sale.

The pony sped through the field and jumped clean out over the post and railing and on to what was then the main Dublin to Cork road. The good horse from the Derby sale decided to follow him and jumped out as well, just in time for a car to come along and wipe him out. The people in the car were OK but sadly the horse had to be put down. Can you imagine? That would have been a tough house to be in that night.

Day-to-day life wouldn't have been nearly that dramatic. They had eleven acres originally, sold a horse for good money somewhere along the way and bought some land out the back that belonged to the Dunnes, a neighbouring farming family. There were another twenty-five acres in that deal and that's where they put the gallop. Five furlongs, all-weather. Dad bought another twenty acres from the Dohertys sometime after, and a strip to connect the whole lot. That was – and is – the family yard in Kill.

Mam didn't come from that sort of background at all. She was one of seven kids, three girls and four boys. She wouldn't have known the front end of a horse from the back before she met Dad. She was born just at the edge of Waterford City in Ferrybank and her father, John Whyte, was a sergeant in the Gardaí. They moved around quite a bit as he progressed through the ranks and eventually ended up in Naas, which is where my parents met. Dad has one sister, my aunt Joan, and she and Mam were in the same class in St Mary's Convent in Naas. These days Joan and her husband Liam live two houses down from Mam and Dad in Kill.

They married in 1976 and Jennifer came along in 1977, followed by me in 1979, Ted in 1980 and Katie in 1984. As kids we lived active lives, basically the same sort of life that country kids everywhere live. When we got up on Saturdays and holidays, we didn't sit in and watch the television. We went out into the yard to see was there anything to be done. We filled the water buckets and haynets and would go to the gallop on the tractor to watch the horses work once all that was finished. Horses were the sun, the moon and the stars. It was a great way to grow up.

My grandfather trained until the day he died, but the earliest memory I have of excitement in the yard was when Barney Burnett was a novice hurdler in 1984 and 1985. He won nine out of eleven races that season and was the leading novice hurdler, culminating in his win at Punchestown. I was five years old, rising six, but he's the first horse I remember well. He was a great hurdler, but he got injured in 1986 and was out for a year or so and never made as good a steeplechaser when he got older. Saying that, he did win a Leopardstown Chase and finished second to Desert Orchid in an Irish Grand National.

Dad rode a fair bit for his father and won plenty of races for him, too. A couple of years ago, we got him a list of all the winners he'd ridden as a Christmas present. He was surprised to go through it and see that the number he rode for his dad came to over 100. He would have always thought it was more like seventy or eighty and assumed he'd ridden way more winners for Peter

McCreery. A win on a horse of your father's always means that bit more. That's how I've always felt about it, anyway.

I only remember seeing Dad ride a race on television once. It was Cheltenham in 1986 and Dawn Run had just won the Gold Cup. I was sitting on the floor at home in Kill with Jennifer, Ted and Katie, bouncing away in her chair. Mam was there too with her mother Claire Whyte who was quite ill with cancer. She died on 7 May 1987 at the young age of fifty-seven. To think both my parents are beyond that now; it's hard to imagine losing a mother that young.

Mam was always around for us and, thankfully, still is. She made sure we never wanted for anything but were never spoiled, either. She's always had a great understanding of people and I always saw her as a very level-headed person. Mam has always had a great ability to stand back from a situation and think it through and if I'm ever in a quandary or a dilemma, she's brilliant for sounding-out. I'd like to think, as I got older, that was one of the things I got from her.

But back then, I was a six-year-old watching the racing on the television. And the very next race after the Gold Cup was the Foxhunters, which Dad won on Attitude Adjuster. Not long after the race was over, the phone rang. It was Dad, ringing to tell Mam that that was him done and dusted. He says himself that he'd been gone for a while but this gave him a nice way to finish it. About an hour later the phone rang again and Jennifer hopped up to answer it. Someone was on the other end, looking for Dad to ride in a 'chase that weekend. Mam took the phone and said, 'No, sorry, Ted won't be riding over jumps anymore.' He was thirty-six and his career as a jockey was at an end.

I think Mam was probably relieved in a way. Dad had never been too seriously injured, although she could tell you stories all day about his falls. There was one at Leopardstown that stands out, from a horse called Little Abbey. Dad broke seven or eight ribs and punctured his lung, and I think it was the one fall where Mam would have been frightened.

But it was before my time and I don't have any particular memory of him being badly hurt. He broke a wrist during the La Touche at Punchestown in 1985 all right but as far as we were concerned as kids, that was fun because we got to wrap and unwrap his bandages. I'd say he didn't think it was as much fun as we did. But to me, Dad was this rock of a man. When he fell, he got up and got on with it. There was nothing soft about him, except maybe his teeth.

He took me to buy a pony from Delaneys outside Fethard, when I was eight or nine. We'd had a pony called Pebbles that I got on my seventh birthday, but he turned out to be a stubborn yoke that wouldn't jump a twig. So Dad took me to get a new one and put me up on this gorgeous chestnut animal with a white face and a flaxen mane and tail. I cantered up the field on him and he was beautiful to ride. He had this big, lobbing canter and rode more like a horse than a pony. We went up and down the field and when I got back, Dad asked if I liked him.

'I love him, I love him,' I said, all excited. So he got up on him and went for a spin to see what he thought and when he came back he said to the fella who owned him that he was a lovely pony and that we'd take him. He cost £1000 though, pricey for a pony in the mid-1980s.

We got back into the yard in Kill and I couldn't wait to get him out of the box. My grandfather was there and he came over to see us as I rode this new pony in the front paddock.

'He's a grand pony,' he said. 'What did he cost?' Dad didn't even give it a half second's thought. 'A monkey,' he said. I looked at Dad and he looked back at me and I sort of knew straight away to say nothing.

'Hmmm,' said my grandfather, 'that's enough, I'd say. Enough for him.'

If Dad ever asks me the price of anything I've bought, I always halve it. And I know well that if I ever ask him what he paid for anything, he does the same.

We called the pony Flash and he was probably our favourite out of all the ponies we had. We all learned to ride on him. My grandfather would even take Katie on his lap as he'd trot up the fields to watch the horses work. As time went by, Ted got a grey pony who, of course, we called Dessie after Desert Orchid. He wasn't so straightforward.

In fact, he was anything but. He was a runaway job, with no manners and stubborn as bedamned. He'd go anywhere and jump anything, but he listened to nobody but himself. You could steer him but you couldn't stop him. The more you pulled out of him, the more he pulled out of you. He actually wasn't a bad pony to learn to ride on, because you had to have your wits about you the whole time. He wasn't that big but he was so free, he'd run away with the twelve apostles. He'd pull and pull and pull. You had to learn how to sit and how to hold because he'd be away on you in a heartbeat otherwise.

I had a terrible fall from him when I was eleven. Alan Fleming is a successful trainer in Surrey now – he trains the good hurdler Starluck that finished fifth in the 2010 Champion Hurdle, among others – but back then he was a young lad working for Dad in the yard. He was only a few years older than me and I got on great with him. The furthest field away up the back, which we called Doherty's top field, was where we put horses with injuries or ones that needed time off. Every evening myself and Alan would head up there with a bale of hay and a bag of nuts for them, the bonus being that we could have a laugh jumping everything on the way home.

Our land divides Kill International Equestrian Centre on one side and Greenhills Riding School on the other so on the way back, we'd jump over one hedge or the other and take a run around the cross-country course on our ponies, jumping everything we saw. It took about half an hour to get back to the yard, jumping all the way. It was great fun – I used to look forward to it every evening cycling home from school.

This one evening though, Mam and Dad had gone to Cork on business and so they were a bit short-handed in the yard. Tony Philips was the head man and when I called in to get Alan, Tony was in bad form and said that Alan would have to stay and help out in the yard and that I could go up and feed the horses myself. Fair enough, I didn't mind at all. Off I went on Dessie, with my bale of hay and my bag of nuts for the horses, which took a bit of managing. Bale of hay in front of me, bag of nuts underneath me. I hacked up to the top field, laid out the hay, poured out the nuts and stuffed the empty bag into the big oak tree up there, then got Dessie and headed for home.

We came flying down the field, running flat to the boards until we got to the first jump and for some reason best known to himself, Dessie refused to jump it. 'Right,' I thought to myself, 'I'll sort you out now.' So I trotted him back up the field to a tree and broke off a branch to give him a few smacks. I pointed him back at this big tractor tyre jump that went out into the next field and had a drop off down the back. Next thing I knew, I was in Naas Hospital.

Dessie had obviously turned a cartwheel, and I'd landed on my head. I have a memory of standing in the field and trying to catch him as he went trotting by me, but after that I have to rely on what other people have told me. Apparently I rode him into the yard with my head down and Greg Behan, who was working there, asked if I was all right. When I didn't answer, he came over to me and saw that I was white as a sheet. He dragged me down off the pony and into the house. I asked him what day of the week it was. 'Thursday, Ruby,' he said.

Our babysitter Mary Byrne was there, taking care of us when Mam and Dad were away in Cork, and she rang Liam Bradley, Joan's husband, and he was over in the van in a flash to take me to Naas Hospital. 'What day is it, Liam?' I said. 'Thursday, Ruby,' said Liam.

We got into the van, me in the front and Ted in the back. Ted's bigger than me and has always looked out for me even though he is a year younger. I'd have been fiery enough at times in school but Ted was always there, ready to stand over me if I ever looked like I was in trouble. He came to the rescue a few times if I got into fights. But this day, on the way to Naas Hospital, he was getting fair pissed-off at me.

'What day of the week is it, Ted?'

'It's Thursday, Rube. And if you ask again . . .'

There were no mobile phones at the time but someone got word to Christy Kinane in Cashel to look out for Mam and Dad driving through the town and to stop them on the road. Christy got them, and his daughter drove Mam back to Kildare and left Dad to head on to Cork. Mam came to the hospital to find me with a cracked rib and concussion. My first riding injury.

Concussion has an upside. Well, obviously a doctor would argue with that and if you can avoid it, you're probably better off living your life never having been knocked out. But if you're going to take a bad fall like that early on, you're as well not remembering it. I don't remember the fall, I don't remember the pain and I was never any way scared the next time I got up on Dessie. I never had any fear.

As I got older, I got more and more to do around the yard. Mucking out, sweeping up, feeding, watering, all the little bits and pieces that keep a yard ticking over. Dad had a good staff in the place and I learned how it all worked from them. Brendan Sheridan was always there, Joe Pearse and Greg Behan, to name a few. For as long as I can remember, no one worked on Christmas Day. There was Dad, myself and Ted, Brendan Brady from the village, another pal of Dad's called Bertie, and that would be it.

On a Sunday it would be half staff. In the yard they worked twelve and a half days out of fourteen – they had Saturday afternoon and a Sunday off every second weekend. To make up the numbers on a Saturday and Sunday at home, the other staff was myself and Ted. There was Katie as well, as she got older.

We knew how to do it and we just did it as our normal, everyday routine. That was the life. It was more or less the same one Dad had growing up, the same as his dad before him and his before him. I was only too happy to take my turn.

My schooldays are always with me. Literally, always with me. Talk about the scars of a childhood! I only need to look down at my left hand to see one from one of my first days at school in 1984. I can date it more or less exactly because Mam was expecting Katie and had gone to Dublin with Dad for a check-up.

I was five and a half so I can't vouch for every last detail of the story, but for some reason I do remember it being a wet morning. I was hanging out of the door of the classroom waiting for our teacher to arrive and had my hand inside, holding the edge of it, just where the latch goes into the doorframe. Next thing, two girls inside the door slammed it, with the top of my thumb caught.

I must have screamed the place down. My aunt Joan and my grandparents had to come and collect me to take me to Crumlin Children's Hospital in Dublin, with my thumb hanging off and me bawling my eyes out. You can still see the remnants of the scar if you look at my left hand, right along the joint of my thumb.

So, not the best of starts. It got better though. I always think it's rubbish when people say your school days are the best days of your life. They're most definitely the easiest but that's not the same thing at all. It was a handy life as far as I was concerned, although by the end I needed plenty of arm-twisting to finish it.

Academically, I was grand. Put it this way – in secondary school, our classes were named after islands and on the back of my entrance exam, I was put into Lambay. Achill and Aran were the bottom two classes, Lambay and Valentia were the middle two and I couldn't tell you what the top two were called. One was Skellig, I think. Anyway, the point is the top classes didn't concern me. Solid. Middle of the road. That was me.

Primary school was in Kill and secondary was in Rathcoole, seven miles away, across the border in County Dublin. I'll never forget the first day in Rathcoole, when about fifteen or sixteen of us from Kill landed into the school on the bus. I'm sure it's the same drill in every school – your first morning, all the first year pupils go into this big assembly hall and your name is called out and you're told what class you're in. All the other classes got called out and in each one there were three or four others from Kill. And who was the only gob daw left on his own? Heading into a class of thirty students knowing no one? Walsh, Ruby (Kill National School).

I nearly died. It was bad enough that I was coming from a small village school where our year and the year ahead would be taught at the same time in the same room. But to be landed in a class with nobody to hang on to for safety on the first day! I walked into Room 23 that morning with my head down and barely spoke a word for a week.

I didn't enjoy secondary school really. I had no real hardship or stress – the opposite, if anything. There was never any massive pressure on me from home anyway. When a report card came to the house, the first thing Dad would look at was the bit where it said general conduct. As long as that said I was well-mannered and was making some bit of an effort, he'd look the other way on the odd 'E' once in a while. As long as when they went to the parent-teacher meeting they were told they were raising a lovely lad, Dad was happy.

Mam was a different story. She'd worry about grades and be on to me to put in a bit more of an effort. But to me, effort was something worth saving for more important stuff than school-work. I learned quickly enough exactly how much I would have to do to get by, and that amount was all I ever did. I just didn't want to be there most of the time.

I hated studying. I was actually pretty good at maths and I loved English, but the other languages were beyond me. Irish was just double Dutch to me and French was even worse. I just couldn't get my head around either of them. In Irish and French exams, you'd be given a piece of text and asked questions about it at the end. My genius scheme for getting through these would be to pick out a word that appeared in the question, find that word in the text and copy out the paragraph containing it line by line, thinking to myself, 'Well the answer has to be in there some-where.' Kind of defeated the purpose of calling that part of the exam 'comprehension', I suppose.

No, school for me was about sport. It was about playing as much of it and getting on as many different teams as I could.

I played everything. If there was anything to get you out of school, I was on the bus. Gaelic football, hurling, soccer, athletics. You name it, I was on the bus. There was always the chance you might get a class off here and there, and if there was even a smell of a half day to go training, I was gone. Out the door and away.

We had a good football team in the school and we actually won a Dublin schools' title in our division when I was in the sixth year. We had great coaches in Michael Higgins and Pat McEvoy who made a deal with us – turn up for training after school on a Monday and you can have a half day on the Friday to go play a match; don't turn up for training and you can stay in class. You got out of it what you put in. I liked that a lot. Never missed a Monday session. Never missed a half day on a Friday either.

I enjoyed football in the school much more than I enjoyed it with the club in Kill. I don't know what was going on in the club but it never felt like the most organised place to be. I'd say, hand on heart, we had about four training sessions in all the time I played. The training was playing indoor soccer in the winter time. You'd get a phone call to say there was going to be a game on Sunday and you might turn up and there'd only be a half a dozen of you.

I got much more out of playing rugby. I started playing in Naas when I was seven and kept at it all the way up along. Ted Coughlan, my mother's brother-in-law, trained the under-tens every Saturday morning. He brought my cousin Karl and me along, and I was hooked from then. I loved it from the beginning, and as I got older I especially loved playing scrum half. You were always involved, no matter if you were on a good team or a bad team. You were always getting a touch of the ball. Or if you weren't, there was always someone to tackle. One way or another, you were always busy.

Actually, that was the main reason I liked playing rugby more than football. I played football matches with Kill where I'd be in the backs and we'd be hockeying some crowd and the ball might squirt my way three times in a half. You'd be freezing or bored (or both) and you'd have some lad on the sideline telling you to stay on your toes, and meanwhile the other team's goalkeeper can't keep the ball kicked out.

Or worse, we'd be getting hammered by some crowd with big midfielders who never let the ball out past them. For years we played against Sallins, and they had this huge fella in midfield who everybody just called Stretch. He seemed three feet taller than everybody else all the way up along the age groups. Every time I turned out on the pitch against Sallins, Stretch was playing midfield. No matter where our goalkeeper kicked the ball, we couldn't get it out beyond him. And if you went to jump with him, you'd only bounce off him.

Rugby is a different game that way. There's a place on the pitch for all shapes and sizes in rugby and everybody's in it together in the one spot on the pitch, fighting away to get the ball and do something with it. I loved all that. I was small and light but I was fiery enough at the same time. I'd tackle anything. That was probably my downfall in a way. I spent too much time trying to crease fellas and not enough working out how to pass off my left hand.

We played North Kildare one day when we were under fourteen. They had this big lump of a lad playing in the second row and he was knocking fellas all over the place when he had the ball, just running through them. I knew that sooner or later he'd have to come my way and when he did, I was damn sure I wasn't getting out of his way. It didn't matter that he had about four stone and two feet on me, I was going to stand in front of him. That's just the way I was; no way was I shirking the tackle. I'd say I made about as much impression on him in the tackle as one of those birds that sit up on an elephant's back, but nobody could say afterwards that I ducked out of the tackle.

I remember going back to Naas that day and wondering who yer man was, the big number four. Turned out that was Bob Casey's last game for North Kildare before he went to play for Blackrock College and then Leinster, London Irish and Ireland. The four stone he had on me then is closer to nine now. I'd probably think twice about making that tackle these days.

I did have my own trial for Leinster, though. Sounds good, doesn't it, like I might be the great lost Leinster scrum half of the age? The truth isn't nearly as interesting. When I was fifteen, the Leinster scouts organised a trials day in Naas and each club for miles around was told to send along around a half a dozen players. So there were lads there from the Curragh, North Kildare and Portlaoise, even as far away as Gorey and Carlow, and we all came along and played two matches apiece in front of the Leinster scouts.

It was bedlam. My uncle Bobby was a coach with Naas and I remember him saying to me that this was a day for thinking of yourself and not worrying about your out-half. I think the same notion was in everybody's head, going out on to the pitch. Everyone trying to be a hero, nobody playing with their head up. Needless to say, I didn't get the call-up afterwards.

Ah, I knew I wasn't good enough anyway. I was a decent organiser who could call a move and get it happening. But I was an average passer at best – OK off my right hand, desperate off my left. I didn't have any great vision for the game and I wasn't going to create any magic for you. Leinster seem to have survived without me anyway.

The idea of sport as a career though would have taken root around this time. Obviously, it would be hard to claim I ever had a notion of being anything other than a jockey but I was hooked on just about every sport. The highlight of the week for me was Tuesday night, BBC 1, *A Question of Sport*. I never missed it. I didn't care what else was happening in the world, I was going to be in front of the television for *A Question of Sport*. When I went on it as a guest years later, I was sitting there thinking to myself, 'Jesus, you never thought you'd make it here.'

And I didn't, not one bit of me. Not back then. Back then, I was more concerned with trying to find a way to convince Mam to let me quit school after the junior cert. I'd done reasonably well in those exams – six honours and three passes – and I was humming and hawing about whether or not I'd go back for the Leaving. Well, I was trying to make it look like I was humming and hawing so that Mam would see me looking like I was humming and hawing. But in my head, I was gone. I'd done a summer at Ballydoyle and worked for Noel Meade by this point. Noel was a big dual-purpose trainer at the time but within a few years, he'd be champion National Hunt trainer in Ireland on multiple occasions. Given that choice, school was only an inconvenience.

Here's how little interest I had in it. The day the junior cert results came out, I didn't even go up to the school to collect them. Instead, Mam, Dad and myself were on our way to Galway because he had a runner called Dunemer in a two-year-old race. We stopped outside Enfield so that Mam could ring the school to get the results. This was mid-September so I should have been in school but no, I was away to Galway with Mam and Dad to watch the filly.

In the end though, Mam convinced me that school was the way forward. There was the option of doing transition year but I never even gave it a thought. But Mam was pretty firm with me and I went back on her terms. 'Look, a couple of years at school is no burden to carry,' she said to me. She was dead right, too. I would have regretted it massively if I hadn't gone back and done my leaving cert and it's the one bit of advice I always give any young lad who asks me. Finish school, you'll be long enough out of it.

Not that I went back and suddenly became a whizz kid or anything. I kept tipping along at my own pace, just doing enough to stay out of trouble like I always had. The only problem was that trouble came looking for me early in my final year. By now I was seventeen, I'd ridden a few winners and I was at the beginning of a season that would end with me as champion amateur. I'd got a taste of the life I wanted to live and there wasn't one other path you could have offered me that I'd have considered taking. These are not the kind of words that fill a career guidance teacher with joy. Especially not in the first couple of weeks of sixth year, when you're after doing poorly in the summer exams.

We got stuck with this career guidance teacher in a 'free' class one day. This lady didn't know any of us. And she started to go around the class and ask everyone what they wanted to do with themselves. I had positioned myself up in the far left corner of the room, hoping the bell would come along for the end of class and save me the interrogation. It was a close-run thing.

'How about you? What's your name?'

'Ruby Walsh, miss.'

'And what plans have you got?'

'I'm going to be a jockey, miss.' (She looked at me as if to say, 'You eejit. Don't be so stupid.')

'You'd want to have a serious think about that, now,' she said, just as the bell went to get me out of there.

The thing was, most of the teachers were happy enough to let me away to do my own thing. They would have known I'd ridden a few winners already, and they would have had a fair notion of what I was doing with my summers and my weekends. I wasn't carrying on some secret life. Still, teachers have to be teachers and I suppose they wouldn't be doing their job if they didn't make some attempt to try and steer you along a conventional path.

There was an almighty row early on in my final year when our year head, Gerry Kiernan, kept me back after class one day and told me he wanted to see my parents. 'This racing lark will have to stop,' he said. 'This is the most important year of your life.' He wasn't talking about my attempt to be champion amateur.

I went home thinking Dad would go mental. Like I said, he wasn't too concerned what the grades were like as long as I behaved in class. It wouldn't matter that I hadn't done anything wrong; he'd think that if he was being called into the school it could only be because I was being a pup. But actually, once he heard me out, it was grand. He could see I was in bad form about the whole thing and he was soon on my side. 'I'm not going back if I can't ride,' I said. 'It won't come to that,' said Mam.

There was a careers evening that night at the school but Mam and Dad had to wait afterwards to speak to Gerry Kiernan. Mam told me later that Dad played a blinder. 'It's like this,' he said. 'Ruby's going to finish his leaving cert but he's going to ride as well. Now, he can do it here or he can go and do it somewhere else. That's up to ye.'

Gerry launched into a speech that he'd given me, about how he'd played minor football for Louth when he was a young fella and had given that up to get a good leaving cert. But Dad wasn't for moving. 'That's fair enough,' he said, 'but Ruby has been no trouble to ye, he's never given you a day's grief since he's been here and this is what he's doing with his life. He's going to do it with your co-operation and that's what's going to happen. There will be half days, we'll all work together, but that's what's going to happen.'

So that's how it was. I got a note to say I could head off at lunchtime every Thursday and I made a deal with Mam that I would spend a half of every Sunday studying. I'd catch up on all my homework on my way to and from racing. That was the plan anyway, and I mostly kept up my end of it. Either Mam or Dad would collect me from the school Thursday lunchtime and we'd be off down the country to wherever racing was on.

One day Dad collected me and we headed off down to Thurles so I could ride a horse of Mouse Morris's in the bumper – the National Hunt flat race that usually closes out each day's racing. Dad had nothing running in any of the races that day but that didn't matter to him at all. Mouse's horse was pretty average and didn't even finish the race but that didn't matter to Dad either. All that mattered was that I was getting experience, learning the game.

So we were in the jeep on the way back up the road and I had my head in a geography book, reading away so that he could tell Mam I did plenty of revision on the way home and what did he do? Only ram straight into the back of a bus in traffic! Looking out of the window, away with the fairies he was. He folded the jeep and left the pair of us stuck to the windshield. All to take me to Thurles to ride in the bumper.

Coming up to the end of school, Mam thought she'd take one final stab at getting me to go to college. I arrived home with forms but I had no intention of filling them in. As far as I was concerned, I was going to work for Willie Mullins as soon as the last bell rang. I had actually been watching the boys in my class filling out their forms and quietly laughing to myself. Away with ye, lads ...

Mam always had a way of getting me to do things, though. She said she'd like me to fill them out, to apply for a few courses just in case. Just fill them out and send them off and sure, you never know what might happen. Keep your options open.

So I did. I filled them out. What I didn't tell her is that those forms that went to the CAO – the Irish college admissions system – told a fairytale at which a five-year-old would make a dubious face. The courses I applied for were all very fine indeed, and that was the whole point. There wasn't a hope of me getting anywhere near the points needed for them. I stuck down veterinary science, which was about 550 points. Not if they gave me the exam papers a week beforehand was I getting anywhere near 550 points. Maybe I might manage to scrape 300. Equine science in Limerick was 410 so I didn't put that down, just on the off chance that the gods took against me and let me do better than I was expecting.

But the great thing about the forms was that you didn't put down the name of the course, you just put down the course code. So all Mam saw was a load of letters and numbers. I showed the forms to her with four courses applied for and she was happy with that.

And you know what? As the years have gone by, there actually have been times when I've regretted not doing a year in college. Not so much for the education but for the social side. When I was out for six months with my broken leg, my girlfriend at the time Gillian Doran – who is now my wife – was in University College Dublin (UCD) and I used to spend a fair bit of time there with her. I loved all that, all the hanging around, meeting interesting people and chatting away. A year of that wouldn't have been so bad.

But that wasn't where I was headed. When the CAO offers came out that August, the postman didn't have to break his back on the way to the Walsh household. I wasn't even there when he arrived. By then, I was gone.

CHAPTER 2

Learning experience

I was always going to head away somewhere to learn more about the game. It was just what you did. There was plenty for me to be doing around home if I stayed, but Dad was keen on me going to other yards to see the different ways things are done. So in the summer of 1994, it was up to Noel Meade's yard in Castletown, County Meath with me. I'd just turned fifteen that May and for the first ten days or so, I stayed with Noel's mother. For the rest of the summer I lived with the McKeevers near Nobber, knocking about with Paul Hourigan, whose father Michael was – and still is, of course – a successful trainer in Limerick, having trained the likes of Dorans Pride and Beef Or Salmon among others.

It was my first long period away from home and I loved every bit of it. The World Cup was on in America that June and we used to work all day and then head to the pub to watch the matches at night. I had never been in a pub to watch a football match in my life. I wasn't even drinking, it was just the adventure of it, I suppose. The weather was scorching that whole summer and I couldn't have had a better time.

I think I was homesick for a bit but if anything I got to love the little aspects of being away from home that made me become more independent. It made me grow up a little, take responsibility for myself.

The work was hard enough but I never felt that way about it. I still wouldn't. If you want to ride horses, you muck them out. Simple as that. Every morning, I was there at seven o'clock, ready to go. Me and three other lads, mucking out from seven until eight, riding four lots until lunchtime and then working on from two until five. In the evenings, we'd ride out a few of Stephen McKeever's horses and that would be our diesel money earned for the lift to work in the mornings.

That summer was mostly pure fun but by the following one it was time to take things a bit more seriously. I was sixteen, I'd taken out my amateur licence and this time I went to Ballydoyle for the summer. Ballydoyle then wasn't like Ballydoyle now. The trainer Aidan O'Brien had just arrived and Coolmore hadn't a massive influence on the place yet. Actually, I doubt if any more than one or two horses in the place belonged to Coolmore at the time.

You'd have to say that, back then, Ballydoyle was a bit run down. It hadn't really been used to its full potential in a few years and Aidan hadn't been there long enough to put his stamp on it. He didn't have the top-class flat horse in the yard that he does these days and mixed through the place were a lot of summer jumpers. The best two-year-old we had in the place was No Animosity – Christy Roche rode him to win a sales race in the Curragh that September. I used to look after a horse called Loshian who was third in the Galway Plate that summer, when Aidan had the first three past the post. But this was before triple-Champion Hurdle-winner Istabraq, even, and well before there were Classic winners at every turn.

This is all hindsight, of course. At the time, I didn't care a bit. I was still green as the grass. The first day I went to Ballydoyle, I got a lift from Naas with Eugene O'Donnell who used to drive Aidan's horsebox up and down the country along with travelling head man Damian Byrne. They had runners in Naas that day so I met him at the racecourse, threw the bike in the back and hopped up in the front with him. As far as I was concerned, this was the life now. Hitting the open road, chatting away with a grown-up, being treated like a grown-up too. Or so I thought.

As we went through Cashel, he pulled in real quick at a garage and said, 'Here, go in there and tell that man behind the counter that you're with Eugene O'Donnell and you need a glass hammer straight away.' Sure of course, I was out of that lorry like it was on fire and away in, the wide-eyed gombeen looking for a glass hammer. If I'd taken half a second to think about it, I might have worked it out. But I was sixteen and innocent. The boys behind the counter just looked at me like I was a fool. I turned and looked out the window and Eugene was falling out of the cab laughing. 'Great,' I was thinking. 'This is going to be a long summer.'

It was mighty though. Seven days a week from seven in the morning to six at night. I was living in digs with Teddy Gould and his family just outside Rosegreen village and it was a matter of getting up at six-thirty, hopping on the bike and cycling the four miles to Ballydoyle with another young lad called Jimmy Barcoe who worked there as well. I was in the back yard – the blue yard, as it was called – with eighteen boxes. You started at box one in the main yard, mucking out, and went around the yard until you were finished. There were seven of us at it – three lads mucking out, three lads with wheelbarrows and one lad sweeping.

We'd ride out at half-nine when Aidan and some of the other lads arrived from his other yards in Owning village, half an hour away. That would last until lunchtime at half-one and we'd then spend the afternoon back with the horses. Clean them, brush them, leave them spotless. Do up their beds, sort out their hay, whatever. Everything done to a high standard, never giving anyone a reason to complain about you. Head home at seven, get your dinner, play a bit of football and early to bed, ready to go again the next morning.

Shay Slevin was the head man at Ballydoyle, and he was tough. You toed the line with Shay – if you pissed him off he'd have you mucking out for the morning, and you wouldn't come near to getting on a horse.

That was what every day was about. Getting to ride out, getting on a horse. Aidan would be over on the hill until half-nine so the craic and the banter would be flying around the yard as we were mucking out, but it would all stop when he'd arrive over. In my head, I'd be waiting for him to come back, having the laugh but working away good and hard so that nobody would have a reason to go to him and say, 'Here, that Walsh lad was acting the goat. Let him stay here this morning.' No way was that happening. Dad always said that if there was nothing to do, pick up a sweeping brush. Always look busy, even if you aren't.

In the evenings, we played a fair bit of football. I ended up lining out for the Rosegreen under-sixteens that summer at right halfback. A fella called Seamie Burke from Cashel had headed away for the summer, so instead of going through the whole rigmarole of transferring over from Kill for two months, I was Seamie Burke until September. We actually won a South Tipperary championship and I played midfield in the final. Can't remember who we beat – I'd say it's probably too late for them to lodge an objection against Rosegreen's ringer now, anyway.

I bucked out of bed every morning that summer, mad for action. Christy Roche would be riding work and that would be all I'd be thinking of on the bike on the way there. Christy had ridden Classic winners and been champion jockey multiple times so he was a legend to me – I'd be dying to get riding a piece of work in the same lot as him, and so would all the other lads. Everybody got to ride a canter but not everyone got to ride work. That was what you were after, day after day. Hoping Aidan would let you give a horse a squeeze and get him off the bridle for a bit. That's what riding work meant. Only the good jockeys got to do that.

There were good lads at Ballydoyle. Adrian Regan lived in the same digs as me and went on to have a successful pin-hooking operation (buying horses specifically for resale) in the USA. Tom O'Leary, who trains the dual Thyestes winner Preists Leap, was there too.

I was a sponge for information. Always have been. When I was only eight or nine I'd be in the back seat of the car with Dad and Brendan Sheridan on the way to the races and there'd always be somebody else there talking racing with them. It could be Tommy Carmody or Mickey Flynn or even Charlie Swan sometimes – any of the leading riders of the time were liable to be in the car. I'd be the little lad in the back, not opening my mouth but taking in every word. So-and-so made a balls of this race; this fella went too soon or jumped out too fast. My ears would be cocked, trying to catch every word like it was gospel.

It was the same story sitting at home on Saturdays watching the racing on television. Dad would be there commenting on whoever was riding and I'd be trying to work out what he meant. I lived for those races and the further I got into my teens, the more able I was to see for myself what was going on. I loved watching a race and trying to separate out the horses that were hanging back for a reason and the ones that were just at the back because they weren't any good. I'd be there wondering why such-and-such was so far back and gradually realising that a horse can only run so far, so fast. It was all about getting the judgement of pace right but I didn't know that at the time.

At Ballydoyle, I'd be listening to every word out of Aidan's mouth. If Christy mentioned that a horse needed to be ridden a certain way, that's the way it would be ridden. If Shay needed a job done before I could ride out, that job was done. Nothing would have to be said twice. All I wanted to do was learn and get on and keep my nose clean so I'd get a ride at the track.

I'd had my first one that May, on a horse of Dad's called Wild Irish. It was three days after my sixteenth birthday and Dad let me ride him in a bumper at Leopardstown. Timmy Murphy and Tony Martin had ridden him before me, but his only win had been in a point-to-point at Naas earlier that year, so there wasn't a whole pile of pressure on me.

Not that I was thinking that way. As far as I was concerned, I just had to do the right thing and I'd be able to get this horse across the line in front. What I didn't know was that you had to have the best horse in the race if you wanted to win. Imagine that! I thought it was all about me and what I did. We came fifth, about fifteen lengths behind a horse of Aidan's called Galetollah.

Still, I thought that if I could only get him in and get him settled some day, I'd win a race on him. A fortnight later, Dad took him to Tipperary and put me up on him again. We walked the track beforehand and I was on to Dad going, 'What'll I do if we turn in here and I'm going well?' He told me to kick on. Drift over to the running rail. Get the stick in your right hand. Set sail for home.

So we got into the race and Wild Irish was going well and travelling OK. I had two horses behind me – Dramatic Venture, ridden by Jackie Mullins, and Step On Eyre, ridden by Willie Mullins. In time, Willie would become a huge part of my life but that evening I didn't know him from Adam. All I knew was that my lad was travelling well enough for me to start thinking we had a chance here. We crept away and travelled into the straight just behind the leaders, so I decided switch out and go for home about a furlong and a half out.

I pushed the button and Wild Irish responded and we were away. I kicked on. Got the stick in my right hand. Set sail for home. Everything Dad had told me to do. Everything except drift in towards the running rail. I left a gap and Willie, like any experienced jockey would, came on my inside. Beat me by a neck.

Disaster. I was sick. I nearly cried. Dad was delighted but I was disappointed. I couldn't believe I'd made such a stupid mistake. I should have gone for the rail as soon as I hit the front and made Willie come out and around me, but instead, excitement got the better of me and I just headed for the line. It's the sort of mistake you'd forgive in any sixteen-year-old jockey on the planet but that didn't stop me being disgusted with myself. It was two months before I managed to get my first winner and that mistake bugged me every day in between.

I know now, though, that this was what that summer was for. Making mistakes, learning from them, trying not to repeat them. I learned a massive amount at Ballydoyle in those couple of months, and not all of them were to do with judgement of pace and riding a finish either. When I learned about wasting, for example, I learned the hard way.

Aidan gave me a ride in the GPT, the big amateur handicap at the Galway festival that July. The horse was called Clear Look and Aidan needed someone to do light on him. Now this horse had run twenty-six times before it won a race, so we weren't talking about Arkle here, but then that first win had come in Killarney a week and a half beforehand so he was entitled to take his chance. It didn't matter one way or the other – if Aidan O'Brien wanted me to do light, I'd do light.

Just one problem. I wasn't sure how to lose the weight. I knew nothing about wasting. Hadn't a bull's notion. Aidan told me a week before the race that I could ride Clear Luck and he would have around nine stone thirteen pounds. So minus my seven pound claim, I would be doing nine stone six pounds. I completely panicked. I hadn't a clue what to do. I'd never been to a nutritionist at that point – myself and Mam went to one in the Blackrock Clinic eventually, but that was a year away yet.

As it was, I couldn't even claim that I was giving my diet any real attention at all. I stayed away from all the usual rubbish and I never went out drinking so my weight stayed fairly constant, but this was different. This was me needing to lose nearly half a stone in a week. There was nothing else for it – I just starved myself for the first few days. Then I started running in a sweat suit, which is basically a tracksuit made out of thick black plastic. I managed to do nine stone six in the end but I doubt if I was at my strongest. Clear Look finished twelfth of fourteen, a long way back.

That July was a good one though, because I rode my first ever winner. Dad had bought Siren Song at Goffs for small money and a few months later he took him to Gowran for a bumper. He was a tricky customer, you could see that in him straight away. He had a 'wall eye', which means that whereas most horses' eyes are fully brown, he had one not unlike a human eye – dark in the

middle but with a white outer. It's not a defect, more a pig-
mentation problem, but you'd always be wary of a horse with a
wall eye. Invariably, there'd be something quirky about them.

Siren Song was definitely a bit like that but he could gallop
when the mood took him. Being away for the summer, I didn't
know him well from the yard but Brendan Sheridan had ridden
him in most of his work and both he and Dad thought he'd go
well. They weren't wrong. He burned down the middle of the
track to come from about seventeenth and absolutely hacked up.
He might not have beaten much but he beat them well.

Not that I had a lot to do with it. I gave him a grand tactical
ride as far as it went and got him there at the right time, but I saw
a video later and in all honesty, I was brutal on him. I've watched
it again since and I'd nearly be embarrassed. I was like an oul' one
up there, physically very weak, all over the place. You think you're
being neat and getting the rhythm right on the horse but really
you're just so raw and unpolished. I can safely say that Siren Song
won that race despite me, rather than because of me.

In fairness, I did better on him a fortnight later in Galway. It
was six days after I'd had to waste for Clear Look and I was a
happier camper altogether. It was the last race on the last day of
the festival and we beat a good mare of Jessica Harrington's called
Dance Beat who went on to win some decent prizes over the
following year and a half. Paddy Graffin rode Dance Beat but my
lad did it well and we won by a few lengths. That was my first
ever winner at Galway, something I've managed to repeat every
year since.

You could say the winners made the work worthwhile but
that was only true up to a point, for me anyway. The way I was
brought up, the work was an everyday thing. It was a way of
life more so than a life choice. They were long hours but

I don't think they did me any harm. I don't think they'd do any young lad any harm.

I know there are such things as child slavery laws but that makes it sound like you're sending eight-year-olds up chimneys. It isn't like that. I see fifteen-year-olds coming into yards now and it's all about filling in the book to make sure no law is being broken. They're only allowed to work from nine to twelve and from two to four and can only do so many hours in a week. To me, that's a load of rubbish. They're laws that give people an excuse to be lazy, that teach them how to get away with doing the bare minimum. It doesn't do them any good in the long run.

It's crazy. I learned to work young, so I knew what work was. You were fit and you were healthy and you went about your day when it was over. If you were sore, you got over it. If you were tired, you coped. When I was at Noel's yard and then at Bally-doyle, you were taught to work, not taught to be lazy. You weren't allowed to be lazy.

I'd have seen all that with Dad, anyway, growing up. The lads who worked hard around the yard were the ones that got the chances. The lads who had their hands in their pockets were left wondering why the other fellas were away at the track in the afternoons, riding races while they were stuck at home changing the hay. The way I looked at it, maybe nobody was passing any remarks on the work I was doing but you could be full sure that somebody would have noticed if it wasn't done.

Racing is a great way of life but it's a tough way of life too and nobody can coast through it. Maybe in other sports you can give a freakishly talented kid an easy ride because he's so obviously going to be a star, but you just can't do it in racing. Nobody gets to the top without the work, and the work is vital for setting the goals and encouraging the drive in a young lad. You'll muck out every box in the yard if it means getting to ride in a bumper that evening.

I got to ride plenty that summer. Dad had a horse called Butler Brennan who he let me ride just about every week. Between the end of May and the end of August, I rode him nine times at nine different tracks. Fairyhouse in May, Leopardstown and Gowran in June, Tipperary, Wexford and Naas in July, Tramore, Dundalk and Kilbeggan in August. Never finished better than third. He was only a cheap horse and he never won a race but winning wasn't the important thing just then.

What was important was getting to go racing. I'd do anything and go anywhere for a chance. I remember the weekend Dad ran him in Tramore, I was down in Kerry with Ann and Michael Hourigan because Paul was riding at the famous flapping meeting down in Dingle in Kerry. Dad rang on the Saturday to say he'd declared Butler Brennan in the bumper in Tramore on the Sunday, and that there were only four horses declared so he was definitely running. A friend of Dad's, Mikey Joe Cregan, gave me a lift from Dingle to Tralee bus station where I got a bus to Cork and then another bus to Waterford, where Mam and Dad picked me up and took me racing. That's five hours' travelling on a Sunday morning just to ride a horse. Butler Brennan finished third.

It was all about experience. Trying to ride races different ways – jumping off in front and setting the gallop, sitting out the back and seeing how much he could improve for giving him a squeeze. Watching how other jockeys positioned their horses, keeping an eye for somebody who was about to head for home, learning which jockeys to track and which to leave off. In those days, I was riding against Frances Crowley and Willie Mullins who were going head-to-head for the amateur's title. The likes of Philip Fenton and Enda Bolger – good amateurs who became successful trainers – and Timmy Murphy who became one of the leading jockeys around, rode in a lot of those races too.

I learned things about race-riding that summer that I still use. Dad told me very early on that I needed to be counting off the seconds in my head as I went from furlong to furlong. In fairness, I'd been doing that since the previous summer when I was riding out at Noel's along with Paul Carberry and Joanna Morgan, but it really came into its own on the racecourse.

Allowing for the time of year and the state of the ground, you should always be running at around fourteen seconds a furlong in the summer, out to maybe sixteen or seventeen on heavy ground in the winter. That was my rule of thumb then and it's the same now. If you're flat to the boards and there's nothing to jump, thirteen seconds a furlong is what you should be doing, but if you're doing thirteen seconds a furlong while jumping a fence, you're going too fast. Fifteen seconds a furlong is about right over three miles. Ideally, in a jump race, you want to be counting fourteen just after you pass the furlong marker. Obviously, you wouldn't have a stopwatch so it's your best guess.

Butler Brennan's career was far from special – we managed a couple of thirds together that summer and Dad sent him point-to-pointing the following spring. But I'll never forget the fun I had with him and the experience I got on his back. By the time I came home from Ballydoyle and went back to school that September, I was getting more and more used to riding in races and other people were starting to give me rides.

One of those people was Willie Mullins. Crimson City isn't a name that will mean a whole pile to many people but I'll always remember her. She was a filly I only rode once and it's probably safe to say that neither of us enjoyed the race at Listowel very much. It was in September 1995 and we finished ninth, a good seventy lengths behind Montelado (who, in fairness, had won twice at Cheltenham and was running a different race to us altogether). But she sticks in my head all these years later because she was the first horse I ever rode for the man who became my boss the following summer and has been ever since.

Willie was someone I didn't know until I started race-riding. I have a vague memory of him being in our house in Kill one morning when I was ten or eleven, probably around the time that Grabel won the International Hurdle in Kentucky. But until that day he beat me on Step On Eyre in Tipperary, he was just a name. I knew he was pally with Dad all right, but then that would hardly have made him unique in racing circles. In my circle he was the one who seemed to win all the bumpers, or at least all the bumpers that Frances Crowley didn't win.

That November, I was at home in Kill on a Sunday morning, messing about in the fields with one of the ponies, when I saw Mam's car coming down in the lane. So I cantered over to see what the story was and Jennifer got out of the car, looking urgent. Willie Mullins had rung from Leopardstown. He couldn't do the weight for the bumper and wanted me to ride his filly.

So I was out of there in a flash. Into the car and away up to Leopardstown to ride this filly of Willie's called Young Fenora. We were tight for time so I had no chance to worry about it. She was pretty free early on but soon settled and was an easy enough ride in the end. I dropped her out, crept away round and, lo and behold, she won. Beat Lady Daisy by a couple of lengths. I later found out that Willie just fancied having a decent lunch that day. Good for him.

And good for me too, because I kept the ride on Young Fenora. Obviously, I realise now that keeping the ride probably had less to do with my silky jockey skills and more to do with the fact that I had my seven pound claim intact. All jockeys starting off in the game have a weight allowance of seven pounds until you ride 15 winners. After that it becomes five until you ride another 10 and then three until you reach a total of 40 winners. Young Fenora had to carry a seven pound penalty in her next race for winning so if Willie took me off, that would have meant a one-stone penalty. But I wasn't sure about that side of it then.

Young Fenora wasn't a bad mare at all but she only ran twice more – in Navan that December and Leopardstown the following January. I rode her both times but our best finish was fourth and there our relationship ended. But from it came one that has lasted.

I had a couple of false starts with Willie though. Or probably what I considered to be false starts. The worst of them was when I rode a filly called Palette for him at the beginning of February. It was a Thursday afternoon and after Mam collected me from school and drove me to the track, we met Dad at the gate.

'Look,' he said, 'that ground is very bad. Go as wide as you can go, stay out under the wings of the fences and don't let anybody outside you.' When I weighed out, Willie said the same. Stay good and wide, keep out of the heaviest ground, don't let anybody down your outside.

I'd looked through the card and done up the form in my head, for all the use it was. Palette had been fourth in a race in Leopardstown about a fortnight beforehand and the field for that race didn't look a whole lot different in quality to the field for this one, so I figured we'd be about fourth again. Honestly, I didn't know much about form or how it worked. I didn't really understand the improvement a horse can make from one race to the next or how it can come on for a run, or any of that stuff.

But Palette was a decent enough filly as it turned out, and as we turned into the straight I drifted out wide and found, a little bit to my surprise, that we were in front and were travelling well. At that time, the second-last fence was on the bend in Punchestown and once you were past that you were into the straight. I thought that we were in with a chance and all I had to do was make a beeline for the inside of the last fence and from there we'd be on our way.

Coming off the bend I could hear someone coming behind me but when I took a look to my left, I couldn't see who it was. But I definitely knew somebody was there. Later, I found out that it was David Marnane on Darakshan, but at the time I was oblivious. Now what I should have done was take a line tight against the last fence and made whoever was behind me come up on my inner. But I must have left a small bit of a gap there because soon I saw a sheepskin noseband appearing at my boot.

Well, I had my instructions not to let anyone down my outside. So I pulled out and kept tighter to the fence and quickened up, trying to get David to come the other side of me. We beat David's horse by a length and I started trotting Palette back, delighted with myself. We came to the gate and I saw Dad standing just inside it. No smile for me.

'You're in trouble,' he said.

'What?' I said. 'What for?'

'You tightened the other horse at the last fence.'

'There wasn't room for him.'

'There might have been. Just say you didn't see him.'

'Grand.'

What had happened was that David, who was a very experienced rider, knew well that the wider you went the better the ground. He had come on my outside and I'd nearly run him into the last fence. He'd had to snatch up and come back around me. And even then I'd only beaten him a length. If I'd been watching it on television, I'd have said David should definitely be given the race and that the lad on the horse in front hadn't a clue what he was doing. But I wasn't, I was at the track. And more to the point, I was in the stewards' room.

It was my first time being there. Talk about daunting. You go in, and there are four people sitting behind a desk – three stewards and a stipendiary steward. The stipendiary steward is the professional, so he's the one who asks all the questions.

Anyone who knew their racing knew I was going to lose the race. Dad was standing outside the door and Willie was in the room with me. David came in and gave his evidence and told them that he been forced to nearly come to a complete stop, otherwise he'd have gone straight into the fence. Then Willie gave his evidence and I gave mine. As far as I was concerned, I was only following trainer's instructions. I'd say I was the one person in the place who couldn't see what was wrong.

We went back outside and left them to deliberate. We were there for ages before we were called back in, so they must have been having some debate. By now, I had a feeling I was going to lose the race but I was completely thrown by the verdict when we got back into the room.

They ruled that it was intentional interference. Now, losing the race I would have understood. Careless riding would have been fair enough. The placings would have been reversed and Palette would have been put second and I'd have learned my lesson. But intentional interference meant disqualification. It meant that Palette was placed last, taking the place money from the owners (not that it was very much, but it was a couple of hundred quid and they were decent lads who I rode for plenty of times again). But worst of all, it meant that I got a twenty-one-day ban.

Twenty-one days! I was sixteen years old. I'd had about fifty rides at most by that time. I'd never been in front of the stewards even once before. And they gave me twenty-one days. In those days twenty-one days meant a flat three weeks, not twenty-one racing days like it does now, but even so. I thought it was the end of the world.

I went back to the weighing room and sat down with my head in my hands. I really thought I'd never ride for Willie Mullins again. Here I was, four winners to my name, my foot in the door with the man who was training every bumper winner in the country and now not only I was after losing him a winner but I wouldn't be able to ride for him or anyone else for three weeks. He'd give somebody else a chance and they'd take it and rack up a few winners for him and I'd be forgotten about. I'd be the fool who tried to run David Marnane into the last fence at Punchestown and I'd carry the stigma of a twenty-one day-ban forever. Talk about teenage angst.

But I really did feel that emotional about it at the time. Dad was going mental too. Willie had to stand in the doorway of the stewards' room to stop him getting inside and telling them what he thought of them. He was raging, and if Willie hadn't held him back and made him calm down, I'd say he'd have got himself in as much trouble as I did.

Thing is, when I look back at it I can only come to the conclusion that someone did me to get to him. I got the ban for who I was, not what I'd done. I don't know what Dad thinks about it and I've never asked him, but it was no secret that some of the things he said on television over the years wouldn't have made him too popular with the authorities. He's been a racing pundit on TV in Ireland since 1984 and for the last few years in England too and eveybody knows he doesn't mince his words.

I know what I did in the race was wrong and I have no problem saying that if I did it now, I'd deserve to be banned for a month. But I was a boy and I didn't realise what I'd done. I didn't know what deliberate interference was. I wasn't that clever. I've always thought since that day that they saw their chance to get at Ted Walsh and they took it.

In the car on the way home, I was nearly inconsolable. There was no point in appealing, there was nothing I could do. Dad told me that my one fatal mistake had been to take the look around as we were coming to the fence, and that made it look like I'd seen the threat and tried to snuff it out. If I hadn't looked, it would have been seen as careless. I'd have got a couple of days' ban and that would have been that. But because I looked, I appeared guilty.

In the end, it didn't turn out to be the huge disaster I expected. I only missed out on maybe five rides through it all and Willie never held it against me. Even on the day itself, he was telling me not to worry about it and I was back riding for him once the suspension was up – I nearly won a bumper on the Tuesday of Punchestown week for him.

Willie hadn't been the only one putting me up on potentially decent horses. Pat O'Leary got me to ride one called Nazmi later that spring and we won two bumpers together – the first in Thurles when we went clear inside the final furlong and the other a month later in Gowran when we came from way back in the field to win. And I rode two winners for Tom Taaffe that May. The first, Dromineer, won a bumper in Navan, and won it well, but the second was a more messy affair. It was my first winner over hurdles but I needed to come through another face-to-face with the stewards before I was able to count it.

I was on a horse called Katiymann in a two-mile handicap hurdle at Leopardstown, almost a year to the day after Wild Irish got beaten at Tipperary. I was coming along as a jockey by this stage. I'd had over seventy rides now and had seven winners to show for them. But Katiymann definitely had a mind of his own and he had a terrible habit of jumping left. We came down to the last upsides Barry Cash who was on a horse called Kephren, and Katiymann did his usual and jumped straight into Barry's horse. When we landed, my horse went away from them on the run-in but we weren't long across the line before they announced a stewards' inquiry.

Into the stewards' room and I gave my spiel. As far as I was concerned, I did all I could to keep the horse straight but he always jumped to the left, so what could I do about it? We were in there for a good while but in the end they came to the conclusion that it was accidental interference and I kept the race. I knew that Vivian Kennedy, Kephren's trainer, was pretty annoyed about it and saying that his lad had been badly hampered and would have won only for the interference.

Two days later Vivian lodged an appeal. Now, this was bad news and it was good news. Bad news, obviously, because there was a chance I might lose the race. But good news because the appeal was held midweek so I got a half day off school. Tom came to collect me in Kill and we headed down to the Turf Club together.

'Now,' he said. 'When we get down here, all you say is what you see on the television screen. You say the evidence is all there. Don't interpret it, don't analyse it, and don't say any more than you have to. Any talking that has to be done, I'll do it.'

Fair play to Tom. I had just turned seventeen about a week previously and I didn't know what was what where these things were concerned – he knew I'd probably hang myself and lose the race if I got talking too much. So we went in and I sat down, hardly saying two words the whole time. I just said that it was all up on the screen they were showing us, and anything beyond that Tom took over and said for me. It worked a treat – the appeal was dismissed and I kept the race, meaning that at the end of my first season I had eight winners to my name.

A couple of weeks before the end of the season, Willie Mullins pulled Dad aside at the races and asked him what I was doing for the summer. At that point, I had no plans at all but I knew what I wanted and that was to go work for Willie if possible. It just so happened that was what he was thinking too. 'Sure, can't he come down to me, so?' were his exact words.

Willie was going to be retiring at the end of the season and wanted me to ride some of his. He'd be retiring as champion amateur, a title he shared with Frances Crowley that year. He had a lot of young horses in his yard and he was looking for a claiming amateur to ride some of them in bumpers just at the time I was finishing up with school for the summer. I couldn't believe my luck.

It wasn't like he was saying, 'Here, you're the man now.' Nothing like that. There were other lads in the yard who'd be riding for him too. Early in that week, he sent James Nash up to Dundalk to ride a favourite and it won handy, so there was no shortage of jockeys for him to use. But still, I thought Christmas had come early.

Cue a second false start to go with the Palette fiasco. The first chance I got was to go to Wexford to ride two odds-on shots on a Friday night. Native Coin at 8–11 and Reeves at 4–5. I'd never ridden an odds-on shot in my life. I was full sure all I had to do was show up.

It didn't turn out that way. I set out on Native Coin and we'd hardly worked up a sweat before the saddle slipped forward, causing me to have to pull her up. On to Reeves then, and I didn't shine on him either. He lost by three-quarters of a length and it was probably my fault. Not the greatest start, then.

That summer was the making of me, though. That was when I really learned about tactics and speed and judgement during a race. Dad would give me lots of advice on style in the saddle as well as everything else. Gradually, I came to learn about each track in Ireland – where to be and when, what to look out for, which bits of track you could get a breather into a horse at, where you should be when you press the button.

I still rode plenty for Dad as well. Just like with Butler Brennan the previous summer, Dad bought a cheap horse called Adaramann for me to ride in maiden hurdles. It was the same drill – he ran him everywhere. Sligo, Tipperary, Limerick, Galway, Kilbeggan, Listowel, everywhere. He nearly could have driven the horsebox himself by the end of the summer.

Adaramann was great horse to learn on because he never let you forget that he was ultimately the one who was going to decide what would happen. He was actually a very good jumper but if you moved on him, he'd change his mind in an instant. And if you got into a battle of wills with him, you'd be the one who'd come off second best.

You could be tanking along down to a fence thinking you were this great horseman, kicking him into it because you'd spotted a nice stride and he'd just refuse to get off the ground until the next stride. It was as if he was looking over his shoulder going, 'Look, you go about your own business back there, I know what I'm doing.' The trick was to sit very quiet on him and keep clicking at him and leave him to do the jumping. It was a good lesson to learn.

He actually gave me my first winner against professionals that July when we beat Charlie Swan one evening in Wexford. I'd idolised Charlie as a kid and here I was beating him in a race on Dad's horse in Mam's colours. Life couldn't get much better.

It didn't, not for a while anyway, because when the summer was over I had to go back to school. The worst thing about it was that I was scared now about the weight I'd surely put on, sitting in a classroom for seven hours a day. When I was at Willie's I was working twelve and a half days a fortnight, I was riding the whole time, and I was active as hell. Going back to school would inevitably mean my weight would creep up and up.

I was weighing myself obsessively by this stage. Every day. And bit by bit, I was creeping up. Ten stone stripped. Ten-one. Ten-two. Little bits of pounds and ounces here and there, purely because I wasn't as active as I had been. In the end, Mam took me to the Blackrock Clinic in September to meet with a nutritionist, Mary McCreery. It turned out to be one of the most important afternoons I ever spent.

I stood up on Mary's scales in my boxer shorts and tipped them at ten-two. She asked me what weight I wanted to be and I said nine stone eleven pounds. 'Grand so,' she said and as I got down off the scales, she wrote out a diet plan for me. I can remember it off the top of my head better than anything I ever learned in a classroom.

A bowl of cereal in the morning. Preferably porridge – not Frosties or Special K anyway – and the only milk I could take was skimmed milk. Connacht Gold butter on any bread I had, because it had the lowest fat. Then I'd bring lunch to school and at ten o'clock break I could have an apple and a mini can of diet Coke or diet 7-Up, like the ones you get on aeroplanes.

For lunch I could have two slices of brown bread, a small bit of meat, Connacht Gold butter, lettuce and tomato. No mayonnaise, nothing like that. When I came home from school at about four o'clock I'd have a Muller Light yoghurt and another diet Coke if I wanted it. If I could make do with just water instead, so much the better.

For dinner, the meat had to be at most four ounces raw. Didn't matter whether it was chicken or pork or steak, as long as it was four ounces before it was cooked. I could have as many vegetables as I liked but only two medium sized potatoes. If I wanted to put a bit of butter on them, I could, but only as half a treat. And on top of it all I had to run four miles every night.

That was my diet and I stuck to it religiously. Between mid-September and mid-November, I lost five pounds and got down to nine-eleven and I stayed on the diet for the whole school year afterwards. I didn't waiver even once. I didn't touch chocolate, didn't eat a sweet, and didn't go near a can of 'full fat' Coke. The only thing I allowed myself was a spoon of sugar in my coffee.

The odd thing is, it sounds like hardship but it wasn't at all. That was the winter when I was in school, seeing everyone else filling out their forms for college and knowing that there was no point filling out mine. I knew what my future was, or at least I knew what I wanted it to be. And more than anything in the world, I wanted it to be in racing.

Horses were going to be my living and this diet was a tiny price to pay. It didn't bother me at all. I wanted to be the jockey who took advantage of the start Willie Mullins was offering in riding some of his good young bumper horses. I wanted to beat Charlie Swan in races like I had on Adaramann that night in Wexford. I wanted to beat all the other professionals too, wanted to hop on the stepping stones that would ultimately lead to becoming one of them.

Most of all around that time, I wanted to be champion amateur. Dad had won it eleven times, Willie had won it six and now, with Willie's backing, I was being handed the ammunition to do the same. If sticking to slivers of Connacht Gold, mini Diet Cokes and four-ounce pieces of meat were going to help me achieve what they'd achieved, I wasn't going to argue. I'd have eaten half those amounts if that's what it would have taken.

CHAPTER 3

Amateur drama

By mid-September 1996, I was motoring. The summer had worked out better than I could have hoped, even allowing for the early mishaps that night in Wexford. I had my biggest win yet when John Oxx let me ride Garaiyba in the GPT at Galway, the big amateur race that Dad hadn't managed to win. Willie provided me with about a dozen winners too – I even redeemed myself on both Reeves (twice!) and Native Coin before the summer was out. Add in the odd winner from outside trainers like Enda Bolger and I was right in the mix for the champion amateur title. It looked probable from early on that it would be between myself and Philip Fenton, although Barry Cash was in the running too.

I was still making some pretty average mistakes though. Desperate ones. One Monday down in Listowel, myself and Philip were on the two horses at the top of the betting – me on West Of Waikiki for Willie and him on Kerani for Edward O'Grady. We jumped off and I had decided beforehand that I was going to follow Philip for most of the way round and then hopefully challenge him in the straight. It worked too – a perfect plan, perfectly executed.

Or so I thought. In those days, a lot of tracks had little markers on the inside running rail after the furlong pole showing distances to the finish line – 200 yards to go, 150 yards to go, 100, fifty. The one small problem was that these distances were only written on the side facing the stands. The jockeys could only see the backs of them. Sure, why would we need to see what was written on them? What possible use could that information be to us!

Anyway, it won't take a genius to guess what happened next. The fifty-yard marker was the last on the running rail but then the winning post was standing upright on the inside of the track further on. I tracked Philip's horse around, made my move when we turned in, kicked for home and rode to the post: the bloody fifty post. Cathy Harrison was between us on a horse called Antics and by the time I realised that we were still racing, she had gone by me. Beat me half a length.

Thank God nobody noticed I'd stopped riding at the fifty marker. It all happened so quick that I was able to get West Of Waikiki going again without anybody passing any remarks. I had only stopped riding for two strides but it felt like an eternity to me. If anyone had noticed, I'd have been looking at another three-week suspension, no doubt about it. Plenty of jockeys have found themselves with unwanted days off because they misjudged the winning post. I could have had no complaints if I'd got a suspension.

I was sick about losing, but sick too about the stupidity of those posts only facing one way. No question, what had happened was my fault, but I couldn't believe that nobody had copped that catching one of these posts out of the corner of your eye in the adrenaline rush of a tight finish might some day confuse a jockey. It took a couple of years – and an awful lot of complaining from the weighing room – before they got round to putting the numbers on both sides.

Poor old West Of Waikiki. I'd ridden him in a bumper in

Dundalk a few weeks previously when Peter Newell had gone blazing away from the start on a horse of his own called Red Radical. I swear to God, he was a furlong ahead at one stage. We pulled him back and pulled him back and nearly got there, as he was getting very tired out in front. But in the end he held on and we failed by just a length. I always felt bad about West Of Waikiki. He should have won at least one of those two bumpers but I lost both on him.

When I made bad mistakes that cost me a race, I always found it hard to forget them. For one thing, I wasn't allowed to forget them – Dad or Willie would always give me a bollocking as soon as they saw me. But as time went by, they didn't have to. I was getting to the point where I knew coming off the course if I'd given something an ordinary ride.

Garaiyba was a perfect example. About a month before we won the GPT together in Galway, John Oxx let me ride her at the Curragh on the Friday night of Derby weekend. There was no pace early on in the race and I nearly found myself having to make it until a horse of Mick Halford's took it up. As we turned for home, I decided enough was enough and kicked on. We were passed – before the furlong pole! – by not one but two long shots. I'd gone far too soon and got another favourite beaten. Nobody needed to tell me who was at fault.

But you learn. You try not to make the same mistake twice – at least, not twice in a short time period in case you get a name for it – and you progress. John Oxx let me keep the ride for the GPT and before the race Johnny Murtagh came to me and told me not to be making as much use of her. 'I know she lacks a gear,' he said, 'but don't ride her like she's slow.'

Johnny is nine years older than me (to the day actually – we have the same birthday, 14 May) and he was John's stable jockey. He was champion flat jockey in Ireland and he'd won a Coronation Stakes and a Breeders' Cup Mile on Ridgewood Pearl the previous year. When he talked, I listened. I was going to hang on to Garaiyba for a bit longer this time anyway after the Curragh fiasco, but Johnny was just making sure. I learned my lesson and we ended up winning well, the biggest win I'd had up to that point. Every amateur jockey wants to win the GPT.

So yeah, there were plenty of mistakes back then but I was still riding a decent amount of winners too and I was battling it out with Philip for the amateur title. That was probably even half the problem in Listowel, the night I misjudged the winning post – I was so consumed by making sure I finished ahead of Philip that I forgot everything else that was going on.

But that was the state of mind I was in back then. This was in September, a full eight months before the amateur championship would be decided, and I was thinking about it every day. My whole life revolved around it. Nothing else mattered – not school, not rugby, nothing. I wanted to do everything I could so that Willie would keep giving me chances, so that other trainers would keep noticing me, so that I could get my nose ahead of Philip and keep it there.

I was still working for Willie at weekends. Myself and James Nash would take it in turns driving down to his place every Saturday morning that winter – James one week, me the next. We made some couple. He still goes on about the time I was driving us in Mam's Volvo one morning and we bought the papers in Kilcullen. He was in the passenger seat with *The Irish Field* on his lap and I glanced over and saw a photo of me on a bumper winner. Well, I wasn't so used to having my picture in the paper that I'd be blasé about it, so I leaned over and told him to hold it up so I could see what they were saying about me.

Bang! Crashed the car. Looked back around at the last second, jammed on the brakes and slapped straight into the back of the fella in front of us. *The Irish Field* was stuck to the windscreen, and James along with it. The damage came to £1400. Couldn't believe it. Neither could Mam. And James hasn't let it go even now.

We spent our lives in cars together back then. Myself, himself, David Casey, Pat Morris, Mark Madden, Tommy Treacy and plenty more, driving all over the country. James, David and I drove up to Galway in 1996 on the Thursday of the festival in James's white Peugeot 405. David was a professional already and myself and James were amateurs, so while the pair of us were heading over there for the bumper, David had a ride in the Galway Hurdle. It was one of Willie's horses, Mystical City, and she got in off a lovely low weight with David still claiming three pounds. She bolted in at 20–1.

Well, we had to celebrate. Out into the Budweiser tent, where everybody was trying to buy David a drink, and then on into town before going into the Corrib Hotel. Galway during the festival is some place. The whole of Irish racing is there and you meet every last man, woman and child you'd want to meet (and plenty you don't). Everyone's in good form and it's easy to lose all track of time when you're in the middle of it, even when you're not drinking like everybody else. Celebrating is hanging around. You can't go on the tear because you have work in the morning and you never know which of you is driving home.

Come three o'clock in the morning, I was asleep in the back of the Peugeot and David was asleep in the front. All three of us were due at Willie's at eight o'clock for work but we couldn't find James. Everybody had seen him and nobody had seen him. We woke at six o'clock to leave, just in time for him to appear out of the dawn. 'Are we right, lads?' he says.

Galway to Carlow at that time of the morning could just about be done in two hours. I'm not saying it could be done keeping to the speed limit, just that it was possible. We had one problem – none of us wanted to drive. This wasn't a matter of who was insured or who had a licence, it was a matter of there being war if we weren't in Willie's yard at eight o'clock. So we settled on tossing coins.

I went first. 'Heads.' It came up heads. Lovely. I was in the back seat before they got the second one tossed. David lost that one and ended up having to drive, Galway Hurdle or no Galway Hurdle. So he set off and myself and James were asleep before we left the car park.

I woke up to the sound of James roaring at him. 'Pull over! Pull over!' I opened an eye and saw the dashboard, lit up like a Christmas tree. Every light on the thing was flashing red. I looked out of the window and saw that we were coming through Freshford, which struck me as odd.

What this all meant was that there was a very good chance that not only had David taken a wrong turn somewhere, he'd done so in a car that was starting to cave in. David reckoned we had no choice though – we were getting to Willie's come hell or high water. He was laughing away to me in the rear-view mirror all the while too – sure it wasn't his car! I'd say James was giving out to him for about fifteen minutes before he finally pulled in at the Rock Bar, just outside Kilkenny.

By now, it seemed like there was steam coming out of every inch of the car. One of the pipes outside the radiator was after bursting. At this point, it was coming up on twenty to eight and we were still a good fifteen miles away from Willie's, with morning

Right Applying for my amateur jockey's licence with Dad and Ted.

Below The Walsh family and friends at the opening of Ruby's Double, a double bank at Punchestown built in memory of my grandfather by Betty Moran.

Dad, Ted and me on Midge in Kill.

With my grandparents, Helen and Ruby.

Riding Roc De Prince at home after his Thyestes win in 1991, Dad's first win as a trainer.

One of my last games for Naas Rugby Club. I am third from the left in the front row.

My first ride, Wild Irish at Leopardstown in May 1995.

My first winner, Siren Song at Gowran Park in July 1995.

Above Dixon Warner (far side) jumps the last at Punchestown in 1997, my first winner over fences.

A young Gillian Doran leads in a young Ruby Walsh on Welsh Grit in Galway in 1997.

Me, Noel O'Callaghan and Willie Mullins after my first Cheltenham Festival winner on Alexander Banquet in 1998.

Papillon battles with Bobbyjo in the 1998 Irish National. Little did we know that the next two winners of the Grand National jumped the fence together.

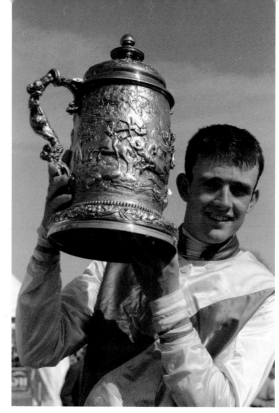

Back before the grey
hair, holding up the
Heineken Gold Cup
won on Imperial Call
in 1999.

Papillon jumps the last
in the Grand National
in 2000.

The faces say it all. Ted and Katie lead Papillon in after winning the Grand National. The man pointing is Brendan Brady.

Inset Dad and Mrs Betty Moran, Papillon's owner, after our Grand National win.

Commanche Court on his way to winning the Irish National just days after Papillon had won the English one.

Rince Ri winning the Ericsson in 2000.

Mam accepting a special recognition award from the INHS committee following Papillon and Commanche Court's National victories in 2000.

traffic in Kilkenny city still to come. So we hopped over the wall and into the back yard of the Rock Bar, got a hose and started filling the radiator. Back in the car and that patch-up job lasted until we were halfway between Kilkenny and Paulstown, where we had to pull in at Paddy's Pub and repeat the dose.

Finally, at about three minutes past eight, James's white Peugeot 405 conked out at the graveyard just up the road from Willie's yard. We had to get out and push it the last 200 yards and we rolled into the yard at five past eight. The poor car never saw road again – James had to get it towed away three weeks later. As for us, we rode out five lots for Willie, hopped straight back into David's car and headed back to Galway for the Friday card. Needless to say, we all came home empty-handed.

That was the life. And I loved every minute of it. James and I were good friends then and still are now, but we were both after the same rides from Willie. We were the two amateur riders in the yard and Willie had about fifty horses in his string, including all the best quality bumper horses. There was great group of us working there, all in or around the same age, and we'd be flat to the boards every morning, riding out these fifty horses. What's better than going to work that doesn't feel like work?

Every day was about hoping for a ride in a race. At the start, you're after any ride at all, good or bad. I was living day to day, ride to ride. But I'd never ask Willie for one. I'd be slow to because I wouldn't want to hassle him. He'd never say who was riding what, not before the declarations were made, and myself and James just waited to see what happened.

Willie could be standing across the yard from me, literally twenty yards away, and I'd still ring racing services to see if Willie had declared a jockey for his horse in the bumper. That's how it was. I was still an amateur so I didn't have an agent to do it for me. It's nearly a rite of passage, the kind of thing every jockey has to do when they're starting out. You'd be ringing racing services every day anyway looking for spares. Or blanks, as you'd call them.

'What's blank in the bumper?' you'd ask. And they tell you, so you'd go off and root through *The Irish Field* directory to get phone numbers to look for rides. It had to be done quickly too, because you had very little time to get your speak in. The declarations would be done up at ten o'clock in the morning and issued at 12.30 p.m. so you only had those couple of hours to find out who had the blanks and try and get through to the trainers. There was no internet in those days, and if there were mobile phones they were the size of hay bales and it certainly wasn't teenage jockeys who owned them. The 'decs' went up on Teletext at around eleven o'clock all right but that was no use if you were out at Willie's yard where there was no television. It was all one big scramble to get a ride.

You didn't always get one, of course. Or if you did, it was often a complete no-hoper. I went through some terrible lean spells that winter where I didn't get a sniff of a winner. I rode a winner on Sheisagale for Tom Foley at Clonmel on 8 December. And then I didn't ride another for a full month. Christmas came and went and I had no winner until Our Bid won for Kevin Prender-gast at Leopardstown on 11 January. When Florida Pearl won the bumper in Leopardstown on St Stephen's Day, James was on his back. Meanwhile, I was in Limerick, finishing third on Ashtale.

And after Our Bid, there wasn't another one for a month again until I won on Clifdon Fog for Jim Bolger in Gowran on 15 February. Jim rang at eleven o'clock that morning; Clifdon Fog won the race at two-thirty in the afternoon.

Nine weeks, two winners. I was getting fairly anxious in between. All I could see was Philip racking up winners while I was at nothing. At least that's how it felt. In reality, he wasn't streaking away or even overtaking me. The day I won on Clifdon Fog we were actually just about neck and neck, with me still two ahead. I was watching every ride he had, though.

Philip and I were competing in races and sometimes we were even competing for rides. Two days before Clifdon Fog, Philip won a hunter chase in Gowran for Enda Bolger on a horse called Dixon Varner to close the gap on me even tighter. I can't remember exactly but I think I was maybe only two or three ahead at that point. It was too close for my liking anyway. But a couple of months later, Dixon Varner gave me my first ever winner over fences. And not just any old winner either – a graded race at Punchestown during the festival.

I wasn't even supposed to be riding him. Enda was training and riding and the pair of us came in and sat down in the weighing room after riding the Champion Bumper. Enda decided he wasn't feeling well. I was sitting just inside the door – where I still sit – and he turned around to me and went, 'Here, you ride my lad in the next.' The next was about twenty minutes away at this stage. He threw me the colours of Mrs Sue Magnier and just like that I had a ride in the race.

No time to think about it, no time for anything but to tie the colours up and go. Out into the parade ring. Met John and Sue Magnier. Got my instructions from Enda – drop him in, take your time, creep away, and see if you can take it up going to the last.

And that's more or less how it panned out. I hunted around on Dixon Varner, kept an eye on a fancied horse of John Costello's called Stay In Touch, tracked him over the second-last, challenged on the way to the last, pinged it, landed in front and won by a few lengths. First winner over fences, first winner at Punchestown, and I hadn't even a ride in the race half an hour beforehand. Just goes to show the part luck plays in these things – since Philip had won on the horse before, Enda probably would have thrown him the colours but for the fact he was already riding a good horse of Edward O'Grady's.

Enda had a huge influence on me around that period. I'd ridden out for him the odd time in Limerick and eventually Dad suggested that I do it on a regular basis because he figured I could learn a lot from Enda. He's so good with young horses, taking them out across the countryside, jumping them over banks, hedges, drains and gates, over anything and everything.

Apart from anything else, it's great fun. Even so, when you're there riding out with him you're there to learn. He would leave you in no doubt at all if what you were doing with his young horses was wrong. He's a good friend of mine now, but at the time I was half afraid of him.

He'd give out to you in a heartbeat and if you had your hands in the wrong place, he'd think nothing of giving them a slap with whatever he had in his hand to make you position them properly. He'd a have a stick or a bit of a branch or something and if your hands were too high over a jump, you'd get a reminder. It didn't hurt but you didn't do it again in a hurry either.

He was an incredible teacher, a real good horseman. He'd be roaring at you constantly to get the horse on the right leg before a jump, to keep it balanced, to sit quiet over a jump. He'd tell you that the key was not to interfere, to let the horse work it out for himself. And because we'd be jumping drains, banks and walls with no definite idea of what the landing was going to be like, you learned how to keep your balance in the right place once you got to the other side. On terrain like that, a horse is going to sprawl plenty of the time or at least land awkwardly and it's up to you to ensure you don't make it worse.

Ken Whelan and John Thomas McNamara were there at the same time and we knocked all sorts of enjoyment out of it. There was nothing we didn't jump, no farm we didn't cross. I was there one Monday on a horse that ended up being called Jim Jam Joey, one of Alfie Buller's that came down from Fairyhouse the previous day. Enda got me to ride him out at around midday and between then and when I arrived back in the yard around half past four, I got seven falls off him.

Myself and Enda had headed off out into the countryside and whatever way he went, we got lost. I didn't think Enda could get lost in the fields of south Limerick but he managed it this day anyway. After a while, we were able to pick out the castle at Rathcannon in the distance and Enda said we'd head for it and he'd be able to find his way from there. But we were after jumping down into a field over a wall that was too high to clear on the way back. Our only other way out was through the field next to it but it had a farmer in it, in his tractor, who Enda figured might not be one bit pleased to see us.

These days, Enda knows every farmer for forty miles in every direction and they're nearly delighted if they see him coming with his horses. He's a real community man and he runs big charity rides in and around Athlacca that raise plenty of money. But back in the mid 1990s, he'd have had to be wary of crossing the wrong farmer by crossing the wrong field. So this day we were out with Jim Jam Joey, we could do nothing but hide under a tree for three-quarters of an hour until the farmer finished what he was at and moved on. We found our way back eventually but I was fairly sore and tired by the time we got there.

Jim Jam Joey was no good then or since but every once in a

while I'd ride a horse out that would go on to make a name for himself. I rode Spot Thedifference when he was a four-year-old and he went on to become a famous cross-country horse around Cheltenham. When Enda first bought him though, he was a bad jumper. I remember Enda even saying he was a bad buy. He rode him in a point-to-point in Listowel and came back annoyed at his jumping. So the following Monday, he put me up on him and off we went together across the fields.

Spot and I took to each other straight away for some reason and we had a great day out. Still had four falls, all the same. At one point, we went to jump a drain just outside Athlacca village and he ended up hanging from a tree stump by his martingale (which, for all the non-horsey people reading, is the tack that we use to control a horse's head carriage). His hind quarters were in the drain, I was in there beside him but his front end was up in the air, suspended by the martingale. I had to scramble out from under him before the martingale snapped and he found his own way out. It didn't do him a bit of harm.

Enda wouldn't make a horse jump anything that couldn't be jumped and even at that, we were jumping these drains just over walking speed. It was all to make the horse think his way around the problem. You'd creep down the bank, let him think about it and eventually he'd skip over the drain and climb up the other side. It was all to get them nimble on their feet. When you'd school over fences, they'd be a lot quicker to move their feet and wouldn't be banging off the fences.

It's a great way of training horses, very old-fashioned and probably unconventional these days. With urban sprawl throughout the country and horses becoming more expensive and staff becoming harder to insure, it's a method that's dying out by the year, which is a real shame. By training horses in that way, you're also training the jockeys who are on their backs. I learned an unbelievable amount about jumping in that year I spent Mondays riding out for Enda. If I'd learned plenty from Dad and Willie about other things, there's no question that that year with Enda taught me an awful lot about jumping.

In the end, Dixon Varner more or less sealed the amateur championship for me that season. After I won on him at Punchestown in April on the Wednesday, I had two winners that weekend in Listowel and then another couple the following week in Clonmel and Dundalk. I rounded off the season by winning on him in another hunter chase in Kilbeggan on 26 May, leaving me eight winners ahead of Philip at the end of the season, thirty-four to twenty-six.

It was a great feeling. I got a great thrill out of going to the National Hunt awards in Adare at the end of the season and knowing, as I went up to get my award from the Turf Club, that here was an ambition I'd set for myself and had gone and fulfilled. Champion amateur isn't an easy thing to win and I definitely didn't think I'd be able to do it so early in my career.

I always knew in the back of my head that some people would have been looking at it and going, 'Sure, why wouldn't he win it when he's Ted's son and when he has all of Willie Mullins's bumper horses to ride?' But to me, that was no way to think about it. I never got anything handed to me because of who my father was and I'd worked my way from the bottom of the food chain at Willie's.

Winning it meant that everything had been worth the effort – the diet, the work, the half days off school, everything. It meant that I'd started to repay Mam and Dad for all they'd done for me and Willie for every chance he'd given me. It meant too that I had a future in this, that if I kept going like I was going I might get to ride against Charlie Swan and Richard Dunwoody more and more, and that I might even get to have a ride at Cheltenham eventually.

By then, I'd had a small taste of what a festival winner felt like, of what it might be to come into the winners' enclosure with the whole crowd going mad and everybody shaking your hand and patting your back and crying and hugging. All thanks to a gorgeous, quiet French horse who came to mean the world to our family. That horse was Commanche Court.

CHAPTER 4

Three Cheltenhams

1996: The love story begins

I don't think I was ever as cold in my life as that first year I went to Cheltenham. It definitely has never been as cold any time I've been there since and I've been there more than most people. I've been in January, November, March, in wind and rain and snow but never was it as Baltic as that first year. And I didn't care a bit.

I'd been itching to go for years but this was the first time I'd been allowed to take the week off school to travel over. Dad didn't have a horse running – we just went. Mam, Dad, Jennifer and me. We got the boat from Dublin to Holyhead on the Monday morning and then drove down to Winchcombe. Mam and Dad rented a house about six miles from the racecourse and their friends, Eddie and Nora O'Connor, stayed with us. I had the couch for a bed for the week. Not a bother for me. It was five-star treatment as far as I was concerned.

The Cheltenham Festival. I was in heaven. Nothing I'd seen on television or heard before from people who'd been there could do it justice. I was in awe of the place as soon as I arrived, just completely blown away. It wasn't so much the look of the racecourse, even though it is a genuinely beautiful landscape. It was more the feeling of being in the one place in the world I would be if I had the choice to be anywhere. I walked around for the whole week taking it all in.

I knocked about with David Casey, who I knew a bit at that stage from the couple of times I'd ridden out for Willie Mullins. I had one bet all week and it won – Willie was riding Wither Or Which in the Champion Bumper so I backed it. I was up on the hill behind the winners' enclosure afterwards, cheering Willie as he came into the ring to this huge reception.

To me, this was unbelievable stuff. A couple of weeks earlier, this man had been standing by my side in the stewards' room in Punchestown, defending me over the trouble I got myself into with Palette. And now here he was, smiling away down below me in the winners' enclosure at Cheltenham. Magic.

I'd be lying, though, if I said I was thinking that I might one day do the same. When I was cheering Willie in, I definitely wasn't imagining myself on the back of some future Wither Or Which. It's not that I was unambitious or anything, more that I would have had a practical enough approach to these things, even at the age of sixteen. I had four winners to my name. If I was standing there imagining myself riding a Cheltenham winner, I would have been getting well ahead of myself. It was fantasy, nothing less.

Think about it. The number of jockeys who go through the place without ever having a winner is huge. Dad had ridden there throughout his career and had managed four, which put him well above the average. Conor O'Dwyer won the Gold Cup that year on Imperial Call – his first ever winner – and then didn't ride another winner at the meeting for eight years. For me to think it was possible there after having had just four winners in Ireland would have been lunacy.

Apart from anything else, nearly all the best Irish horses in those days were sold to England. Jennifer remembers Dad telling her when Imperial Call was being led in to make sure she enjoyed an Irish winner of the Gold Cup because it could be a lifetime again before we saw another one. For me to think seriously of riding a winner at Cheltenham one day, I would probably have had to be prepared to move to England. I couldn't be thinking about that sort of thing back then. I didn't know what the future held. I was more concerned with skipping school for the week and enjoying the experience for what it was.

We went home on the boat on Friday morning and I went back to school on the Monday. I can't remember if I got given out to or not. The teachers might as well have been giving out to the wall if I did. That one hit of Cheltenham had me hooked for life.

1997: Commanche

We'd had good horses around the place when I was a kid but they were horses for the grown-ups. Barney Burnett had won nine times from eleven runs in 1984 and 1985 and was the champion novice hurdler. Roc De Prince had won the Thyestes in 1991. These were horses that were in the yard that I knew well enough but I could never say I was involved with them. I was just too young. Commanche Court was different though.

Dad had bought him in France from Nicolas Clement for Dermot Desmond a few months after he'd won the 1996 Austrian Derby. When he came to the yard I used to ride him out quite a bit. There was a hill gallop in Straffan where Dad used to work him twice or three times a week and I'd go over with him first thing in the morning to ride work before Mam would arrive and take me to school. When it looked like he was going to be a proper horse, the effect he had on the place was massive.

He won a juvenile hurdle at Leopardstown in early February 1997 and we thought he was good. Then he won another one in Punchestown a fortnight later and we knew for a fact he was good. Dad knew it. Norman Williamson had ridden him both times and he knew it too. People started talking about him for the Triumph Hurdle. He was on the front of *The Irish Field. The Irish Field!* For a horse of ours to be on the front page of *The Irish Field* was a huge thing.

That whole winter and spring, the mood of our house was very often dictated by Commanche's mood. If Commanche Court didn't work well in the morning, there was no conversation in the evening. This horse was the whole place. This horse meant everything because he had potential. Nobody knew what that potential could lead to and that was the whole point. He could be anything. What he was going to do could be the making and breaking not just of that year but of a couple of years for the yard.

Dad would have been under pressure as a result. Not that he'd show it very much but he'd have too much knowledge of history not to be under pressure, if that makes any sense. Because he has such a good memory for horses, and for good horses especially, he would have known exactly what it meant to be going to Cheltenham with a horse that had a live chance. It had been a while since we had a real good horse in the yard but you could sense Dad knew what he had on his hands in Commanche. He would have been backing himself to do it right, to do the horse justice by getting him to the race intact and in shape.

Nine days before Cheltenham, I rode him work in Leop-ardstown after Sunday racing. He worked with Guest Per-formance, a Dessie Hughes horse that was heading over for the Champion Hurdle, and it was a serious piece of work. He went a proper gallop from the beginning and the further we went, the better Commanche travelled. He galloped all over Guest Per-formance. You couldn't see that and not be convinced he was in with a shout if he travelled over OK.

Going to Cheltenham that year was so different to the year before. In 1996, I was on an adventure. I was seeing Cheltenham through a spectator's eyes, walking around in wonder at this place that I was falling in love with. This time was more serious. I went over on the horse aeroplane for the first time, leaving Dublin airport on the Monday with Commanche, Theatreworld, Istabraq and Finnegans Hollow on board.

That was some collection of talent on the one plane. Finnegans Hollow was going very well in the Supreme Novices' Hurdle when he fell three out and slapped Charlie Swan on the floor; Theatreworld finished second behind Make A Stand in the Cham-pion Hurdle and Istabraq had his first Cheltenham win in the Sun Alliance Hurdle.

Commanche wasn't running until the Thursday so we looked after him in the stables just as if he was at home in Kill. I say 'we', but actually on Tuesday Jennifer, Ted and Katie did what needed to be done. I wasn't much use to anybody. That was because I spent the morning making my first ever trip to a place I would come to know very, very well over the years. Cheltenham General Hospital.

I'm not even that sure what happened. All I know is that I went into the stables on Tuesday morning to muck out Commanche and next thing I was panned out on the floor. I must have come up to his hindquarters and startled him. I ended up colliding with either the door or wall. One way or the other, I ended up out cold. That morning I spent a few hours getting seen to in Cheltenham Hospital and felt like a right tool. I suppose it gave us all something else to think about rather than fretting over Commanche. I still rode him out Wednesday morning though. He walked around the place like he owned it.

Thursday came and I led him up. Jittery as hell. Me, that is. Not Commanche. Commanche was grand. Norman got up on him and headed out on to the track and myself and Ted went and stood in the grooms' stand. I'd never known nerves like it. The sweat was absolutely pouring from my hands. Ted's too. This was everything. This was Cheltenham. Nothing was bigger.

The Triumph Hurdle was a bit more of a lottery in those days than it is now and with twenty-eight horses you weren't guaranteed to get the run you wanted. We all had different views from where we were. Mam said afterwards that when she saw him turning in with a chance, she was happy. Win, lose or draw from there, Commanche had done his job. Fair play to her level-headed nature – that's why she's the boss.

The rest of us weren't so calm, not by a long way. When Norman turned in, myself and Ted started edging off the grooms' stand. He jumped the last in a line of four along with Circus Star, Shooting Light and L'Opera, which was our cue to start running up the woodchip walkway in front of the crowd. And when he passed us with Norman in full flow, the two of us were running for all our lives, roaring and jumping and shouting like a pair of jackasses.

He won by a length and the place went wild. First race on the Thursday, and the only Irish winner all day as it turned out. It was incredible, just beyond words. Ted and I ran up past all the other horses that were coming down to catch him and lead him back down past the crowd. We got to the parade ring and gave him to Pat Desmond and she led him in. We were walking on air. Dad was in tears and he wasn't alone.

They could have called off the rest of the races that day and we wouldn't have noticed. The Gold Cup was a few races later and I'd say it's still the only Gold Cup I've missed since I was a kid. I was in the vet's box with Commanche as he gave a sample for a drugs test, no more than a couple of hundred yards away from the winning post, and I still didn't know what won it until later that night.

That was the start of our big days with Commanche. He came back to Cheltenham for a Stayers' Hurdle, a Cleeve Hurdle, an Arkle Chase and a couple of Gold Cups. He won some serious prizes at home as well and gave us some great days out at Leopardstown, Navan and Fairyhouse. He even stuck around long enough to give Katie a few of her first rides over hurdles. But it's hard to say that any day was better than the day he won the Triumph. That was something, it really was. Best day of my life up to then, no doubt about it.

1998: The great Alexander

I left home that summer. Once the leaving cert was over and done with, once we'd all agreed that there was no danger of any university finding a place for me, I headed off down to Carlow and moved into digs at Kay McCullough's house along with Mark Madden and Robbie Walsh. Mark was working at Willie's with me and Robbie was in Paddy Mullins's yard. Willie was getting more horses into the yard, but as far as we could see there weren't too many more staff about the place. We were riding out nine or ten lots a day for a while. Loving it too.

We played indoor soccer on Tuesday night. And I mean night. Ian Almond (aka Busty, because he had a nosebleed on his first day, and since horses who get nosebleeds are called bursters, Ian got a nickname that has never left him) lived locally in Ballinabranagh and we'd start playing at ten o'clock, play for an hour, and then his parents Faith and Ally would have tea and sandwiches ready when we got finished up at eleven. I'd be awake for hours after it and wouldn't be half slept by the time I'd have to get up again the next morning, but we never got around to changing it. It was the same again the following week and the week after and the week after.

We put a five-a-side team together that summer and won the stable lads' tournament in Kildare town, beating a load of teams from the Curragh. George McGrath was the assistant head lad at Willie's and he played in goal. Brendan Flynn played at the back, with myself and Robbie in midfield and David up front. All the other teams brought subs on and off but our only sub on the sideline was Ian and he wasn't up to much, so we played away every minute ourselves. For a crowd of National Hunt lads to come up from Carlow and beat all these local flat yards was a bit of a coup.

That was the summer I started to get to know a girl called Gillian Doran pretty well. She was a cousin of Willie's and was part of the same social circle as us – we were the same age, went to the same places and knew the same people. She actually worked in Willie's yard for a summer and then came riding out at weekends when she started college in UCD. We became good friends and always enjoyed each other's company. In time, we'd move past that phase but for now we were just friends.

Myself and David used to go to Punchestown on a Tuesday morning to ride in schooling races for Willie. We'd be in work for eight o'clock, ride out two lots, then hop in the car and head away to Punchestown for ten. We'd ride six each there and leave around lunchtime and head back to Willie's for another four in the afternoon. They were long days but out of one of them came the great Alexander Banquet.

You never saw a lazier horse in all your life. The first time we came across each other, he was this big sloppy four-year-old who was absolutely bone idle. He would do nothing for you. The first time I got on his back in Punchestown I had to kick and slap and drive him out of the parade ring, never mind around the track. Not a very promising type at all.

But then I rode him in a bumper in Gowran Park in the middle of February where I bucked him off in front and made all the running. Every time I asked for something he responded and in the end he won quite well from what turned out to be some very good horses. Native Upmanship finished fourth that day and the race also had Glazeaway and Ferbert Junior in it. If you came back to that bumper a few years later, you'd have found a field that had won an awful lot of prize money in the meantime. Native Upmanship, especially, went on to great success for Arthur Moore – he won a Powers Gold Cup, a couple of Melling Chases at Aintree and finished second in two Queen Mother Champion Chases as well.

A few weeks earlier, I'd won a bumper at Leopardstown on Joe Mac for Christy Roche. He'd been Philip Fenton's ride originally but Philip had had a fall and the ride had come my way. I guess because I was champion amateur and I was keeping up a decent strike rate, I was getting more and more chances. As a result, I'd ridden most of the good bumper horses in Ireland that winter, and to me there was no doubt that Joe Mac was one of them and Alexander Banquet was another.

Actually, the one I thought I got the best feel from was trained by Paddy Mullins, a horse called Siberian Gale who I'd ridden at Leopardstown that Christmas. That was some day, the first time I ever rode a double. Not just that, an across-the-card double into the bargain. It started with me driving to Limerick to ride a horse for Dad called Scoss in the first, a maiden hurdle. And then Michael Ryan, who owned him, gave me a lift in his helicopter to Leopardstown for two bumpers later in the afternoon. This was it, I was a real jet-setting jockey now – Limerick to Leopardstown through the skies, the executive way. I won the first bumper too – on Strong Son for Willie – and then headed out on Siberian Gale.

But I didn't shine on him, of course. There was no pace in the race and he ran far too free. The double should have been a treble but we got beaten by half a length by Colm Murphy on Moondigua. The jet-setting jockey had to find a lift back down to Limerick to get his car and then he had to drive it home, cursing himself over the one that got away. Funny though, if anyone asked who I thought was the best bumper horse I'd ridden that season, my answer was Siberian Gale.

But in the end, Mr Mullins didn't send him to Cheltenham. Christy was sending Joe Mac all right, and Willie was sending Alexander Banquet in the hope that he could train the winner of the Champion Bumper for the third year in a row. I was riding most of Willie's bumper horses but I didn't expect to stay on Alexander Banquet for the festival. Richard Dunwoody had won on Florida Pearl the previous year and the word was that he was looking for the ride, so I just presumed that would be that.

To be honest, I was reasonably OK with it too. The way I looked at it was that I was still an amateur and had two rides booked for amateur races at the festival anyway, plus two more for Dad. I'd won a beginners' chase in Thurles on a Mouse Morris horse called Thatswhatithought the previous December and he was running in the four-miler. Dad was running Papillon in the Kim Muir as well as Scoss in the Triumph and Commanche in the Stayers' Hurdle. I was delighted. Four rides at Cheltenham!

Willie had been using me quite a bit more and more throughout that season, though. He'd had a horse called Native Darrig in the yard for a couple of years on whom I'd won a few amateur flat handicaps through the summer at the Curragh, Leopardstown and Tralee. After he won the good handicap hurdle in Listowel that September, Willie decided to bring him to England for the good handicap hurdles through the winter. The Murphys Hurdle in Cheltenham (now known as the Greatwood). The Fighting Fifth in Newcastle. The Tote Gold Trophy in Newbury. And for whatever reason, he left me on him.

I knew nothing about riding in England. I didn't know the tracks or the form or most of the jockeys. But the things I knew, I loved. Or at least I loved the idea of them. Small, stupid, simple things like packing a bag for two days instead of one. Making sure I had my passport where I could find it. Getting Mam to make sure she taped BBC or Channel 4 all day in case somebody like John Francome mentioned my name at some point, even in passing.

Native Darrig didn't win any of the races, although we had every chance in the Fighting Fifth but got outpaced between the second-last and the last and finished third. It was no disgrace, I suppose, and after the Tote Gold Trophy (sixth, never in contention) there was talk of him running in the Coral Cup. But as with Alexander Banquet, my thinking would have been that Willie would be putting a professional jockey on him.

I was about to be pleasantly surprised. One of the things I most admire about Willie is that he does his own thing. I didn't know his views at the time but I've come to learn since that he has a deep conviction when it comes to bumpers. In Ireland, they're for amateur jockeys only and that's how he likes it. The way he sees it, bumpers should be for not only the horses of the future but the jockeys of the future too.

If a young lad is breaking his back every morning mucking out stables, the least Willie thinks you ought to be able to use him as an incentive is a ride in a bumper. Do that often enough and even if he turns out not to be much of a jockey, chances are he'll stay in the industry in some capacity. That way, the whole show keeps rolling along. That's why he likes bumpers being confined to amateurs in Ireland and why he'd like the same rule to apply in England too. I couldn't agree with him more.

Even so, if Dunwoody was looking for the ride on Alexander Banquet, it would have taken more than just a stubborn streak to say no. He'd have needed the say so of the owner. That was an odd situation in itself, because although the hotelier Noel O'Callaghan owned Alexander Banquet, he'd actually leased out ownership of him for a season in a raffle at Leopardstown the previous November. But the guy who won the raffle, a Mr Martin Swarbrick, was a mystery figure to me. I rode Alexander Banquet a dozen times, twice in 1998 when this chap owned him, and I never met him once. He wasn't even at Cheltenham the day of the Champion Bumper.

So in the end, Noel O'Callaghan had the final 'yea or nae' on me. It turned out to be a yea. Willie told me at Leopardstown on the Sunday evening ten days before Cheltenham that I'd be keeping the ride on him and on Native Darrig. I couldn't believe it. I've never forgotten the chance the pair of them gave me that year and I never will, either.

These days, it's nearly automatic that one of Willie's horses will go off favourite in the bumper because he's won it so many times. But although he was just after winning it two years in a row, Alexander Banquet still was only about fifth or sixth in the betting in 1998. Joe Mac was a banker in most people's eyes and I suppose you couldn't argue with them on the form in the book.

But Willie had Alexander Banquet revved up for the race. He did a load of short, sharp, fast work with him. There was no danger of him not staying, the danger was that he'd be too laid back, too sluggish. Willie hadn't given him a minute's peace trying to get the fat off him that winter. It was an incredible training performance.

Over to Cheltenham, then, and I had my first festival ride on Papillon in the Kim Muir. He ran no sort of race really, finished about mid division. Papillon could be a moody sort when he wanted to be and I think he took a notion against Cheltenham. Norman had ridden him there to win a good two miles five furlong race that January, a real hard race that he'd only won by a head in the end. For one reason or another, he never ran a good race at Cheltenham again, never finished better than sixth. In that Kim Muir, I just couldn't get him to go about his business. He ran lazily and hung in behind the horses in front of him and I couldn't get him out. I guess at eighteen, I wasn't as tough a customer as Papillon.

But it was a first Cheltenham ride and at least it was done and dusted now. That was the Tuesday and I had three rides on the Wednesday. Native Darrig finished fifth in the Coral Cup without ever really threatening and Thatswhatithought ran on for second in the four-miler. A fifteen length second, but second all the same.

They were both decent enough results, especially for Thatswhatithought since he was a 20–1 shot. So I went out in the bumper reasonably happy with my day's work.

Hand on heart, I didn't think we would win. Actually, that's the wrong way of putting it. It was more that the thought of winning hadn't really crossed my mind. I was too naive to think we could do it. Joe Mac looked like a proper horse and I knew from riding him in Leopardstown that he had unbelievable cruising speed. With Conor O'Dwyer riding him, you were talking about a Gold Cup winning jockey on a serious horse.

Willie is at this game longer than me, though, and he thought we had a chance. He knew the work he'd put into Alexander over the previous few weeks and how fit he'd gotten the horse. His one worry was that if we didn't get a good position where he could see what he was doing, he might revert to type and go to sleep.

'Be ready at the start,' he told me in the parade ring. 'Watch out for it. This isn't like the bumpers at home where everybody tries to get a position for the first furlong and then everyone settles down. These are professionals. It will take three, three and a half furlongs for the thing to settle down. Get out handy and into the race. Then see what happens.'

Down to the start and I was clicking at him and jizzing him up as we circled. Letting him know we were here for business and not out for a pick of grass. I bucked him off smart when the tapes went up and let him stride along until I found a position. Then he travelled like an absolute dream. I couldn't believe it. We passed stands and turned up the hill to the left and I was in about fourth place.

Heading down the back was when it kicked in. Before the race, I wasn't considering winning so I wasn't afraid of it. I hadn't taken any time to think about it or to try to understand it. I hadn't wrestled with the meaning of it or even really wondered what it would be like. I went into it with no pressure. While I wasn't the young boy standing on the hill behind the winners' enclosure anymore, I wasn't any sort of big shot either. I still would have imagined that a Cheltenham winner was a far off, distant dream. It definitely had been three minutes earlier, anyway.

But now we were heading down the back and as we started to climb the hill Alexander Banquet was upsides in front and was travelling really well. We had a real, genuine chance of winning the race. We cantered to the top of the hill and when we turned to run down, I started to let him quicken. I knew he'd stay all day and didn't want to be outsprinted. But after we raced through the wings of the second-last hurdle, Conor came up on my outside on Joe Mac and I could see he was going well too. So I decided to ask Alexander for whatever he had left. He had plenty.

It was nip and tuck with Joe Mac as we passed the last hurdle, but as soon as we met the rising ground, Alexander found more. Stuck his head down and galloped all the way to the line. I stuck mine down as well and didn't lift it until we were past the post. These days I would know well if I'm two or three lengths ahead and I'd be able to stand up and enjoy crossing the line but when you're eighteen and you can't believe that this is really happening, you keep your head down and you ride every last inch of the course.

I nearly wouldn't have the words for what I felt just then. Sheer disbelief would be closest to the mark. We turned around and walked back down the chute past the stands and the crowd were so good, so appreciative. They're always a good crowd at Cheltenham, even when they haven't backed a winner, and this was my first taste of what it felt like to tip the cap at them and say thanks.

I got back to the parade ring where I met Mam, Dad, Willie and Jackie and it was all like being in a dream. It nearly didn't feel real. Conor O'Dwyer and Charlie Swan were over congratulating me, James and David too. They knew as well as I did that this was an unlikely winner. I'd ridden Alexander Banquet out all through that winter and to look at him work and look at Florida Pearl work, you couldn't believe one would follow the other in winning at Cheltenham. Chalk and cheese.

I stayed around for the next day and had two more rides – Scoss, who tailed off badly in the Triumph Hurdle, and Commanche Court, who was sixth in the Stayers' Hurdle. I talked to anyone who wanted to talk to me, shook everybody's hand that was for shaking. At one point, I caught a bit of Channel 4's coverage and they put up a graphic on the race for leading jockey at the festival. Right down at the bottom along with Richard Dunwoody, Charlie Swan and Norman Williamson, I saw the name of Mr R. Walsh. I enjoyed that, got a real kick of pride out of seeing it up there.

Racing never lets you lose the run of yourself, though. If I had any notions about getting cocky or thinking I had Cheltenham cracked now, I got my answer slowly, painfully and gradually. It was another four years before I saw my name in that graphic again.

CHAPTER 5

Willie

Willie Mullins has been my boss since I was seventeen but I'm fairly sure I've never actually heard anyone call him boss. Or chief. Possibly Mr Mullins the odd time but definitely not 'guvnor' or anything like that. Willie is, was and always will be Willie. He walks into the yard and it doesn't matter whether you're an owner who's had a dozen horses with him or a fifteen-year-old boy looking for a job, he's Willie.

The older I've got, the more I've come to appreciate the amount of skill and knowledge he has for understanding horses. Willie is a brilliant judge of a horse, purely on observation alone. If an outsider came and watched him for a morning on the gallops across the road from his yard in Closutton, they'd go away none the wiser really as to what makes him so good. They'd just see him standing there in the middle of the circle, with his dog Sybil at his ankles, giving short, quiet instructions to whoever was riding out each particular horse.

Everything is done on his eye alone. Nothing is written down. You ride past him, he asks you how it felt on the first gallop and he tells you what to do or what he can see. That fella is a bit too light so you're not to do any more with him. Or that fella is too fat, so work him a bit harder. He does it all off his eye alone. He's not there with a notepad and pen, just his eye, his brain and his memory.

He's an incredible man. He's also probably the worst time-keeper in Europe. You could be on the gallops waiting for him and one of the lads will text him saying we're ready to go and he'd text back, 'one min.' We'd all be thinking, 'Yeah, right,' knowing well it would be closer to ten by the time he'd be out.

I've lost count of the number of times we'd be going racing in England and he'd ring me, asking if I knew anyone going through Dublin Airport just then who could check him in so that he wouldn't miss a flight. It's at the point now that, if I'm riding one of Willie's horses in the first race on any card and I come out of the weighing room to find him standing there with the owner in the parade ring, I'd nearly be thinking to myself that there must be something up with the horse.

But a good man to learn from. He was a very tactical rider, a good judge of pace and timing. As the years went on he started to trust me more, mostly obviously with Native Darrig and Alexander Banquet at Cheltenham but in other, smaller, more subtle ways too.

I rode a horse for him at Navan one day called The Next Step. Not a bad horse at all, one that eventually won a decent novice hurdle at Punchestown and beat Rooster Booster and Risk Accessor in doing so. But this day in Navan he still hadn't won his maiden and in the parade ring beforehand, Willie told me to drop him in seventh or eighth and see what happened.

When we got down to the start it became clear that there was no pace in the race and none of the other lads were that keen on making it. 'To hell with this,' I thought, and so I bucked him out and made all the running. Charlie Swan came after me on Park

Leader but he hit the second-last pretty hard and my lad galloped on to the line.

Even though we'd won, I wasn't completely sure of what kind of welcome Willie would have for me when we came back in. I'd done the exact opposite of what he'd asked me to do, after all, and I didn't have enough experience of defying him to know for sure how it would go down. But when I got there, he had a big smile on his face. Didn't say a word about the tactics.

I guess that day stands out for me because I knew from then on that I had licence to try things out off my own bat if the situation called for it. I knew he wasn't going to eat the head off me – win, lose or draw. That's not to say he wouldn't give out to me. He'd still do that to this day. The bollockings could range from a quiet 'That wasn't your finest hour …' to a quizzical 'What was that about?' or to a disappointed 'What in God's name were you at?!' Possibly stronger. But now I'm long enough in the tooth that I usually get in ahead of him (or Dad, or Paul Nicholls who I ride for in England now, for that matter). I generally hop off the horse and hold my hands up when I've made a mess of a race.

If a jockey learns no other lesson as he goes along in his career, he has to keep one thing in mind above all others. The trainer knows the horse better than you do. Always and forever. It doesn't matter how much schooling or riding out I do on a horse, or how many races I win on it or lose on it, the trainer knows better than I do. I often have to remind myself of that. Willie never says it but any short amount of time spent in his company will always teach me it again.

But more or less from that day in Navan, our relationship gradually became one where we arrived together on how best to try to win on different horses. He'd ask what I thought I'd like to do and sometimes I'd say that I wanted to be handy and up with the pace. Other times I'd have picked out the best ground on the outside or whatever. He'd then suggest what he thought and we'd come to a plan. If it didn't work out, so be it. There was always next time.

We've shared brilliant days over the years but often it's been his attitude on some of the worst days that has made me admire him even more. You can't train as many horses as he does without losing some from time to time and the way he handles that sort of loss has always been a lesson worth learning.

'It's outside the back door,' he says. It must be an old Irish country saying because it's one I've heard different people use over the years whenever a horse has died. It's a kind of moving on phrase, a 'life goes on' sort of thing. Basically, the thrust of it is that if you have a pet dog that gets hit by a car and dies, you bury it in the back garden and a week later you're over it.

But if, God forbid, it had been a toddler who had got hit by the car, you'd bury the toddler in a grave and you'd spend a lifetime trying to get over it and probably failing. So although every dead horse is a terrible thing, his attitude is that we have to keep in mind that it could be a lot worse. Be thankful that it's outside the back door and not inside.

I came to terms with the delicate life of horses at a pretty young age. I remember we lost a pony when I was about fourteen. Bertie, we called her. I was out riding in the fields with Katie and as I galloped across a wooden bridge the pony slipped and you could hear her hind leg crack. I knew straight away what had happened. And what had to happen. Katie went back to the house to send for the vet and we could do nothing else but wait there with this poor little pony, knowing she would have to be put down. Not a day I like remembering very often.

The first time I had to hold a horse as it was being destroyed was on a racecourse when I was working for Noel Meade in the summer of 1994. I went racing to Gowran and David Marnane was riding a horse called Rocket Dancer which had the misfortune to break his two front legs turning into the straight. I'd ridden this horse out a few times at Noel's so I knew him a little bit. I ran down to him and David had the saddle off by the time I got there. I held his head until the vet arrived and destroyed him.

I've been lucky enough as the years have gone by not to lose too many on the racecourse but it wasn't that way at the start. A few months after I had my first bumper ride on Wild Irish at Leopardstown, Dad sent him to Limerick for my first ride over hurdles. We were heading away from the stands when all of a sudden he lost his action completely. I hadn't a clue what was happening – I hadn't heard a crack or anything – but Brendan Sheridan was behind me on a horse called Willies Surprise and he shouted at me to pull up quick. He had broken a hind leg, a sad end for poor Wild Irish.

About a year later I rode another horse of Dad's in the Ingoldsby Chase at Punchestown. It was my first ride over fences. Alligator Joe had always been a good horse for Dad – he'd won an Irish Lincoln on the flat in 1992 at the Curragh and a few chases under Garrett Cotter in 1995. The Ingoldsby was his first run back the following season and since it was an amateur jockeys' handicap, Dad let me ride him. We were going well too, in front coming to the second-last. But he fell and broke his hind leg, just like Wild Irish had done.

I couldn't believe it. First ride over hurdles and first ride over fences and neither horse had made it back to the unsaddling enclosure. It was desperate luck both times. But you take it on the chin and you move on. It's outside the back door.

I know that sounds heartless to some people. I know it sounds cruel. But it's a fact of racing life that, in all the centuries humans have been taking care of horses, nobody has been able to come up with a workable, repeatable, humane way of saving a horse with a broken leg. So the only caring thing to do is to end its life as quickly as possible.

There actually is a way of doing it but the success rate is so tiny and what you put the horse through is such an ordeal that those who've been involved in doing it don't really think it's all that humane. You can put screws or a staple in a horse's leg but you can't put a plate in it. You basically have to drug the horse for six months and suspend it from the roof of a stable. It's a process that's fraught with danger for the horse because any amount of complications and side-effects can occur.

The big problem is that you can't explain to the horse not to put any weight on the broken leg. Say you break your leg – the doctor puts you in a cast, gives you two crutches and tells you not to put any weight on it for six weeks. You know to put your weight on the other leg until it's fixed. The problem with a horse is that when it lies down, it has to use all four legs to get up. It can't carry a leg like you'd carry a leg. That's why you have to suspend them from the roof.

It's a tortuous process and there's no guarantee of success at the end of it. All the money in the world won't guarantee you any of this will work. Look at Barbaro, the brilliant American horse that won the Kentucky Derby by a mile in 2006. His owners were multi-millionaires, the horse himself won over $2millon in prize money and they spent nearly nine months trying every operation under the sun to try to fix his hind leg. In the end, they had to admit defeat.

It's a desperately sad thing to see a horse being killed on a racecourse. It's sad for the jockey but it's worse for the stable staff.

I'd only been in Noel Meade's a couple of weeks when Rocket Dancer was destroyed but it was still traumatic. Imagine what it's like for the stable lad who's had a longer relationship with a horse, someone who's looked after him every day for a couple of years.

You have to understand the mentality of someone working in a yard. Nobody's in it for the money – they'd be much better off working in a factory if they were. It's a labour of love. If it hadn't worked out for me as a jockey, I know well that I'd have ended up working with horses in some capacity and I'd have surely been in that position at some stage.

You work with horses because you love them and you love that life. You come to have favourites in any yard, horses you treat like pets. You feed them, muck them out, ride them out, keep them stocked up with water, brush them over, everything. You'll spend long stretches alone with horses, even find yourself talking to them half the time. Then you send them off to the races and just hope that they come back.

When they don't, it's very sad. These days, if a horse I'm riding takes a fall and is in obvious trouble, I'll look up and down the track to see if I can spot his groom running towards us. They always do. If I can at all, I'll cut them off and try to stop them getting behind the screen to see the vet do his work. There's no point leaving them with that image in their head. Let them remember their horse on the good days.

You never get used to seeing a horse destroyed. You just don't. It's possible to do it by lethal injection but that can take longer and it can be quite messy on occasion. In saying that, I've never agreed with using a humane killer if it's close to the stands or the public enclosures. I'm a firm believer that if a horse has to be put down anywhere near the public, it should be done by lethal injection. Racegoers don't need to hear a shot ring out just yards from them. The screens going up bring enough attention to the whole sorry scene.

But in general racing people have the same attitude to it. If you have livestock, you have to be prepared for having no stock. A dead horse is a terrible thing but it's not the worst thing in racing. It's not worse than a jockey dying after a fall or a stable lad getting killed riding out. No way.

I was champion amateur for a second time at the end of the 1997–1998 season, again relying on Willie to provide a lot of the ammunition. I rode forty-four winners overall, seventeen of them for Willie and six for Dad who was coming into a beano period with the horses in the yard at home. Bumpers were still my bread and butter but Willie was giving me chances in hurdle races too and I won a couple of decent hurdles on a horse called Welsh Grit in the summer at Galway and Tralee.

Sometimes, the whole thing just felt like one great big adventure. One day in early December, I rang Arthur Moore about a ride on a horse he had entered in an amateur chase in Clonmel that week. He said he was sorted already for it but asked would I have an interest in doing ten stone that Saturday in the William Hill Hurdle at Sandown Park, on a horse called Major Jamie. Now, he was mostly asking about the ten stone but all I heard was Sandown and Saturday. This was the big handicap hurdle of the day in England, with £35,000 to the winner, and I was being offered a ride in it – yes, sir, I most certainly would be up for it, thank you very much.

Once it sank in that I had to do ten stone, I started wasting. To the absolute pin of my collar, I was. I got the flight to Heathrow on the Saturday, along with Dad and Conor O'Dwyer who was riding Grimes for Christy Roche in the same race. Landed in

Heathrow and I thought I was going to die with the thirst. My tongue was stuck to the top of my mouth. I bought a bottle of water to tide me over but my stomach was nearly begging for mercy by now.

When we got to Sandown I weighed myself and tipped the scales at nine stone thirteen pounds. I went into the sauna to lose another pound. And it was in there that I met Mattie Batchelor for the first time.

Ask any jockey who rides regularly in England for a character in the weighing room and one of the first names they'll say is Mattie Batchelor. Guaranteed. He's full of one-liners, yarns and stories. I didn't know him at all before that day but I got into the sauna and he was there, rabbiting away, and next thing I knew, an hour had gone by. I was having a great time, not really saying very much but enjoying every minute of Mattie. Russ Geraghty was in there too and he went out and won the Tingle Creek Trophy later that afternoon on Ask Tom.

Anyway, after an hour of this, it struck me that I should probably get out and go about my business. Weighed myself again. Nine stone nine. I'd lost four pounds in an hour. That was crazy, three pounds more than I needed to. I wasn't light-headed or dizzy after I had a cold shower but it was still too much. A real novice's mistake.

But I got away with it. Funnily, one thing I've learned about wasting is that if you're involved at the business end of a race, you won't feel in the least bit weak. You'll ride a horse forever if it has a chance to win. But if your horse hits a few obstacles or starts tailing off, you'll feel a lot more tired and drained. It's all just pure adrenaline.

Major Jamie got involved all right. I popped him off in fifth or sixth place and he travelled like a dream, arriving down to the last just in front of Nahrawali which, by pure coincidence, was Mattie's horse. He jumped a bit to his right over the last hurdle and bumped into Nahrawali but kept on to win by three parts of a length. My first winner in England.

Or so I thought. Just before someone from Channel 4 interviewed me (I can't remember who), they announced a stewards' inquiry. Damn. Into the stewards' room. Gave my side of it. Mattie thought his lad had been impeded, I maintained we'd done nothing to hamper him. The contact was accidental. The stewards came down on my side. A phone call slightly chancing my arm on a Wednesday had led to a 25–1 winner on live television in England on a Saturday. How could you not love a life like that?

On through Christmas then, and the double across the card in Limerick and Leopardstown. And then Cheltenham and Alexander Banquet, all the while keeping the number of winners ticking along. There was hardly a cloud in the sky as far as I was concerned. The amateur title in the bag from a long way out, and it looked like Dad was going to let me ride Papillon in the Irish Grand National on Easter Monday. He was top weight and had finished fourth the year before as a novice with Charlie Swan riding him.

He'd had that bad run-in the Kim Muir at Cheltenham and as a result of that, expectations weren't very high going to Fairyhouse. And even though he pinged the first few fences, expectations went even further out of the window when Druid's Brook fell in front of us at the fourth; we hit him broadside on and almost came to a complete stop. We went from fourth or fifth place back to around nineteenth.

I don't know what it was about Fairyhouse, but Papillon used to absolutely love it around there. Fair play to him, he got back on the bridle straight away and jumped for fun. By the time we'd done a full circuit, he was back up to about sixth and was enjoying himself. Ears pricked, happy out. I was getting excited myself when he jumped to the front at Ballyhack. We got to the sixth – last and Jason Titley arrived on my outside on Eton Gale, trying to up the tempo.

Of all the races down through the years that I would love to take back and have another swing at, this would definitely be well up in the top five. And if I got another go at it, the exact point at which I would do something different would be right here, where Jason came to challenge.

You know how sometimes you watch a boxing match where one of the fighters is looking to turn it into a brawl and you can hear the coach of the other telling him to duck and move and play it smart? I needed someone in my ear right at that moment, telling me to relax and leave Eton Gale off. But I didn't have the experience to do that and when Jason upped the ante, I went with him.

That's the best way I can find to explain what in God's name possessed me to roll on a bit with Papillon six fences – six! – from home in the Irish National. I just didn't have the confidence to let Jason away and ease Papillon back. Instead we got involved in a race. And Papillon won that race by the time we got to the third-last, where Eton Gale was a beaten horse. But sadly that wasn't the race I needed to win.

In my head I had it won at that point. I genuinely remember thinking, 'I'm going to win the Irish National.' All I thought we had to do was stay upright. We shortened into the second-last and popped over it. And it was only when we got to the other side that I saw Paul Carberry land beside me on Bobbyjo.

To me, they'd come from nowhere. Now we really did have a race on our hands. But Paul was coming with all the momentum on his lad and although mine was battling his heart out, the effort he'd put in racing with Eton Gale told in the end. Bobbyjo won by half a length.

I was as disgusted with myself that day as I've ever been. I think we should have won the Irish National and it was totally my fault that we didn't. The horse ran a cracker, the jockey had had better days. Dad was delighted with the run, as it happened, but I was nearly in tears. He didn't give out to me or say one cross word but I felt that if I'd only sat off Eton Gale, let him take me down to the second-last and passed him then, Bobbyjo wouldn't have beaten us.

When you ride like that, someone like Paul will always be following waiting to pick you off. He'd have only been waiting to do to me what I should have been doing to Jason Titley. Fair play to him, he won it well and went on to take the English Grand National the following year. My day in the sun would have to wait.

Come the end of the season, it was decision time. Stay amateur or turn professional. As with just about everything I've ever done, there were only a few people whose thoughts I wanted to hear: Dad, Willie and Enda Bolger. None of them ever turned professional and Dad has always said he regrets not doing it. Things were different in those days because the bottom weights were lower than they are today and there would have been a dismissive attitude towards someone like him who could do ten stone four at a stretch but hadn't a hope of getting down to nine-seven, ever.

It's not as severe now but I still thought I was maybe going to be a bit heavy to be turning pro. I was tall enough for a jockey (still am) and I was ten-four stripped and could take a few pounds off that if I needed to. But Dad told me not to worry about it, that it wouldn't be any great hardship for me in the long run. He was fairly anxious that I do it in the end. 'Don't get to my age and be annoyed at yourself for not having a go,' he said.

Enda thought I should stay amateur and said the amateur championship was there for me for the next few years if I did. Willie had an army of bumper horses and Enda had plenty of hunter chases that I could ride, and point-to-pointers too.

In the end, it was probably more a question of timing than anything else. For all my worries about my weight, I was probably always going to turn professional at some stage. If it was going to be OK by Willie, then I was going to do it. When I asked him what he thought I should do, he gave me the answer I was hoping for. 'Do it,' he said. 'You'd be mad not to.' So that was that. A comprehensive 2–1 win for the pro camp. I couldn't have argued with the result, even if I'd wanted to.

I got going very quickly as a professional, even though I went into it not really knowing what to expect. After thirty-four winners in my second amateur season and then forty-four in my third, I figured that if I was able to put together, say, forty-five to fifty winners as a pro, that wouldn't be a bad first attempt. David Casey was in Willie's yard as well and at best I thought we were going to be sharing the rides. That meant that to get anywhere near the fifty mark, I was going to have to get a lot of rides from outside trainers, which is where my big sister came in.

Jennifer was working in Racing Services, so she was already a sort of inside line for me when it came to finding rides. I'd ring home from school looking for the declarations, checking if Willie had any bumper horses running the next day and what was available elsewhere if he had nothing for me. She'd just naturally be keeping an eye out for me, would know straight away where the blanks were and would go and sort it out.

From there, I guess it was probably a natural progression that

I should take her on as my agent once I turned professional. My only other option really was Ciaran O'Toole who was the big agent for a lot of jockeys in Ireland – he had David Casey, Paul Carberry and Norman Williamson on his books among others. But I knew straight away that I'd always be the number one call on Jennifer's books and wouldn't have to be elbowing other jockeys out of the way for rides if I were to use her.

Mind you, if I remember rightly, it was she who came to me saying she'd like to do it rather than the other way around. One way or the other, it was one of the best decisions I ever made. A professional jockey is only as busy as the quality of his agent and Jennifer works her socks off for me.

In those early days, it was all about getting rides and she found some real good ones for me. Big yards, small yards – it didn't matter, Jennifer found me winners. As the years passed and I started going to England a lot more, she added travel agent to her portfolio of skills as well as advisor and organiser. She deals with trainers and press so that my mind can be kept clear. When it really comes to the crunch and there's an awkward phone call to be made, we discuss between us who'll make it. Sometimes I'll do it, more often than not Jennifer will.

She was crucial in those early days. I got loads of rides and started working away, getting a winner or two most weeks. As in my amateur days, my first winners were for Dad. At the start of June I rode Datem to win a maiden hurdle in Tramore and then the first winner over fences was a fortnight later when a horse called Mcilhatton won a Beginners' Chase in Kilbeggan.

I was riding against the big boys now. Dunwoody, Charlie, Norman, Conor, David. And Paul Carberry, who was back home after a stint in England. In every race I was coming up against fellas who'd been at this a while, who knew all the tricks. While

I was holding my own, I was still conscious of looking like an amateur.

I knew people were saying that Ted's son had no jumping experience and that it was a bit of a gamble to put me on some of their better horses. I was still only nineteen that year, still very raw. Developing a riding style took a while, for instance. At the start, when you're an amateur, you're trying everything in the hope that something will work. I did loads of things when I was sixteen and seventeen that I wouldn't now, purely because now I know the game better. But back then, I had somewhere between half a notion and none.

I would often use other jockeys as a guide to get me into a race. My whole philosophy would have been based on picking someone who I knew would have an idea of the right pace and just following them. I'd never tell them what I was doing, although they probably knew anyway.

In those bumpers when I started out, I'd obviously pick Willie if he was in the race and follow him. If anyone knew what he was doing, I could be fairly sure Willie did. I'd watch him and see that he was taking his time, picking his spots here and there. I'd use him to drag me along to about half a mile from the finish and then make my decision on what to do. It wasn't very scientific – and it went wrong plenty of times – but it was the best I could think of at the time.

As the years passed, I got more confident. I started picking my own routes, deciding my own tactics, refining my own style in the saddle. I'd ride a fraction shorter, try my best not to look so agricultural. It didn't always work.

I'd watch videos of myself and be embarrassed at how ungainly and awkward I looked. Siren Song is a perfect example. After the euphoria of riding my first winner had passed and I took time to actually look at a replay of that bumper in Gowran, I was appalled. I remember being really disappointed and thinking to myself, 'Jesus, I don't even look like a jockey.'

I know now that I was being hard on myself. When you're so intent on riding a winner and you haven't won a race before, it's natural that style goes out the window. But when I watched that replay, I was thinking to myself, 'Surely now I'll change my hands. Go on Ruby, change your hands. Change your hands, for the love of God!' I did eventually. I should have done it about ten to fifteen strides earlier but I got there in the end.

I looked like Benny Hill on a horse in those early days. I find it hard to watch replays now. They're nearly like childhood photos that your granny would take out to embarrass you. I was getting it right sometimes when it came to placing horses in the right place at the right time to run as well as they could and I was always able to hold a horse so that it knew I was in charge. But when I look at the style now, I just cringe.

The worst of it was that, in my head, I wanted to be Dunwoody. That's who Dad always said I should copy because I was more or less the same height as him. Even from the time I was riding ponies, he'd be on to me. 'Sit like Dunwoody. Fold over. Sit quiet, sit quiet, sit quiet.' He was my hero as a jockey from very early on. In my eyes, he was just the best there was. I wanted to do everything he did on a horse and I wanted all the success it brought him.

But the older I got, the more I appreciated the different things a jockey needed. I came to realise that Charlie was better tactically than Dunwoody, even though he didn't look as neat in the saddle. But then, Charlie was better tactically than everyone. He was ahead of every jockey he ever rode against. Maybe there were stronger jockeys over a jump and maybe there were jockeys who looked more stylish but nobody was better than Charlie for winning a race when he had no right to.

Charlie made very few mistakes. He won races with his head. He rode an enormous amount of winners in Ireland when there wasn't that much racing here and the reason was that he was outstanding mentally. He had that edge on everyone else because he just knew instinctively what to do.

That was the one major thing that came as a revelation to me as I gradually went from a promising amateur rider to a fully-fledged professional jockey. I realised that race-riding is a lot more to do with your head than with your body. Starting out, your only experience is what you see on the television or at the races. The rides that stand out to the naked eye are naturally the exciting ones, races where a jockey keeps working on a horse and gets it up on the line to win and everybody turns around and says fair play to him.

But most of race-riding is actually in your head. It's a series of mental tasks rather than one huge physical one and brains will beat brawn every time if you use them the right way. Your physical strength might only win you one race in 100, if even that. It's in your head that you can have the greatest effect as a jockey. Until I saw up close how Charlie Swan won so many races, I didn't really know this.

It's not so much the ability to control a horse mentally either. It's more the ability to keep the horse relaxed for as long as possible, to save as much energy as it possibly can, leaving it free then to exert all the energy it has left at the right time. But you are the one who has to make the judgement as to when the time is right to do that. That's what the job is. It's about thinking it out.

Once in 100 races you will be able to haul a lesser horse to win a race through brute force rather than judgement and skill. And that one time will be because someone else in the race has made a mistake. They went too soon or their horse found less off the bridle than they thought it would. Or they left it too late and the line came a half a length too soon for them. All the while, you were rowing away on your lad and he found that little bit more for you and you won. Afterwards, everybody will say you did some job to get him over the line in front. But you didn't really. The jockey on the better horse handed you the race.

This was all stuff it took me a while to learn but I was having a magic time learning it. I had a brilliant summer and by the time the season got going in earnest that winter, I was actually nine winners clear of Paul Carberry in the jockeys' championship. Jennifer was getting me plenty of outside rides to take advantage of – winners from small yards count the same at the end of the season as the ones from the big ones. I rode a double in Clonmel at the start of September on horses for Paul Lenihan and David Hanley and another in October in Down Royal for Tom Taaffe and Frances Crowley. Both Dad and Willie had horses that were flying too.

The biggest feather in my cap came in November when I rode two Grade One winners back-to-back in one afternoon at Fairyhouse. Alexander Banquet had come back fit and healthy from his summer break and Willie had sent him hurdling with big things expected, as there always is with any Irish Cheltenham bumper winner. He won his first two – with me on his back at Fairyhouse and then with David in the saddle at Punchestown a fortnight later – although he was still as lazy as ever and he idled once he got to the front.

Willie put me back on him for the Royal Bond at Fairyhouse and I knew well that his best chance of winning would be to make sure I wasn't on my own for too long in front. Going to the last, Paul was a length or two clear on a good horse of Noel Meade's called Cardinal Hill. But if we knew one thing about Alexander Banquet, it was that he was tough out and battled all the way from the last to the line to win by a head.

The next race was the Drinmore and I rode Promalee for Frances Crowley, a horse I'd only ridden once before in a novice chase in Naas about three weeks earlier. It was a very open race but just about every Irish jockey who was anybody was riding in it. Dunwoody was on Inis Cara for Michael Hourigan, Paul Carberry was on the favourite Feathered Leader for Arthur Moore, Tony McCoy rode Foxchapel King for Mouse Morris, Norman was on another of Frances Crowley's called Moscow Express.

I was already on a high after winning the Royal Bond and then I went out and got a great ride from Promalee. He travelled beautifully, took it up two out, jumped the last in front and won well in the end by three or four lengths.

That was a huge day. First of all, to be trusted with horses that had serious chances in the first really big Grade Ones of the season was a massive vote of confidence. Then to get the tactics right on both horses and win for Willie and Frances after they'd given me the chance meant that they had all the more reason to keep their faith in me as the season went by. I'd started in June hoping for between forty-five and fifty winners for the year – Promalee was my forty-ninth and we were only at the end of November.

These were two high-profile races live on RTE on a big racing Sunday. It meant that getting on a better class of horse was going to come that little bit easier now and that was going to help with the race for the jockeys' championship. When I won on Colonel

Yaeger in Cork the following Saturday, I started December with fifty winners, only a couple ahead of Paul who was having a brilliant season himself. But I had a treble in Navan the Saturday before Christmas that put me four clear.

Once the New Year came there was the usual Irish cold snap, causing us to lose a few days' racing, so to keep me occupied, Dad suggested that I go to Ditcheat in Somerset to do some schooling for Paul Nicholls, the word Ditcheat would have meant more to me than the name Paul Nicholls. Dad had always been friendly with the landlord there, Paul Barber – whether it was through buying horses for him or recommending ones he should take a look at – and we'd been over there on holidays a few times when we were kids.

It was Dad's idea to go, just for something to do, really. Dad's thinking would always have been that a new experience like that couldn't do any harm. I wasn't going over touting for a job or anything like that but it would have been in Dad's head that something might come out of it eventually. It would be a good connection to make at least.

The first time I met Paul was at Leopardstown a couple of years before. I was walking the track ahead of riding a horse of Dad's called No Mistake in a hunter chase and he was doing the same before he ran Belmont King in the Hennessy Cognac Gold Cup and See More Business in the big novice chase. I knew of him but I didn't know him. In fact, I was probably delighted to see Dorans Pride beat Seemore that day, happy to see an Irish horse beating an English one.

Anyway, I went over to Paul's and stayed for two days at the start of February. I rode out a few in the morning for him and schooled one of his called Earthmover, which I ended up riding at Cheltenham a few weeks later. But as far as I was concerned, it was what it was and no more. A few days' work, a contact made in England and home again. It wasn't the beginning of any master plan. If you'd tried to tell me on the plane back to Dublin where it would all end up, I'd have had some laugh at you.

You'd have got the same response if you'd waited those few weeks and told me after that year's Cheltenham. Talk about a reversal of fortune from the previous year. Seven rides, of which Earthmover was just one of a string of horses that never performed. I rode him in the William Hill Chase and had to pull him up before the last after he jumped badly the whole way around. It was symptomatic of the week – Wither Or Which, Alexander Banquet and Papillon all ran below their best.

So I had no winner and what made it worse was that I ruined the chances of the only one that came within an ass's roar of winning. Balla Sola was an ex-flat horse of Willie's that I'd won on in Thurles that February in his only run over hurdles. He hadn't beaten very much that day but he'd won by a mile and I couldn't believe the speed of him between obstacles. Willie sent him straight to the Triumph Hurdle without another run.

Coming down the hill at Cheltenham, I couldn't get over how well he was travelling underneath me. He really pinged the second-last and was full of running, so I decided to set sail off the bend. Of course, as I know well now, the bend on the new track at Cheltenham is a hell of a long way from the last hurdle and by the time I got there, Balla Sola was starting to tire and Mick Fitzgerald was only getting going on Katarino. I was flat to the boards and he wasn't moving a muscle. That's when you know for sure you're in trouble.

Katarino won by eight lengths in the end, as an 11–4 favourite is probably entitled to when it's 8–1 the rest of the field. But that didn't change the fact that I'd gone an hour too soon on Balla Sola and never gave him a chance to getting a stiff two miles. Looking back, we probably wouldn't have won but we should have been a very good second. It was an ordinary ride.

But you get over these things and you move on. Heading to Punchestown, I more or less had the jockeys' title sewn up. I was lucky enough then to be offered the ride on Imperial Call in the Heineken Gold Cup. It was three years since he'd won his Cheltenham Gold Cup but it was still some opportunity and after I rode him work the Friday beforehand, I thought he had a huge chance. Dunwoody was on Florida Pearl, McCoy on Dorans Pride and Richard Johnson was over to ride Escartefigue for David Nicholson. All good horses, but I knew that on his best form Imperial Call would have a great chance.

He loved it that day in Punchestown. It was one of those days when you know a horse is just loving every minute. He bucked out, made all the running, jumped from fence to fence and bounced off the good ground. I couldn't believe the feel I was getting off a horse that was supposed to be past it.

He landed quickened up to the fourth-last, pinged it, did the same at the third-last and second-last as well. In those days the second-last at Punchestown was on the bend so once we jumped it and set sail for home, I took a look over my shoulder. Basically, I was looking for McCoy and Dunwoody to see where they were. I nearly had to look twice. I was about twelve lengths in front of Florida Pearl and I couldn't see Dorans Pride at all.

'This race is over,' I thought to myself. 'Just don't fall whatever the hell you do.' So I eased him up on the run down to the last and sat quiet on him, expecting him to go short and just pop it. I nearly had a heart attack when he went long and I was left there with as loose a hold on the reins as you could get. For all that I'd worried earlier in the season about trying to look professional in the saddle, this was about as amateur as I'd looked all year. But the horse was fine, not a bother on him and we hacked up.

That was the biggest win I'd had up to that point. On top of it, I ended up being leading rider at Punchestown. I didn't even know I'd done it either, because I'd only ridden two winners all week and thought surely to God somebody would beat that. But in the last race for professionals on the Friday, I rode a mare of David Keily's called Triptodiks in a handicap hurdle and finished second on her. We were walking back in when Dunwoody came trotting up beside me on The Barge after finishing down the field.

'Where did you finish?' he said.

'Second,' I said.

'Fuck it!' he said and he rode off. I didn't know what was up with him at all until somebody explained to me back in the weighing room that the second place had counted towards leading rider and meant that I'd just beaten him on placings. I had no idea. Delighted!

I was on top of the world. Leading rider at Punchestown and then, a couple of weeks later, champion jockey at my first attempt with ninety-six winners. I couldn't believe it. I really couldn't. What I couldn't believe above all was that it had actually been so easy. This game was a piece of cake as far as I was concerned. I'd worked hard but I'd never considered it work. Nothing to it.

It's funny to look back on yourself as a twenty-year-old. It's not that I was stupid or ignorant or blasé about things. I just didn't have the experience I do now. I still don't consider what I do for a living to be work. A job? Yes. Work? No way.

But otherwise, my attitude to racing has completely changed. It's not a piece of cake by any stretch of the imagination. It's not easy. It's a cold, hard game that can be very cruel and very hard to deal with. The difference between that twenty-year-old and me is that he had never been injured.

That was about to change.

CHAPTER 6

Agony to ecstasy

Pardubice is a nice little town about seventy miles east of Prague in the Czech countryside. It's all old buildings and narrow cobbled streets, the kind of place you see in spy films or advertisements for Eastern European beer. It's also the home of the Velka Pardubicka, otherwise known as the Czech Grand National, a famous old race that's been going since the 1870s. The race is over four miles and two furlongs on the second Sunday in October every year on a course that crosses banks, ditches and fences and generally provides everyone who rides in it with a bit of a thrill.

I'd ridden in it in 1998 on a horse of Mark Pitman's called Superior Finish. It wasn't what you'd call a success. Richard Dunwoody was riding Risk Of Thunder for Enda Bolger, so much as in my early days as an amateur, I decided to follow one of the only two jockeys in the race that I knew. Paul Carberry was in it too but he was dropping out, so I followed Richard.

The sixth fence at Pardubice is like the Canal Turn at Aintree only in the opposite direction – instead of going ninety degrees to the left, the field turns ninety degrees to the right. Risk Of Thunder was in the lead and myself and Superior Finish were lobbing along behind him, so when Dunwoody cut down the angle of the fence I followed in his wake.

Risk Of Thunder jumped it beautifully. Superior Finish didn't. Instead, he refused and ran down the fence, colliding with a Czech horse that was coming on our inside. Risk Of Thunder bounded off in front, myself and the Czech jockey went flying into the fence and Superior Finish set off a chain reaction that must have brought down fifteen or sixteen horses, including Paul's. I scampered in behind a big tree that was at the corner of the fence and watched the carnage unfold. Twenty-six horses started that race and only seven finished.

Sadly, one of those seven wasn't Risk Of Thunder. Dunwoody had been left with a huge lead after the turn and only a few horses had managed to pick their way through the mayhem to follow him. He must have been a fence in front at that stage but then he came to fences nine and ten which were close together with a roadway between them. Risk Of Thunder jumped the first one all right, he took a stride and for some reason decided to turn left. He did it so quickly that Richard was thrown straight out over the fence all on his own.

That's what the Pardubice was, though. A weekend away and a good old-fashioned cross-country race where anything could happen. Charlie Mann won it in 1995 with It's A Snip and I suppose after that people started thinking it might be worth travelling over and giving it a try. There weren't many banks races around for horses of the type that Enda trained so this was as good a place as any to go to find success. But on top of that, it was good fun.

By the following October, I was having another decent season at home. David Casey had gone to England to ride for Oliver Sherwood so I was pretty much first choice for Willie. I knew that once the winter came, that would mean the likes of Alexander Banquet, Micko's Dream, maybe even Florida Pearl since Dunwoody had to retire because of ongoing injury problems. But I was doing OK in the summer without them – I rode Moscow Express to win the Galway Plate for Frances Crowley in July. All was rosy in the garden.

That was until 1 September, when I went to Dundalk to ride a horse of Dad's in a handicap chase called Sir William Wallace. He was no star but I'd won on him in Wexford a couple of months before and he went off as favourite in Dundalk. Anyone backing him didn't get much of a run for their money though because we fell at the first. Worse, I bounced off the firm ground and broke my collarbone.

Believe it or not, that was the first time I'd ever broken a bone of any kind. I'd been knocked out in a fall from my pony as a kid all right but hadn't so much as cracked a finger before this. The doctor said I'd be out for four weeks but I made it back in three to ride Three Rivers for Willie at Listowel. Maybe I was too enthusiastic because I ended up getting a two-day ban for use of the stick on him.

Anyway, the long and short of it was that the ban was going to cover the following Thursday and Saturday, which just happened to be the weekend of the Pardubice. Enda said he was bringing Risk Of Thunder over again and was taking another one called Shannon Fountain with him as well. Shannon Fountain would go as a travel companion but also so Enda could enter him in one of the earlier races. That way, I'd get a feel for the track before the big race. Happy days.

A gang of us decided to make a weekend of it. Gillian and I were going out with each other by now and spending plenty of time together whenever we could. She was in third year in UCD and I was in Carlow but I often went to Dublin to see her during the week and we met up at weekends when she came home as well. A trip away to the Czech Republic was too good an opportunity to pass up.

Two good friends of mine, Mark Madden and Mark Power, came as well, Jennifer too and a friend of hers called Jennifer Mullen. We said we'd fly to Prague via London on the Saturday morning, go to Pardubice, stay Saturday night, go racing on the Sunday and then head back to Prague for a big night out and home on the Monday. We nearly missed the connection in London, having to run the guts of a mile through Heathrow Airport. Turns out we should have walked and let the plane off.

The town of Pardubice was from another age. I hadn't really noticed it the first time around but they were decades behind us – the television in the hotel was an old push-button one that didn't even have a remote control. But since everything was dirt cheap and we were young and innocent and away from home, we didn't care at all.

Sunday came and we went to the track, which was in the middle of an army base. The dressing room was like an old GAA (Gaelic Athletic Association) clubhouse you'd see belonging to some junior team that nobody cared too much about. It was small and dingy; the toilets were half broken. The stables were these barns out the back and as you walked past them to go and stand on the scales (the weighing room was 100 yards away from the dressing room for some reason), you couldn't help but notice the big army presence. There were fellas dotted through the hedges with big machine guns slung over their shoulders. That wasn't something you saw with army lads around the Curragh.

Enda ran Shannon Fountain in the earlier race and my instructions were to go and get a good look around and learn anything

I could about riding the track. But once we set off, he was very keen. I was pulling and dragging out of him to try to get him to settle but he was running away with me the whole time. Thankfully, he was jumping the way all of Enda's horses jump, from fence to fence without a care in the world. So much so that actually by the time we jumped the second-last, we were lying third behind two Czech horses and not in a bad position at all heading for the final turn.

The only problem now was that he was hanging right on to the running rail and I couldn't get him to come away from it. Just as we came to the point in the bend where you turn in sharply, the running rail was open where it should be connected and a loose rail was jutting out. Because there were banks and hedges to jump, I was riding a little longer than I would usually and this meant that the rail was coming right for my shin.

I only had a split second to think by now and couldn't get out of the way so I braced myself. I knew I was going to get a slap of this thing and that it was likely going to hurt a bit. But I thought the worst that would happen was it would send my leg flying backwards and I'd be unseated.

I was wrong. Horribly wrong. The rail cracked my shin dead centre and sent my leg right up the side of the horse before it swung back into the iron under its own momentum. Purely out of instinct, I went to press my foot into the iron to get some purchase and fell clean off that side of the horse. Lying on the ground, I could feel my right foot flapping at the end of my leg. I didn't need to have had much experience in broken bones to know that I was in big trouble.

It's weird, the things that pop into your head. A few years earlier, I had read Peter Scudamore's autobiography. He describes a scene in which he breaks his leg in a fall and the ambulance comes and takes him to hospital. They get him there and he goes through absolute agony as they try to pull his riding boot off his broken leg. This was all I could think of lying on the ground in Pardubice. 'Take the boot off now while I'm still warm because it'll be easier.'

I thought I was being clever, thinking way ahead of the game. Of course, what I didn't consider was that in Scu's time they didn't have zips down the back of their boots and that's why it was such an ordeal to get it off him once he got to the hospital. That sort of logic escaped me just at the moment. I zipped off my boot and took off my ankle pad and waited for the ambulance. I'd say the medical staff took some look at it when they got to me. Why has this mad Irishman gone and taken off his boot?

Anyway, within a few seconds Dad appeared. He'd been standing on the infield watching the race and came running over. I was in agony by the time he got to me.

'Are you all right? Are you all right?'

'No, I'm not. My leg's broken.'

'It couldn't be broken, it's just sore.'

'No, no, it's broken, I know it is.'

'Here, try and stand on it . . .'

I did, but as soon as I put any weight on it I came down like a ton of bricks. The ambulance arrived and put me on a stretcher. And when I say ambulance, I mean one of those little old Volkswagen camper vans. It almost wasn't long enough to fit the stretcher. On the way to the hospital I was wondering what sort of place I'd end up in but I needn't have worried – it was the one modern facility in the whole place. They even had a television on up in the corner showing the big race. Ken Whelan got the ride on Risk Of Thunder and finished second after Dermot Cox allowed him to get off Dennistown Thriller.

They were brilliant in the hospital. They x-rayed it and put on a back slab cast and gave me a couple of the old style wooden crutches to use. Luckily for me, J.P. McManus was in Pardubice to see Risk Of Thunder run. Sean Connery owned the horse but J.P. had some sort of involvement too and he owned Shannon Fountain as well. He offered to fly me back to Shannon in his jet. Dad and Jennifer jumped in as well.

(A quick story: The others came home on the horse plane that night. Along with our own crew were David Cox and Sarah Hogan, Enda Bolger's first wife who was always very good to me. Now, a horse plane is basically a normal plane with everything taken out to make room for the horses. They leave a few seats but very little else. As a result, the flight is not the smoothest or most comfortable in the world. Gillian showed me her diary and she describes coming home that night as one of the scariest trips of her life. Mind you, it can't have been that bad – she was sitting in the cockpit drinking champagne with Jennifer Mullen most of the way, the two girls trying to calm their nerves. Meanwhile, I was lying on the couch in the back of J.P.'s jet.

However rickety it might have been, their trip had a happy ending. Mark Power and Jennifer Mullen had never met before that weekend but they must have bonded over the trauma of coming home on the horse plane. Whatever happened, they ended up getting married. So did Gillian and I. Although I still owe her a night out in Prague.)

Mam was waiting to collect us at Shannon airport when we landed and next morning we went to Cappagh in north Dublin to see Mr Bill Quinlan, the orthopaedic surgeon. I'd first met Bill a few weeks earlier when I'd broken my collarbone and while he'd been a great help, I had hoped not to see him again for a good while. He's a sound man and a great surgeon but if a jockey is getting friendly with an orthopaedic surgeon, it's usually not a good sign. Sadly, we're great friends these days. He knows just about every bone in my body all too well.

Bill has always been the same since the first time I met him. He has these massive hands that he comes at you with and the first time he does it, you're kind of bracing yourself. But all he does is he feels around the bone, checks the x-ray, tells you what's wrong and puts your mind at ease. 'That's grand, come back in three weeks and we'll take another look,' he says, regardless almost of what the injury is.

He's gone above and beyond the call of duty for me so many times. Basically, if I'm looking for him, it's not to make an appointment for Tuesday week at a time that's suitable. It's because there's a bone pointing the wrong way and I'm more than likely already in the car, en route to his surgery. He fits me in between appointments and out of office hours and nothing is too much hassle for him.

The morning after we got back from Pardubice, he saw me straight away and was delighted with the job they'd done in the Czech Republic. There was great interest throughout the hospital in Cappagh in the x-rays and the treatment I had received because, if I remember right, the doctors in Pardubice had all served their time as young doctors in Cappagh. Bill told me not to worry, that it was going to be fine, that I would be able to come back as good as new if I gave it time. He put me in a cast from my toes to my hip and told me to come back to see him in three weeks. And when I did that, he did the same again. After six weeks, he cut the cast down to below my knee.

For all that time, my mother was my ambulance driver. And Jennifer went from agent to chauffeur for a while as well. I doubt I was much company. It was my first real taste of disappointment, the first time I had to sit and do nothing only feel sorry for myself and think of how badly done-by I was. Barry Geraghty and Jason Titley were riding most of Willie's horses for him now and I'd be sitting on the couch with plaster up the whole length of my leg, watching them win races that I should have been winning, sulking at the cruelty of life.

To be fair, Willie was brilliant with me through it all. He probably rang me once a week to see how I was getting on and we'd talk about how the horses were running. Gillian was great too. She was studying agricultural science in UCD and I got great enjoyment out of heading to Dublin to hang out with her. I lived the life of a student for a while – sat in on lectures, forged my way into the sports bar, all that carry on. I even bought a pair of combats to wear (although I wouldn't wear them now if you paid me). I remember thinking that this wouldn't have been such a bad life after all. Then again, I was only there for a visit.

Funnily, I didn't put on any weight even though all I was doing was sitting around all day. The routine I'd gotten into three years before, after Mam and I met Mary McCreery in the Blackrock Clinic, had obviously settled my weight at a certain point. I didn't feel any temptation to graze away for the day out of boredom.

To this day, I don't get hungry unless I'm active. If I'm just sitting around the house, I could go the whole day on a couple of cups of coffee. Sometimes, I'll have dinner in the evening just for the sake of it rather than because I feel like having a meal. It's odd, I know, but any time I've been injured over the years, I've always lost weight to begin with. If I've put any on, the most would have been seven pounds.

I got the cast off in the run-up to Christmas and Bill told me that the leg was structurally fine but that I was effectively lame. 'You can work on it and build it back up,' he said. 'But I can't guarantee it won't break again if you try to rush it.' Now, it was sore and I still had to walk with a crutch for a while over Christmas but this was the news I wanted to hear.

I was mad to get back riding. Couldn't wait. I was pushing the whole time because there were such good horses out there for me. Florida Pearl had won the big James Nicholson race in the north with Paul Carberry riding him and Christmas was coming with big chances on offer all over the place.

But eventually I had to admit defeat. I was standing in the parade ring in Leopardstown with my crutch in my hand when Dad's horse Rince Ri beat Florida Pearl by a neck in the Ericsson on 28 December. Conor O'Dwyer rode Rince Ri, Carberry rode Florida Pearl. I was delighted for Dad but I knew that one way or another I'd missed out on the big Christmas prize. Also, any shot I had at retaining the jockeys' championship was gone at this stage.

I couldn't help myself. I had to get back riding. Even just schooling and riding out, just to get a feel for it again. The Pardubice had been on 10 October and by now we were getting into January. Three whole months down the drain. I had never spent that long out of the saddle.

So I persuaded Dad to start letting me ride out again. I was probably saying that my leg felt a bit better than it actually did because it was still pretty sore. After a few days, we went to the Curragh and he let me school Shiny Bay, who was pretty much as safe a horse as you could get. We were to jump eight hurdles but Shiny Bay stepped right on top of the fifth and turned a cartwheel, firing me into the ground.

I stood up and felt the leg buckle a little bit under me. It didn't go, but it hurt as bad as it had at any stage since Pardubice. A real shooting, stabbing pain. I got back on Shiny Bay and tried to carry on but I couldn't really ride and definitely couldn't jump a hurdle on him so I trotted back to the horsebox in agony.

I got into the car and drove the dozen or so miles to Kill. My head was spinning. I was after spending three months doing nothing and we were about eight or nine weeks away from Cheltenham. This couldn't be happening. I didn't deserve this! The only thing to distract me from the unfairness of it all was the pain I got any time I moved my right foot. That meant I needed somebody to drive me to Dublin. Jennifer was in the house when I got there and she got the job.

I met Bill in Blackrock a few hours later. It turned out I had reopened the fracture slightly. It was a small enough thing, but I was going to have to go through the whole rigmarole again. Bill put on a cast – only up to the knee this time, which was something at least – and told me it would be six weeks before I'd be fit to go again.

All I wanted to do was cry. This was a disaster. To be within touching distance of coming back and then go back to square one right in the middle of the season was the worst thing I could have imagined happening. I had moved back home with the leg before Christmas and had actually used the time off to buy my first house in Carlow. It would be something to look forward to when I was back on my feet. But I couldn't move into it yet because I was stuck to the couch again.

I'm pretty sure I did cry at times. I was starting to realise very quickly just what a precarious life a jockey leads. Champion amateur, champion jockey – none of it matters if you can't get from the living room to the kitchen without crutches. And no matter how much Willie or Dad did or said to assure me that I'd be right as rain soon enough, I didn't know that for certain. I didn't know how well I'd heal or how strong I'd be.

I didn't know either if I'd be able to slot right back in with the horses I'd been on before. Maybe their owners would be happy with the lads who'd been on them in my absence. Maybe they'd think that I was delicate or something if I couldn't come back from a broken leg within a couple of months. Maybe people would forget about me altogether. It all sounds very dramatic but these are the things that go through your head when you have nothing to do all day only think about what you're missing out on.

In the end, the second time around wasn't so bad. It was only about five weeks before I was out of the cast and those weeks had given the bone time to heal properly. So when I went back to ride work, it was good and strong underneath me. I eventually got back racing at the start of March in Tramore. The first one back was one of Dad's called Make My Day in a two-mile maiden hurdle. Finished third. Needed further.

I'd missed so much in the five months. It's not just that you miss the winners, although obviously that's a big deal. But you miss the day-to-day knowledge you pick up just by riding in races. You miss the little nuances of each horse, both the ones you ride and the ones you ride against. It means that you're playing catch-up all the way when you come back, that you're at a disadvantage to all the other jockeys as soon as the tapes go up. Physically you're fine but form wise you're on the back foot. I have learned over the years to be more aware when I'm injured, to watch more racing and keep myself in the loop.

The one advantage you do have is that nobody is as hungry as you are. I was mad for action in those weeks. It was like I was starting from scratch again. I'd ride anywhere for anyone. Bit by bit I got my sharpness back and the Saturday before Cheltenham I rode a double in Navan – the first for Dad on Gabby Hayes, the second for Willie on The Next Step.

I went on to Cheltenham but I had no winners, which was predictable enough. There was no point going there hoping for miracles. The ground that year was good to firm and that was always going to be a bit too quick for most of my horses. Alexander Banquet was my best chance all week in the Royal and Sun Alliance Chase on the Wednesday, but he jumped a bit high over a few of his fences and gave away ground. If there'd been a bit of an ease in it, he might have done the business but as it was, Jim Culloty pulled away from us going up the hill on Lord Noelle and we finished second.

Commanche Court had been brought down three out in the Arkle but he was a beaten horse by then, ditto Rince Ri who made a bad mistake at the same point in the Gold Cup and sent me to the floor. I wasn't overly upset by the lack of success. Mostly, I was just happy to be back.

Plus, I had something to look forward to now. The Sunday before Cheltenham, I went to Leopardstown and rode a winner each for Dad and Willie. But in between times, I finished third on a horse of Dad's in a two miles four furlong handicap hurdle. It was his best run of the season by a mile and he definitely seemed to be enjoying the quicker ground. Dad came away delighted and said he'd have to talk to the owner to see what to do next. The owner was Mrs Betty Moran. The horse was Papillon. And what he did next changed my life.

Mrs Moran is a family friend from America, going back years, back as far as when my grandfather was training and she had horses with him. These days, she and Mam are holiday buddies, regularly heading off on trips all over the place together.

She always had one or two with Dad, including Wild Irish, and when he was killed in Limerick after breaking his hind leg the horse she bought to replace him was Papillon. It was pure coincidence obviously, but Papillon grew up from there to be my first ride in the Grand National five years later. The world turns in funny ways, I suppose.

Actually, for a long time Mrs Moran wasn't that keen on running Papillon in the English National. There's hardly a National Hunt owner alive who doesn't love the idea of having a horse in the National but they're naturally very protective of them too. After Papillon had finished second to Bobbyjo in the Irish National in 1998, Dad mentioned sending him to Aintree the following year but Mrs Moran didn't really like the idea. Too big a risk, she reckoned.

But once Bobbyjo went and won it then, I think Dad decided to himself that he'd work on trying to convince her for 2000. And when Papillon responded so well to the quicker ground the day he finished third in Leopardstown just before Cheltenham – beating Bobbyjo in the process, as it happened – Dad only had one intention.

As soon as Mrs Moran agreed, I allowed myself to get excited about it. Through all the broken bones and all the frustration of the winter, the hope of a ride in the National had been one of the things that kept me going. We'd always known that not only had Papillon ability but the trip would be no problem to him and he'd love jumping the fences. The more we thought about it, the more we fancied our chances of a decent run at least.

All the same, I wasn't going over to Liverpool thinking about winning. Only an eejit would head into any Grand National thinking like that, never mind your first one. So much can happen, not just in the race itself but in the lead-up. Believe me – I know. This is coming from a man who broke his arm an hour before he was due to ride the favourite in the race just this past year. But even back then, I knew there was no point counting chickens. We were going there with a shout but that was about as bullish as I could get. I was more thrilled with the idea of actually having a ride in the race at all.

You have to remember that Irish jockeys really didn't get that many spare opportunities to ride in the National back then. Bobbyjo had been the first Irish winner of the race since the 1970s. It wasn't anything like the Irish beano it became in his aftermath, so there weren't hordes of Irish horses going there every year to take part. And although Aintree was a good festival with quality races and good prizes on offer, the fact that Irish horses had had such a bad record in the place for so long meant that fewer and fewer of them went over each year.

So basically, unless you were attached to an English yard, it was nearly unheard of for Irish jockeys to get a ride. There was no hope at all of getting a phone call out of the blue in the run-up to go over and ride an English horse. When the Carberrys won the previous year with Bobbyjo, I was watching on television along with most of the other Irish jockeys in the weighing room in Wexford.

I had been to Aintree a few times already – I was nine when got my first look at the place. Myself, Ted, Dad and Brendan Brady went over in 1989, the year Little Polveir won. I was there three years later as well when Dad ran Roc De Prince and Charlie Swan rode him but finished well down the field. I'd even been as a jockey in 1998 (when Earth Summit beat Suny Bay) when I rode in the bumper for Jonjo O'Neill and in the Foxhunters' for Edward O'Grady. But to be going with a ride in the National was something else altogether.

Dad was brilliant with me all week in the build-up. I had moved into the new house in Carlow by then, but on the Monday before the race I came up home to Kill for the evening and myself and

115

himself sat down in the living room and watched the last nine Grand Nationals on video together. He wasn't instructing me or dictating what I should do, just sitting there watching with me and asking what I thought. All he could do was get Papillon ready and once the race started it would be up to me. He knew that if I worked out for myself the best way to ride the race, so much the better.

So I kept an eye on the winner from the start each time to see where they went, to try and pick out a pattern. It seemed to me that they were nearly always prominent over the first few fences and then never really out of the first dozen once it all settled down. They'd positioned themselves mostly right in the middle, if anything more inside middle than outside middle, apart from when it had come up soft and they'd gone wide to find the good ground. We were fairly certain Aintree was going to have nice, good ground that Saturday so that's what we settled on – get a good start, a clear run to the first, somewhere between the middle of the track and the inside rail.

Racing is racing, though. And the Grand National is the Grand National. We both knew that it was pretty unlikely that I would get the run of the race like that. You can make a plan for getting to the first fence at Aintree but there's every chance that plan will be null and void within a few seconds of the tapes going up. There are forty horses and forty jockeys and one starter and everyone has their own agenda. There was no point assuming that Papillon and I were going to get our way just like that.

So we decided that if I couldn't pop him out towards the middle-inner, I'd sit wherever he travelled best, see how he took to it, settle him in and ride the race after that. And if Dad had one instruction above all, it was to hang on as long as possible before setting sail if I was in front. He always talked about Crisp

Fadalko (right) winning the Melling Chase in 2001, my first ever winner for Paul Nicholls.

Jumping the last on Papillon in 2001 after A.P. McCoy and I had remounted. Although we were a mile back, A.P. still had to beat me home on Blowing Wind!

Commanche Court can't go with Best Mate (4) in the Gold Cup, 2002.

Azertyuiop jumps the last in the Arkle in 2003.

Kevin O'Ryan, Gillian and me at Epsom on Derby Day, 2003.

Riding work at Willie's – me on Florida Pearl and James Nash on Royal Alphabet.

Mam, Dad and me after I won leading rider at Cheltenham in 2004.

Dad congratulates me after winning the 2005 Irish Grand National, beating his horse Jack High into second.

Hedgehunter jumps the last on his way to winning the 2005 Grand National.

Patrick Mullins greets Hedgehunter and me after crossing the line at Aintree.

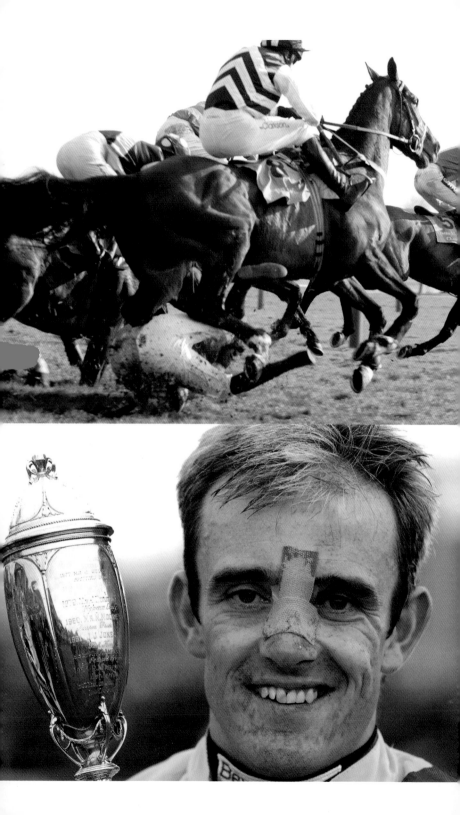

First day back after the crushed vertebrae in 2006. This was ten days before Cheltenham and thankfully I walked away unscathed.

Opposite page

Above Not content with beating me all those times, Moscow Flyer decides to give me one last kicking in the 2006 Champion Chase.

Below After winning my third Kerry National on Bothar Na in 2006. The bandage covers a kick in the face I got riding out that morning.

At Gillian's parents' house on our wedding day, 3 July 2006.

Kauto Star on his way to his first victory in the King George VI Chase at Kempton, 2006.

and Richard Pitman and just the heartbreak of seeing that horse beaten after running his heart out for so long. Whatever happened, I was to hang on. Don't go too soon and empty out after the elbow.

But that was it. That was the full extent of the conversation about the race between us. Between then and Saturday, he and I hardly mentioned it to each other more than a couple of times. By now, there was a bit of a buzz building up around Papillon – I think Dad had told every last man, woman and child in Kill (and probably Kildare) to back him. But we carried on as if we were oblivious to it all. At dinner on the Friday night, we never mentioned the race even once. We talked about anything and everything under the sun but nothing to do with the Grand National.

I have no doubt that was a deliberate move by him. He knew I'd be thinking about the race constantly anyway so he'd have seen his job as trying to keep me calm about it all. I'd been to walk the track and drop my gear into the weighing room on Friday morning and I'd hung around for the day even though I had no ride. Dad wanted it so that when I arrived at Aintree on the Saturday, it was as close to just another day's racing as possible.

It worked too. The day felt completely normal all the way along. I went up to Jennifer and Katie's room that morning to pick them up so we could share a taxi to the racecourse. As I waited for them to get ready, I flicked through the *Racing Post* and had to roll my eyes when I saw we were number 13. 'Well that's that anyway,' I joked with the two girls. 'Sure, we've no chance now.'

We got to the track and I saw that the price had been tumbling all morning after he was tipped up in the *Racing Post* by Pricewise, so much so that it looked like he might even go off as favourite. I just shrugged at the idea. It meant nothing to me, genuinely. All I could think of was that this was the Grand National and that the odds of even getting around were pretty slim. If anyone asked me I always said he was a good bet at 66–1 or 40–1, those kind of odds. But I didn't feel any more or less pressure once he was gambled down to 10–1. It changed nothing.

I was excited, but more by the experience of the day than anything else. I'd already walked the track so there was no need to walk it again. Once I'd had a quick sweat, I threw on the colours and settled in beside Barry Geraghty and Paul Carberry in the weighing room and watched the BBC coverage of the day, just like I would have if I was a teenager sitting at home in Kill. Chilled out. Relaxed.

When the time came, all the jockeys filed out of the old weighing room through all the crowds and the cameras and into the old parade ring. The horses were there by now and when I looked to see if I could pick out Papillon, I cracked into a smile when I saw Katie leading him up. She was wearing this huge sponsor's jacket that was way too big for her – she was only fifteen and a small fifteen at that. All I could see was this Martell Cognac jacket with number 13 on the sleeve taking Papillon around the ring.

I went to find Mrs Moran and Mam and Dad, chatting away amongst themselves as ever. Dad was keeping everything real upbeat, making it all enjoyable. Just another day at the races. Mrs Moran was delighted to be there and herself and Mam were talking about what a great thing it was to be part of, what a brilliant occasion and all that.

Then Dad turned to me, shook my hand and said, 'Now, enjoy yourself. Just ride him like the horseman you are.' Those were the instructions, simple as that. Just ride him like the horseman you are.

I got up on Papillon and walked out on to the track and got in order for the parade past the stands. I was still pretty calm about everything. When we got to the start and all forty horses began to circle, I found myself beside Paul Carberry on Bobbyjo and Jason Titley on Micko's Dream. Not a bad place to be at all, I thought. Both jockeys had already won the race. Bobbyjo knew his way around and Micko's Dream was well-fancied after winning the Thyestes for Willie when I was out with the broken leg. When the starter got us all to stand in a line, I was more or less right where I wanted to be – around six or seven horses from the inside rail.

But everything went out the window as soon as the tapes went up. There was a huge cheer and then it was all a big charge down to the first, a complete frenzy. We jumped off well and got in a nice position. If anything, I got a better start than I wanted because we jumped the first in about third place. Micko's Dream was on my inside and I could see him going at the first.

I couldn't believe how smoothly the start had gone. It had worked out exactly as we'd hoped it would on Monday night. I couldn't have been better placed and Papillon was loving the fences. He had no choice in the matter because they were coming at him so fast.

If anything surprised me about the race, that was it. This is a race that lasts ten minutes but you get no time to look around you or take in the scenery. It's a bit of a trek from the third-last to the second-last and from the water jump to the first on the second circuit but otherwise the fences come to you in a flash. You can't switch off or lose concentration because there's so much happening.

There was no hope of that with Papillon. He never put a foot astray and just travelled and travelled. He sailed out over Becher's, got a bit close to the Chair but jumped it no bother and pinged the water jump. He was enjoying it nearly too much because as we passed the winning post and went out on to the second circuit, I started to think that maybe we were a bit too prominent. We were third or fourth at that stage, just a length or two off the pace that was being set by Mick Fitzgerald on Esprit De Cotte and Dicky Johnson on Star Traveller.

To my mind, this was too close to the front but Papillon didn't care. I was pulling at him and dragging him to try and get him to come back a little but all he saw in front of him were those six fences down the side at the start of the second circuit. And he just took me from fence to fence. Travelling like that, I was beginning to think we had a serious chance by now.

At the Canal Turn, he put in an enormous leap on a real long stride. It was a beautiful jump, a wonderful jump. At nearly any other fence at any other racecourse in any other race in the world, you'd be delighted with a jump like that. But this was the Canal Turn at Aintree with not much more than a mile left to the finish of the Grand National and we needed every yard of ground we could save. We went straight on instead of at an angle and ran a bit wide, losing our position. I remember thinking right at that second that if we lose this now, that's where the mistake was.

But this was our day. As we came down towards the next, we could see that the cones had been put out in front of the inside section of it because there'd been a jockey down on the far side of the fence. What it meant was that the whole field had to move out to the right-hand side of the fence and that nobody could jump it on the inner. All of a sudden, we were in the perfect position. It was as if we'd meant to jump wide at the Canal Turn, like we'd known it was coming. We didn't – it was pure pot luck. So much for being number 13.

We got to the last ditch and we jumped it in the lead, just ahead of David Casey on Enda's horse Lucky Town and Norman

Williamson on Mely Moss. We crossed the Melling Road in front. In front! I started talking to myself, calming myself down. I had to snap out of it quickly enough because I looked up to see four loose horses coming back down the track towards us. They were a fair bit away but I was afraid they'd get in our path before we crossed the Mildmay course on to the National track and headed for the second-last fence. I roared at David: 'What about the loose ones!'

If he answered, I couldn't hear him. There were a couple of loose ones around us anyway so he was probably more worried about them. Anyway Lucky Town faded away as we jumped the second-last, leaving it so that as we came to the last, it was just myself and Norman left.

I remembered Dad telling me to hang on to him. That's all I was saying to myself as we jumped the last. Don't kick. Whatever you do, hang on to him and don't kick too soon. I gave him a couple of flicks of the stick going to the last but it took all the restraint I had not to hit him again until we passed the elbow. But that was the plan and I was sticking to it.

We got to the elbow a couple of lengths clear and all of sudden, he lugged a bit to his right and pricked his ears. Not good! A horse's ears flop forwards and backwards when he's paying attention to the person on his back. If his interest is taken by anything other than the person on his back, he pricks his ears and turns them in that direction. It means he's watching something else. Maybe it's something in the crowd, maybe it's a photographer beyond the rail, it could be anything.

In Papillon's case, it might just have been the whole spectacle that's laid out ahead of you when you come to the elbow at Aintree. You run right into the mouth of a crowd that, as far as the horse is concerned, wasn't there a few seconds ago. Something caught his attention anyway because he pointed his ears in the direction of it and veered a bit to his right. Norman took advantage of the gap on my inside and drove Mely Moss through. 'Oh, no,' I thought. 'Jesus Christ, no.'

The time for hanging on to him was gone. It was now or never. I took the stick into my right hand and got to work on Papillon. And fair play to him, he stuck his head down and started to gallop again. For about 100 yards past the elbow, it was a real ding-dong between myself and Norman but once Papillon got going again, he started to pull out that bit more. I knew that the water jump on the inside track was about fifty yards from the winning post and by the time we passed it, I could feel Papillon putting a length between us and Mely Moss.

I remember thinking to myself, 'This can't be happening.' But it was. We were about to win the Grand National. Hand on heart, that fifty-yard run from the water jump to the line was the first time I'd contemplated winning the race. Throughout the winter with the broken leg I had known that Papillon was there and that maybe I'd get to ride him in the National when I came back. And that given a bit of luck, he might get himself around and run into a place. But winning was just never a consideration until that point. Maybe it goes back to the fact that Irish horses didn't win the National – there was just no way to believe that it could be done.

There aren't the words for what you feel at a moment like that. I know a book is supposed to put into words the emotions that go through someone just then and I could write here that I experienced unbridled joy and excitement and delight. And it would all be true, I did experience those things. But it wouldn't capture it, not really. My mind was racing and yet I was thinking of nothing.

I was twenty years old, winning the Grand National at my first attempt. After six months out with a twice broken leg. Doing it on my dad's horse. Looking up to see my brother Ted coming running towards me with tears in his eyes. And then Katie coming with tears in hers, followed closely by Jennifer. Hearing the crowd cheering and clapping and shouting my name. Shaking hands and taking congratulations from the best jockeys in the sport. I was in disbelief as much as anything.

Ted came up alongside the horse and just put his arms around my waist and hugged me. We waited for the rest of the field to file back in and headed down the walkway last. Just as we passed the entrance to the stable yard, I spotted Dad in the crowd. He was in tears. He'd ridden in the National a few times but never got beyond Becher's. I knew well what this meant to him. Greatest day of my life.

I've never witnessed anything like it since. Every day is different obviously but this was special. The faces in the crowd as I came back in. Mam. Mrs Moran. Gillian standing over in the corner beside the number one pole.

Grand National day comes and goes in a blur anyway but it's total chaos when you end up winning the race. You can't stand still for a second. You do a press conference. You talk to the BBC – in those days Sue Barker was doing the interview. You stand for the presentation. You get your picture taken a million times. All the while, you're moving and running from pillar to post. Loving every minute, trying to take it in, knowing there isn't a hope.

We filled a minibus with everyone who had come over from home that morning. Gillian and myself. Ted and Jennifer. Joan and Liam. Brendan Brady, Jen Mullen, Matt Mitchell, Joe Gibbons and Peter and Paula Whyte. All friends and family. We headed off to Manchester Airport.

Mam and Dad stayed in Liverpool with Mrs Moran that night and came home the following morning. Papillon came home in Willie's lorry with Micko's Dream, and Katie stayed with him the whole way. The rest of us got to Manchester Airport ready to celebrate. Champagne all round. But the poor lady in the airport café was standing there with empty hands by the time we arrived. 'Sorry, lads,' she said. 'All I have is chips.' Champagne and chips it was.

If the day was a blur, the night was worse. We spent it in the Old House pub in Kill village, which was wedged to the door by the time we got there. I arrived and Gary Hutchinson and Mark Watts, the lads who worked for Dad and who both would have ridden Papillon work all through the winter, came running to congratulate us.

It was dawn before we left it. Our house was home to everyone for miles around that night and the following morning there were bodies strewn everywhere. At one point, the doorbell rang and I got Kevin O'Ryan to go answer it. These days he's a big shot jockeys' agent but on that Sunday morning he was the eejit who answered the door to Sky News in his boxers, looking like yer man in the film *Notting Hill*.

It was a great day. Every news camera was there through the day – RTE, BBC, every radio station. Mam and Dad arrived back mid-morning with Papillon. People came from all around to congratulate us and to share it with us. I went to bed for a while in the afternoon before heading out to the Old House again that night.

It was special being there, both that night and a few nights in the weeks afterwards. I've never been a big drinker – it wouldn't take much to get me off the bridle – but the Old House was a place that I spent a fair bit of time when I had the broken leg.

There were plenty of evenings that winter when I'd be bored stupid sitting in the house and I'd head down there and play cards with Ted and Brendan Brady, Bertie and Mick Johnson and the other regulars. To sit there half the winter feeling sorry for myself and then come back in the springtime having won the Grand National was a great feeling. I think they wore out the tape of the race, playing and replaying it.

Any time I watched it again, I just had to smile at what an easy ride it had been. Papillon was such a wonderful horse who had really made it easy for me. He was as good a ride in the Grand National as you could possibly have.

We enjoyed it for a couple of days but life keeps moving on for Grand National winners, the same as it does for everybody else. I remember a few days later being down at Willie's riding out one of the mornings and somebody saying, 'Welcome back to the real world.' I smiled and shrugged and went, 'Yeah, cheers.'

But there was no such thing as going back to the real world from the feeling I had. I don't mean that I was in trouble of losing the run of myself or getting notions above my station or anything like that. It's just that in a way, I could never be brought down to earth from something like this. Winning the Grand National with Dad was pure heaven. Nothing that happened from then on could ever take from it in any way.

CHAPTER 7

Moving on up

There's no getting away from it – winning the Grand National makes you public property. We'd seen it with the Carberrys the year before, how a father and son team winning the biggest race in the sport becomes a story that's easily understood and easily covered by every last bit of the media. We were on the front page of every paper in Ireland and England on the Sunday and plenty of them again on the Monday. The flecks of grey were starting to come through in my hair with perfect timing right around then.

To be honest though, we were in a bubble of celebration and good humour. Being on the front, back or middle of the papers meant nothing to me at all. And anyway, people were more interested in Dad than in me. He'd been the face of racing on RTE for so long that people related to him straight away and were delighted for him. Day after day in the weeks that followed the race, we got bags and bags of post into the house. Letters, cards and faxes congratulating us, and Dad especially. They made a pile the height of the kitchen table before Mam could sort them out.

Sometimes a batch of horses come through a yard at the same time and they're the making of the place. To have Papillon, Rince

Ri and Commanche Court under his care all at once was brilliant for Dad. As much as anything, it was a reward for his faith in them. Papillon hadn't won a race in over a year before the National – he ran no race in the Champion Chase in 1999 and finished lame in the Irish Grand National that year too. Plenty of people thought that either his best days might be behind him or that he was just that bit quirky. But Dad always knew he was a very good horse and was happy that he'd get on the right side of the handicapper eventually.

Then there was Rince Ri. He'd won the Ericsson at Christmas with Conor O'Dwyer riding him and would again the following year with me on board, as well as a Powers Gold Cup at Fairy-house. He was a serious horse, one of the best Dad ever had. To this day, I think there was maybe even a Gold Cup in him in 2000. Dad isn't so sure but I think we were a bit unlucky with how it turned out.

Rince Ri was going well in that race coming to the third-last behind Florida Pearl, Looks Like Trouble and Gloria Victis. We made a small mistake at the fourth-last but recovered well and were right there with a chance coming to the next. But Rince Ri hit the top of it, pecked on landing and bounced me out over his ears. I got unseated. I tried to hang on for dear life and was nearly upside down hanging off him at one point but it was no use. After about fifteen yards, I gave up and let my feet touch the ground. It was UR; unseated rider.

All jockeys hate being unseated because it basically means you fell off the horse. At least if the horse falls, you couldn't have stayed on anyway. Now, there are times when you get unseated and there's not a whole pile you could have done about it. Some-thing might have cut across you or your horse might have pecked and thrown you on landing. Gravity won't have any mercy when that happens. But that day I think if I'd ridden him a bit differently, I might have been all right.

I was nearly in tears afterwards because I felt it was my fault. Poor Gloria Victis ended his life at the next fence and Looks Like Trouble beat Florida up the hill but there was no persuading me that day that Rince Ri wouldn't have been in the shake-up. I came off the track full sure I'd cost us a Gold Cup.

Dad told me not to worry about it, that he didn't think he would have won anyway. He was probably right but I was raging with myself all the same. In the back of my mind, I was worried that the six months off had taken away a bit of sharpness. Getting unseated at that fence was something I was sure wouldn't have happened if I'd been riding all through the winter. But as time went on, I realised you could get unseated anywhere at any time.

But then came Papillon and the Grand National and those doubts were swept away. On the Thursday after the National, we went to the Curragh with Commanche Court to do a piece of work with him ahead of the Irish National. I'd ridden him at Cheltenham in the Arkle but he'd been brought down by Frozen Groom at the third-last and we weren't sure whether or not he'd get the trip.

The piece of work he did that morning along with Total Success was unbelievable. He just blew us away. We were on a high after the weekend anyway but this was getting unreal. We came away from the Curragh that day saying, 'Well, if this fella stays, he wins.' All his form that season had been over two miles or two miles five furlongs. He'd come fourth in a four-horse race over three miles in Navan the previous February and had won a three-mile hurdle at Leopardstown at Christmas 1998. But that was a while ago now. The Irish National is run over three miles five furlongs so this was a step into the complete unknown.

Well, he bolted in. He was only a novice – this was his first win over fences, believe it or not – and he jumped and travelled like a veteran. I couldn't believe how easy it was in the end. There was plenty of pace in the race with Edmond and Lancastrian Jet keeping it going up front. Mouse Morris's horse Foxchapel King tracked them all the way and was the big danger turning in.

But I couldn't get over how well Commanche was going once we straightened up before the second-last. We landed upsides and left Foxchapel King behind. Jumped the last on our own and galloped away up to the line. Commanche couldn't have been more impressive.

Inside sixteen days, Dad and I had won the English Grand National and the Irish Grand National. No trainer had ever done that in the same season before. Tommy Carberry had done it as a jockey back in 1975 all right but nobody had managed it as a trainer. It made up for some of the bad luck Dad had had as a jockey in the race back in the 1980s – he'd come second one year and fallen the next while leading at the second-last. But that was all forgotten now.

He obviously felt we were on a roll because he entered Commanche in the Heineken Gold Cup at Punchestown just nine days later. This was a serious race that had Danoli, Dorans Pride and Micko's Dream in it, along with some good English horses like Stormyfairweather and Addington Boy. I suppose Dad just thought we may as well chance our arm seeing as things were going so well.

His line to the press afterwards was: 'When your luck is in, your cow will calve – and have a bull as well!' It was definitely in that day because we were struggling to keep up with the pace down the back straight and surely wouldn't have won only there was big pile-up at the third-last that probably should have brought us down as well.

But Commanche was an amazing horse and such a quick thinker. Micko's Dream was in front over the third-last but he fell and brought down Dorans Pride in the process. Stormyfairweather swerved to the inside and left us with nowhere to go. Without a pause, Commanche landed the far side of the fence and jumped over Micko's Dream in the one movement. He'd tried to do the same thing in the Arkle when Frozen Groom fell in front of us but hadn't managed it because Frozen Groom was half up to his feet and he took us to the floor. No problem to him this time, though – up and out over Micko's Dream as if he was a schooling fence.

I couldn't believe it. I was all over the place and nearly fell off but Commanche was cool as you like and galloped on to the next fence. Even at that, we were lucky to win in the end because in swerving to miss Micko's Dream, Mick Fitzgerald had gone off the track and had to take drastic action on Stormyfairweather to get back inside the next doll. By the time he righted himself, Addington Boy had gone on with me in hot pursuit. We challenged at the last, landed in front and stayed on well to win.

That was an incredible month. You could never have another one like it. Papillon was my fifth win after coming back from injury, Commanche Court was my sixth. Just like that, the winter went away. I rode three winners for Willie at Punchestown to cap it all off. That festival has always been very good to me but given what the months before had been like, it was especially kind in 2000.

That month opened up a whole new life for me. I got noticed more than before. I got more rides, more chances of good rides and winners. I got opportunities that I honestly never thought would come again during the injury. It sounds a bit over-dramatic but when you're sitting at home day after day, cursing your luck and wondering what the future holds, you have no foundation for your confidence.

It's so hard to stay positive. You almost have to grieve to get it out of the way. That goes the same for now as for then but that was my first proper experience of it and there were days when I just didn't know what to do with myself. I'd get so filled with doubt as to where I was going and what I was doing. The uncertainty over what it would be like when I got back riding was probably the worst part of it.

The actual pain itself is nothing. Or at least it's nothing serious, nothing long-term. You'd swap the uncertainty for pain every day of the week. You know the pain is going to go away and that the bone will heal eventually if you take care of it properly. I bought an exercise bike and rode it for an hour and a half each day so that I could feel like I was helping it along and keeping myself some way fit.

But you can do nothing about the uncertainty only worry and fret. Especially that first time when you're young and you're only starting out and you know nothing. You don't know how strong you're going to be when you come back. You don't know who's going to stand by you. You don't know whose stock is going to rise when you're away.

That year, I went to Cheltenham wondering how many rides I was going to have. I was going over with a few of Willie's and a couple of Dad's but that was that. There was no chance at all of getting an Irish outside ride that year and rightly so. I had just spent six months on the sidelines. What trainer is going to tell a jockey who's been riding his horse all through the winter that he's jocked off now for a twenty-year-old who's been in a cast or on crutches all that time? Nobody is. Nobody should either.

Willie was there for me and I'll always be grateful to him, for that and for so many other things. But you need a big horse to launch you back into the game and I got two of them. I was blessed. Papillon and Commanche Court came along at the perfect time and got me back in action. They got my confidence going again and got the ball rolling.

Once the new season started, I was mad for action again. Went everywhere, rode everything. Willie had his usual army of good horses on the go and I started getting back on a few of the rides I'd lost during the injury. Conor O'Dwyer had ridden Balla Sola in the Champion Hurdle but once he went chasing I got back on him and as the season wore on we won a couple of novice chases. And then there was Florida Pearl.

Florida Pearl has to go down as one of the best horses that ever went through Willie's yard. Definitely as classy an animal as I ever saw come through there. When you rode him to work, he gave you this brilliant feel. He'd gallop away like a dream for you and feel like a superstar underneath you.

But once we got to the racecourse, Florida and I just had no luck together. He was the best horse in Willie's yard and I was Willie's first jockey and yet we never won a race together. Not once.

Think about that. He won his first race for Willie on St Stephen's Day 1996 when James Nash won the bumper at Leopardstown on him. He won his last race in February 2004, the Irish Hennessy at Leopardstown, with Richard Johnson on his back. All in all, he ran thirty-three times for Willie and his owners the O'Leary family, winning seventeen of them. And I wasn't in the saddle for even one of them, even though I was working for Willie all the way through.

It's actually comical when you go through it. It was mostly pure bad luck all the way around. When I started out, he was Richard Dunwoody's ride and Dunwoody rode him to win the Cheltenham Bumper in 1997 and then the Royal and Sun Alliance in 1998 and the Irish Hennessy the year after that. Then he retired.

Florida's first run back in the 1999 to 2000 season was to be the James Nicholson in Down Royal on 6 November. I was to ride. This was a big deal – Florida was the star horse in the yard and I was getting my chance on him. Then Pardubice happened on 10 October and Paul Carberry rode him instead. They won handy. I was sitting on the couch in Kill looking for a cat to kick. Not that I could have kicked it very far with my cast on.

When he won his second Irish Hennessy the following February, it was just a few days after I'd broken my leg for the second time while schooling Shiny Bay. I hadn't expected to just be handed the ride anyway since I was only working my way back but still, it didn't improve my mood any. Paul kept the ride for the Gold Cup in the race where I was unseated from Rince Ri.

Florida came second to Looks Like Trouble that day when he just didn't quite stay up the hill, and Willie ended his season after that. But come November, he was back and ready to go for the James Nicholson again. Paul got a bad injury that September and was out for a few months but Willie had decided that I was going to take over the ride on him for that season anyway. So we went to Down Royal and I was all set to finally have a go.

He ran terrible, fourth in a five-horse race behind Looks Like Trouble, Dorans Pride and Inis Cara. All good horses but on that day they looked a different league to Florida, even though they obviously weren't. He never jumped, never travelled, never threatened. Felt like a different horse altogether than the one I rode at home.

We put a line through that run and went again in December, this time in the John Durkan at Punchestown. Native Upmanship beat us by a head. This was more like the Florida Pearl I knew. He jumped a lot better and just got touched off in a close finish. So it was encouraging. But I still had not won on him.

Over to Kempton Park for the King George VI Chase, then, that Christmas and we were second again, this time behind First Gold. We were well beaten that day but it wasn't a bad performance at all. You could definitely see he was back to something approaching his best and Willie said afterwards that he'd go to the Hennessy again and then the Gold Cup.

The Hennessy was on 4 February. The day before it, I went to Naas and all was going well – I had a winner in the second race on Killtulagh Storm for Willie. But in the three-mile handicap hurdle that day, I was riding Hollybank Buck for Tony Martin when Battery Park slipped and came down on the flat right in front of me and brought us down. I was knocked out cold but I was a lot better off than Willie Slattery who was riding Battery Park and who ended up in hospital for a long time afterwards.

I tried my best to brush it off when I came round. I met Mam and Dad before I went into the medical room and although I hadn't a clue where I was or what I was saying, I thought I was making sense. Dad said to me: 'Look, tell them you're not riding for the rest of the day. You're riding Florida Pearl in the Hennessy tomorrow.' So that was my line. Dad told me afterwards he had to tell me it five times before I'd remember it. I was walking into the room muttering under my breath: 'Florida Pearl in the Hennessy tomorrow, Florida Pearl in the Hennessy tomorrow ...'

The doctor asked me how I was and I tried to come across as nonchalant as possible. 'Yeah, grand, yeah. I'm going to give the rest of the day a miss. Not going to ride anymore today. I've got Florida Pearl in the Hennessy tomorrow.'

I thought I'd gotten away with it too, until that evening I got a phone call at home in Kill from Walter Halley, the senior Turf Club medical officer. I'd fooled nobody. I was stood down for seven days. Dicky Johnson got the ride on Florida the next day and of course he won, beating Alexander Banquet by a couple of lengths. Three Hennessys in a row, three different jockeys. None of them R. Walsh. I know I had no divine right to win on him but this was getting ridiculous.

As Cheltenham approached, it emerged that Dicky was going to keep the ride for the Gold Cup. As it happened, Cheltenham was called off because of the foot and mouth scare but when Florida won the Heineken Gold Cup in Fairyhouse that April, Dicky was on board again. When he came back the following season, Paul Carberry rode him to win the John Durkan at Punchestown and Adrian Maguire won the King George on him.

The next time I rode him was in the King George in 2002 when he went over to try and repeat his success of the previous year. But to no avail. We came fourth, well down the field behind Best Mate. I guess it just wasn't meant to be for Florida and me.

Still, Florida Pearl aside, I had a decent season in 2000–2001 and was champion jockey again by the end of it. Rince Ri won the Ericsson that Christmas, Commanche nearly won the *Racing Post* Chase at Kempton in February and Micko's Dream took some big prizes near the end of the season too. But everything was overshadowed by the loss of Cheltenham.

Going a season without Cheltenham is like going a year without Christmas for people in racing. When the foot and mouth outbreak first hit the news that spring, nobody knew for sure what the implications would be. When it got to the point where the government was requesting that Irish people not travel to England for Cheltenham, we were heading into unknown territory.

I was happy enough to toe the party line like everybody else if I had to. Well, maybe not happy enough but prepared to stay at home like everybody else once all the Irish horses were barred from travelling. But that was before I got a call from Paul Nicholls asking if I would ride See More Business in the Gold Cup. Mick Fitzgerald had won the race on him in 1999 but was being claimed by Nicky Henderson to ride Marlborough and Paul was offering me a ride in the Gold Cup on a former Gold Cup winner.

Not only that, but Seemore had to have a serious chance. Fair enough, he was getting on a bit by then at the age of eleven, but he'd won the Pillar Chase that January by a distance. With the Irish horses out of the running, he was the favourite in most books for the race by this point.

It's not every day you get a phone call asking if you want to ride the favourite in the Gold Cup. So I said I would. To avoid being any sort of threat, I said I'd go over and ride Seemore for Paul ten days before the festival and stay there until it was over. I'd even stay on afterwards if it wasn't safe for me to travel home for fear of what I might be carrying. If it meant living in England for a few weeks or even a couple of months until the scare passed, then so be it. I didn't mind. Anything to ride the favourite in the Gold Cup.

As soon as it got to the media, though, all hell broke loose. Some government minister was in the papers saying he had very serious concerns over the signal it sent if the likes of me and Barry Geraghty rode in the festival when everybody else was making the sacrifice and not going. That night, my phone went mental with people ringing me looking for a comment. I didn't answer it. I remember looking at it at one point and seeing that there were twenty-four missed calls.

In the end, it was a story for a day and no more. Within twenty-four hours, the festival was pushed back by a month. Not long after, it was found that some infected sheep had been grazing near the racecourse itself and so the whole thing was cancelled for the year. A terrible shame.

But life moves on. By the time the Grand National came around, we were all allowed to travel again and Papillon went over looking for a repeat success. That was the year Red Marauder came through the quagmire to win in the rain and the muck and the dirt. That was a desperate day, a real slog.

Papillon hated soft ground at the best of times and he wasn't enjoying himself this day. But he was honest and tough so he kept plodding away and we were actually going all right, pottering away in our own time. It was a totally different race to the previous year. It was about finding the best ground and surviving until you could get into the race over the last couple of furlongs.

I had walked the track that morning and thought that the best ground was on the outside so that's where I stayed. A good thing too, because it meant I avoided the melee at the Canal Turn the first time around that wiped out half the field. I didn't even ride to come at it at an angle or anything, just jumped straight over it to where the freshest ground was. So I was oblivious to just how bad the carnage had been behind me. I knew a few had gone but I didn't know how many.

We tootled along up past the winning post for the first time and there were loose horses everywhere. I hadn't looked around to see how we were getting on because I was more intent on trying to get Papillon to travel better. He wasn't going well and I was squeezing him and squeezing him trying to get him into it.

But when I did take a look, I realised there were only about half a dozen horses left in the race and that we were in with a shout. I knew he'd stay and not many of the rest of them could definitively say that about their horses.

But then just as we came to the third fence second time around – the big ditch – past the stands, one of the loose horses intervened. He got to the ditch in front going to jump it, changed his mind at the last minute, jammed on the brakes and fell into the drain. He stood up and started running down the ditch, wiping out A.P. McCoy on Blowing Wind in the process. I was a couple of lengths back and had a little more time to try to swerve around him but he went to change direction again and came to another stop. Papillon jammed on the brakes and fired me into the ditch.

I was raging, absolutely going mental. I was standing inside in the ditch, fit to be tied. By God, I was sore. Two Grand Nationals in a row would have been something special. I got out of the ditch to see A.P. standing there looking off into the distance.

'There's only two standing,' he said.

'What do you mean?' I said.

'Beau is after unseating Carl Llewellyn. That means there's only two left in the race.'

'Well, sure come on, so. We'll go again.'

'Do you think?'

'Sure, why wouldn't we?'

So the pair of us ran back about half a furlong. Papillon and Blowing Wind were standing side by side at the back of the second fence so we caught them and remounted.

'We'll head down here together, now,' I said.

'We might get in trouble,' he said.

'There won't be a thing said. We'll just potter around together, keep each other company, nothing too dramatic, right?'

'Right, fair enough.'

So we went along, slow as you like, just cantering around, popping the fences. The race was long over at this stage and Red Marauder and Smarty had finished first and second. We were way behind; I mean minutes back up the course. But there was no danger of us hurrying. It was only between us for third and fourth. Papillon had no interest in racing after being remounted and I had no interest in pushing him.

I didn't know A.P. that well but we just hunted around with me shouting at him to wait on me. When we got to the second-last, he was looking to make sure he was going to finish third. So I asked him again to wait for me until we jumped the last. He hung on and we jumped the last together but no sooner were we the far side of it than he was away. That's how it finished – Blowing Wind was third, Papillon was fourth. That's A.P. for you. The man has to win. And nobody said a word to us about remounting.

So, no repeat for Papillon then. But I did have one winner at Aintree that weekend, a good one to get at the time and a very important one considering all that has happened since. The weather on the day before that Grand National hadn't been nearly as foul, although the ground had come up pretty soft when it rained early in the morning. After coming over on the Friday the previous year just to walk the track and get a feel for the place, this time around I had three rides, all for English trainers. And thanks in part to the soft ground, one of them did the business to give me my first ever winner for Paul Nicholls.

Fadalko was a very decent horse on his day, a French import owned by Sir Robert Ogden. He'd always liked a little bit of cut in the ground and had finished second to Stormyfairweather in the Cathcart at Cheltenham the previous year, and again to Flagship Uberalles in the Tingle Creek earlier in the season. A.P. McCoy had ridden him in the Tingle Creek that time but of course Martin Pipe had first call on A.P. so he wasn't available.

Paul had been looking around for someone to ride as first jockey for his yard. He had been on to me during that spring, looking to see would I be interested in coming over and joining his team at Ditcheat full-time. I got a letter in the post one day from Paul Barber on behalf of Paul Nicholls and his owners, offering me a full-time job as first jockey. They would pay me a retainer of £30,000 a year and, since they knew how attached I was to life at home in Ireland, they said I could nominate two Irish horses that I'd be allowed to ride at any time on any given day in any race. The catch was that I'd have to move to England full-time.

It was a seriously good offer. Paul had won the Gold Cup a couple of years before with See More Business and was pushing Martin Pipe every step of the way in the trainers' championship, getting closer to him with each season. You could see that he had some proper horses in the yard too, like Call Equiname (although he was never the same after winning the Champion Chase), Ad Hoc, Shotgun Willy and another young one from France called Azertyuiop who was being talked about as having a big future. To be asked to be part of that future was very flattering and my first instinct was to be excited about the idea.

Then I thought about it a bit more. The thing was, Willie and Dad had plenty for me to ride at home. Good horses too. Fair enough, I could choose two of them if I decided to go but in my head that was no choice really. Was I going to pick Alexander Banquet and Commanche Court but not Papillon or Rince Ri or Micko's Dream? That sounded like more trouble, more headaches than it was worth.

Still, I could probably have put up with that end of it if it had come right down to it. It was the idea of moving to England that was the real problem. I just didn't want to do it, for any number of reasons. At heart, I'm a home bird. I love living in Ireland and working here. I love having family around me and the friends I had made.

I had real ties in Ireland that I didn't want to break or even strain very much. Gillian and I had been going out for a few years by now and she had started a good job here. She had been with me since I was an amateur and had helped me all through the broken leg and everything that had happened. Moving to England would have either meant her moving over with me, which wouldn't have been very fair on her, or us carrying on a long-distance relationship for a while. Was it worth bringing that extra pressure on ourselves?

I looked around to see what advice I could get. I asked Dad and Willie obviously and while both of them said they wouldn't stand in my way if I wanted to go, they both thought it sounded like something I could do without. 'Do you really fancy the hectic life of being full-time over there?' was how Willie put it to me.

Dad wasn't that pushed on the idea. It didn't matter that he was very good friends with Paul Barber, he would look out for my interest first and foremost. And to him, there were plenty of opportunities in Ireland for me still. Willie's horses were flying and so were his. I was twice champion jockey and there was decent money to be made here without having to rely on a retainer in England, no matter what size it was.

We were just coming to the beginning of a boom in horse ownership in Ireland around that time. The building trade was doing well and that brought a lot of people into the game that wouldn't have been there before. With the economy growing, you could see more and more syndicates getting involved. The knock-on from that was that more sponsors got interested and prize money went up across the board and when you added all that up, it meant that a lot of good horses that would have gone to England in the past were now being bought and kept by Irish owners and Irish trainers. I didn't want to leave that behind. I didn't need to either.

I asked Conor O'Dwyer what he thought. He wasn't crazy about it either. A jockey's life in England is a hell of a lot busier than a jockey's life in Ireland. I've never been one bit afraid of hard work but England is a big place with racecourses the length and breadth of it (not to mention Scotland and Wales). There's a lot of driving involved, a lot of long hours and you're on the go every day. I'd have no problem living in England at all but working there as a full-time jockey is a tough life.

In the end, I decided not to take the job. There were plenty of reasons but I guess near the top of the list was the fact that I couldn't see myself walking out on the job in Willie's yard. This was early 2001 and I'd been with him since 1996. He'd stood behind the sixteen-year-old who got a twenty-one-day ban on Palette and the eighteen-year-old who hoped to keep the ride on Alexander Banquet in the Cheltenham Bumper even though there were professionals who were after it, and the twenty-year-old who broke his leg twice and had been out for six months. I couldn't turn my back on him after that.

So I decided against it. I wrote back to Paul Barber saying 'thanks but no thanks'. We kept in contact – hence the offer from Paul Nicholls of the ride on See More Business in the Gold Cup that never happened – and I arranged to meet them at Aintree to say it to them in person. I told them that it was a very kind offer and that I appreciated the chance they'd be giving me. But I loved my life in Ireland and would be staying there for the foreseeable future. I said too that I'd be delighted to ride the odd one here and there for them when I wasn't needed at home.

That was how Fadalko came about the day before the National in the Mumm Melling Chase. Sir Robert Ogden asked for me to ride him and when Paul put it to me I was delighted to say yes. The big Grade One chase on Grand National Friday in Aintree and a first prize was £74,000? Bloody sure I'd be happy to take the ride.

Fadalko did it beautifully on the day. It was over two miles four furlongs and he had that bit more stamina than the rest of the field, helped as well when the favourite Tiutchev went at the first. I rode him handy all the way around and then pressed the button after the third-last. He won well in the end, by fifteen lengths or so.

Three weeks later I went over to ride two for Paul at the Whitbread meeting in Sandown, Fadalko and Ad Hoc. I might not have been keen on a full-time job but I wasn't a fool either. These were two proper horses in big races on the last Saturday of the season in England. He still hadn't nailed anybody down as his stable jockey yet so I filled the gap for him that day.

Good thing I did too, because Ad Hoc won the Whitbread Gold Cup. He was another Robert Ogden horse, this one a former point-to-pointer from Ireland. He'd finished second in the Scottish National for Mick Fitz the previous Saturday but had a reputation for being an unreliable jumper at times. Paul's instructions were to just switch him off and creep away round. He didn't put a foot wrong for me the whole way. He jumped really well and when I asked him to go just after the Pond Fence he gave me plenty in response. We ended up winning by the guts of twenty lengths.

Unfortunately, we missed out on a nice double when Fadalko

was touched off in the two-mile Celebration Chase by A.P. McCoy on Edredon Bleu. A.P. had made all the running and I'd sat in behind him, tracking him all the way. It turned into a great race, a real battle to the line between the pair of us. I thought I had him too – and so did A.P. – but he won by a short head in the end. I ended up getting a one-day whip ban for my troubles.

A one-day ban is nothing at all really, a day off more than anything as long as it doesn't clash with a big meeting. But it can still be very annoying when you get it. Myself and A.P. had been involved in a great finish on Fadalko and Edredon Bleu and both our horses had kept going all the way to the line. We were ten lengths clear of another of Paul's, Desert Mountain, back in third. We'd given the public a good spectacle and there wasn't a hint of damage done to the horses. And yet I got a ban.

The whip problem is an image problem and it starts with the word itself. Whip. Whipping. You hear it and you think ugly thoughts straight away. You get a harsh image in your head of the skin of an animal being torn at or lashed. But what we use isn't a whip at all. It's a padded flexible stick.

I've heard some people say that if you took away the whips, the same jockeys would win the races. And maybe that's true, but only if those jockeys are clever enough not to get up on the wrong horses. The simple truth is that certain horses just find more because of the whip.

Take Cooldine, on whom I won the RSA Chase at Cheltenham in 2009. That's a horse that keeps plenty for himself unless you are able to use your stick and let him know what you want from him. What would Brave Inca have won without the whip? Or Hardy Eustace? Harchibald might have a couple of Champion Hurdles to his name but instead the other two are the ones who got the glory. And did it take anything out of them? Of course it didn't. They lived very long and very happy racing lives and retired as heroes of the game.

At Cheltenham earlier this year, my sister Katie rode her first festival winner on Poker De Sivola but her use of the whip on the run-in got her a four-day ban. Now, she may very well have used the whip more times than she was supposed to on the run-in, but there was no way she should have got a ban in my mind. Her horse kept finding, which to me, ought to be the standard.

Nina Carberry, whose horse she beat on the run-in, got five days. But the two girls are not butchers. What the stewards did was reduce horse health to a numbers game. They said that the girls went over the permitted amount of times they could hit their horses coming up the hill. I don't envy the stewards their jobs for one minute because they're given no leeway to make a judgement call. But anyone who knew the difference between right and wrong when it comes to horse welfare knows that Katie and Nina didn't harm the horses at all. The stewards were only working by the letter of the law. There are great stipendiary stewards in England that are tied up by rules and prevented from using their better judgement.

In Ireland, it's different. It's not so much about the numbers at home, it's more about the manner in which the whip is used. It's about how rather than how many, if you like. Any time I'm pulled in by the stewards, I always say the same thing. In my eyes, somebody who gives a horse two smacks of the whip when it has no chance of finishing in a place is using it excessively. That is a far worse crime than somebody continuing to use it on a horse that's running forward, responding each time.

That isn't what the rules say but they're the rules I ride by. They are my rules and I won't be changing them now. I've got plenty of whip bans down the years but I don't think anyone would regard me as someone who is overly hard on horses. Put it this way – I'll never be in the stewards' room for a horse that finished fifth. I'd say I average about two whip bans a year, a few days each time. That's two from the guts of 750 rides every season. It's nothing, really.

Overall, whip rules are a very good thing. They make jockeys rely on their skill and their strength and there's no doubt that wasn't always the case in the past when fellas used to thrash away for all they were worth. I just wish they were applied with a bit more common sense.

All was rosy in the garden going into the 2001–2002 season. I had twice been champion jockey and had access to some decent rides in England from time to time too. I made a reasonable start to the season too, enjoyed the summer well and was all set to drive on through the winter months. And then I got injured again.

I'd been doing so well. Injuries are always going to happen but since I'd come back from the broken leg, I hadn't had anything too serious. A cracked thumb here, a broken finger there. Those are the most common injuries for me, purely from falling with the whip in my hand. When I fall off a horse, I don't have time to let go of the stick before I hit the ground. So I'm forever spraining and cracking thumbs but there's not a whole pile you can do about them other than strap them up and get ready for the next ride. They'd never keep you out of a race.

Broken wrists are different. A broken wrist needs a cast and that will keep you on the sidelines for a few weeks. Near the end of October 2000, I broke my right one when a mare of Willie's called Sophoronia fell at the third-last with me about a dozen lengths clear in a handicap hurdle in Cork one Saturday. Home and hosed we were, until she stepped on this hurdle three out.

The old familiar routine. Racecourse to local hospital – Mallow this time. X-ray. Broken bone confirmed. Cast on. Met Bill Quinlan on the Monday in Cappagh. Out for four weeks. No big deal.

This next one was a lot more serious. I had a clean run all the way until Listowel in September 2001, and then on the first day of the festival we were just past halfway in a nineteen-runner handicap hurdle. I was riding a horse of Eric McNamara's called Johnny Ringo and we'd just passed the stands when suddenly it all got very tight coming to the next hurdle. The horses on the inside pushed out, the horses on the outside rolled in and I was completely squashed in the middle. I had no room and nowhere to make room and Johnny Ringo just dived into the middle of the hurdle, flipped over and came down on top of me.

It was a terrible fall, one of the worst I've ever had. I was in agony on the ground. The pain was unbelievable, much worse than when I broke the leg in the Pardubice. I had no idea what was after happening or what I'd broken, but it was ferocious pain. I thought my femur was broken. I was sure it was smashed.

To make it worse, the racecourse response was a shambles. It was the one time in all the falls I've had all over Ireland, England and beyond that I've been disappointed with the medical care and attention. Every other time has been great, without fail, and I owe medical people across the countries a huge amount of gratitude for what they've done for me down the years. But this day in Listowel was a nightmare.

Everything took so long. They couldn't tell what was wrong with me, hadn't a clue what to do with me. I told them I needed to go to the hospital, that my femur was smashed and needed treatment straight away. But they wanted to bring me to the ambulance room first. In Listowel, this meant crossing the track, going through the crowd, heading to the little ambulance room, getting diagnosed, putting me back in the ambulance, heading back out through the crowd, going back across the track and out on to the road to try and get to Tralee General Hospital.

The ambulance crew and doctor really wanted to bring me to the medical room but I was giving out to them, telling them I needed to go straight to the hospital and to quit messing about. We were already in the middle of the track so there was no point wasting time going back to the medical room. I'm sure I used stronger language than that but it was no use. I'd say that from the time I hit the ground until the time I entered Tralee General, nearly an hour and a half had passed.

This ambulance I was in was useless to me. They didn't have the right stabilising equipment to keep me supported on the stretcher so I was shifting all over the place. Not good when every movement hurts. They hooked me up to a drip to rehydrate me, but instead of hanging it up over my head, they left it on the ground beside me. So instead of getting fluids into me, the bag started filling up with my blood. I asked them for painkillers and they said they didn't have any. This was a cardiac ambulance. Pity I didn't have a heart attack, maybe then they could have done something for me.

When we got to the hospital, they rolled the stretcher out of the back of the ambulance and dropped it straight on the ground. I roared with the pain. I was definitely on to far stronger language by this stage. They took me into accident and emergency and I finally met somebody who knew what he was doing. There was an Australian doctor who I'll never forget (I couldn't tell you his name, but whoever you are, Aussie Doctor, you'll always be a hero to me) and inside two minutes he told me I had a dislocated hip. It had come clean out of the socket so that one leg was a good few inches lower down than the other. I was screaming that it was my femur but he was cool as you like.

'Nah, mate,' he said. 'You've dislocated yer hip.' I didn't care what it was, I needed the pain to go away quickly. He obliged by injecting me to knock me out. By the time I woke up, the surgeon Mr Murphy had put it back in. The relief when I woke up and the pain was gone was huge.

I stayed in Tralee General for three days before being transferred to Dublin in another (less traumatic) ambulance. Bill came to look at the hip in St Vincent's Hospital and was delighted with the work Mr Murphy had done. He told me I'd be out for eight weeks. The fall had happened on the Monday and I was home in Kill on the Friday, determined this time not to let an injury get me down.

I decided to go on holiday instead. Dad was going to the Breeders' Cup in the USA with a few friends so I got together a few of mine and we went as well. It was in Belmont Park in New York that year and because it was so soon after 9/11, the flights were sold for half nothing and the hotels were the same. It was the first time I'd ever been to a Breeders' Cup and we picked a good one. Johannesburg won the Juvenile for Mick Kinane and Aidan O'Brien that evening.

We had some night of it. We finished it off by going for breakfast in McDonald's in Grand Central Station at six o'clock in the morning. There, we got talking to this couple from Clare. The girl was fairly hammered and wanted to know the story with the crutches. I told her I'd got a fall off a horse and dislocated my hip. She asked was the horse all right and I said no, sadly, the poor horse had been killed in the fall.

Well, she lit into me! Started giving out yards to me in the middle of Grand Central Station at six in the morning, attacked me for killing the horse. I couldn't get a word in edgeways. Her boyfriend calmed her down in the end and we headed off to find our beds.

It was a great holiday though, just what I needed. I was back racing by the middle of November and actually had a winner on my first ride back, a maiden hurdle in Clonmel on a horse of Dad's called True Blue Victory. The second winner I rode when I came back was for Willie, on Joe Cullen the following Saturday in Punchestown. Normal service resumed.

But I still kept up the English connection through that winter. At the start of December, we brought Commanche Court to Newbury for the Hennessy Gold Cup and I picked up a few spare rides on the rest of the card that day for Paul and for Mark Pitman and Richard Hannon. The following Saturday, I went over to Sandown to ride Fadalko in the Tingle Creek. And the Saturday before Christmas, Willie sent Adamant Approach to Ascot for a big handicap hurdle race and I rode Ad Hoc while I was there. I didn't have many winners but it was great to be getting rides at meetings like these.

I occasionally rode for some other trainers in England as well, including Paul's big rival, Martin Pipe. In fact, it was on a Pipe horse that I finally got another Cheltenham winner to add to the one on Alexander Banquet four years earlier. Blowing Wind was the horse that A.P. had been on when he and I remounted in the previous year's Grand National.

At Cheltenham, he was one of six Pipe horses on the Mildmay Of Fleet, a twenty-one-runner handicap on the Wednesday just before the Champion Bumper. He'd actually won at the festival before, the County Hurdle in 1998 with A.P. on his back. It turned out to be a cracking race, with about half a dozen of us jumping the last in a bunch. My lad stayed on the best up the hill to win by a length and a half from another Pipe horse Lady Cricket, the favourite who had A.P. on board.

I came close in a couple of races at Cheltenham that year. Adamant Approach was travelling like a winner coming to the last in the Supreme Novices' Hurdle. He was a rising star in Willie's yard and had won the Pierse Hurdle at Leopardstown that January, the only time I've ever ridden the winner of that race. This should have been another for him but he fell at the final hurdle and Like-A-Butterfly raced away up the hill.

Then there was the Gold Cup, top of the list of races in my career I'd love to have back so I could take another crack at it. Commanche Court hadn't won since the Heineken Gold Cup in Punchestown in 2000 but he'd been unlucky along the way. We really thought he was going to have a serious chance in the Gold Cup in 2001 after finishing second in the *Racing Post* Chase that February, so that was another reason to be gutted when Cheltenham was cancelled. By the time we came over in 2002, he was flying completely under the radar. I think he even went off around 25–1.

The way he jumped and travelled, you wouldn't have thought for a second he was a 25–1 shot that day. He was brilliant all the way through – jumped like a stag, never missed a beat and as we turned at the top of the hill, we had only See More Business and Best Mate ahead of us. Joe Tizzard was on Seemore, Jim Culloty was just behind him on Best Mate with me in third just outside them. Perfectly positioned.

And then somewhere between the third-last and second-last I decided to go for it. On paper, it wasn't the worst decision in the world. This was Best Mate's first Gold Cup and nobody knew whether or not he'd get three and a quarter miles. He'd never won over three miles and Commanche had won an Irish National.

So it was feasible that if I kicked, we would outstay him.

Things pop into your head during a race and you make snap decisions. The job is to filter through them and pick the right one and I didn't do that this time. In the space of a few strides, I got it into my head that my lad was definitely going to stay and nobody could be sure whether Best Mate would. So I set sail.

But when I look at the video of the race I just want to scream at myself. When I moved up on Jim's outside, I should have kept him there in the pocket. All I needed to do was ease forward a bit so that I was level with Joe's boot, maybe just a half a length down. That would have left Jim with a decision to make. If he stayed where he was, he risked not getting a run and if he had to come out to go round us, he'd have lost ground.

I should have kept him there in the pocket, sat on Joe's boot down to the second-last, kept him tight against the rail so that Jim couldn't come up the inner and taken my chances from halfway between the second-last and the last. Instead, by going so early, I opened up the race. Seemore moved out as Commanche went by him and that left Best Mate with a straight run up the inside.

To make matters worse, Commanche got the second-last just a little bit wrong. He was a bit long at it, and when I pushed him for the stride he half-pricked his ears and fluffed it. He landed on it and took a few seconds to get going at the back of it. By then, Jim was away and clear and although Commanche stayed on well up the hill, Best Mate won by a length.

Now, obviously Best Mate went on to be one of the best Gold Cup horses of all time so I can't say for sure that Commanche would have won if I'd hung on to him a bit longer. It's very possible that even if I'd kept Jim in the pocket going to the second-last, he'd eventually have pulled out and come around me and Best Mate might have beaten us anyway. You never know. What I do know is that the way I rode Commanche wasn't the best way to win the race that day. I made the wrong decision at the wrong time.

But you move on. A few weeks later, I was in England again, this time for the Lesters, the big awards evening for jockeys. We had a fine night, plenty of craic and slagging. The next morning I was lying in bed when I got a phone call from Jennifer saying that something was happening with Timmy Murphy on a plane home from Japan, and that Paul Nicholls was asking if I would ride for him that week. There was a meeting in Cheltenham on the Thursday and then the Scottish National meeting in Ayr on the Friday and Saturday. I said I would.

That was in the middle of April. By the end of the summer, Paul and I had decided we'd be seeing a lot more of each other.

CHAPTER 8

A new arrangement

I landed at Prestwick Airport the following Friday morning to a message on my phone telling me to ring Jennifer. When Paul Nicholls had rung for the first time that week, nobody was really sure yet what was happening with Timmy Murphy but since then he'd said he was going to take a while away from racing to get himself right. That meant that Paul was looking again for a full-time first jockey at Ditcheat. He'd offered it to me a second time but I still wasn't up for moving countries.

When I rang Jennifer back, she had news. Paul thought Barry Geraghty might be the man for the job. They hadn't come to terms yet or sat down to discuss the ins and outs of it, but it was on the table for him. What that meant in the short term was that a few of Paul's owners wanted Barry to ride their horses that weekend, which was fair enough. So Barry got the ride on Valley Henry and Shotgun Willy and I rode the rest.

I ended up having a great weekend. I hit the post with a couple on the Friday but came back and rode a four-timer on the Saturday, the last four races on the card. Three of them were for Paul and the other was the Scottish National itself on Take Control for Martin Pipe. That was a great race – we just got up in the last few strides to chin Shotgun Willy on the line. It denied Paul a five-timer but he went away happy enough with the four winners he got that afternoon – my three plus Valley Henry who won the Future Champions' Novice Chase.

I rode another winner for Paul the following Saturday in Sandown on Moving Earth to wrap up the season. As far as I knew, Barry would be going to work for him now. Barry and I started out at more or less the same time and this was a big job that he well deserved. He'd won the Arkle on Moscow Flyer at Cheltenham that year and had recently become the latest in the line of jockeys who weren't me to win on Florida Pearl, first at Aintree and then at Punchestown.

But within a short while, it turned out that Barry wasn't going to take the job either. He had plenty going on in Ireland the same as I did, riding winners for just about every trainer in the country. Moving to England didn't seem to suit him any more than it did me. You'd be hard pushed to say he made the wrong decision either, because by the end of the following season, he'd had five winners at the Cheltenham Festival and had won the Grand National on Monty's Pass for Jimmy Mangan.

So I spoke to Gillian about it one night. There had to be a way of doing this. Jennifer got out the racing calendar and went through it to see what days there was racing in both Ireland and England. I asked Dad what he thought and he suggested that maybe if we sent Paul a list of the days I might be available and included the Saturdays on it, then maybe we could find a compromise. The Saturdays were the crucial part. Racing here was often fairly ordinary on Saturdays but it was the big day of the week over there.

I had a chat with Willie and asked him how he would feel about it. I'd still be available to ride for him on Thursdays and Sundays so I wouldn't miss out on most of the big races for his better horses. And when it came down to a clash, say at Cheltenham or Aintree, I'd make an honest call.

I don't know how keen Willie really was on the idea but fair play to him, he went along with it. 'Fair enough,' he said. 'If that's what you want to do.' He didn't have to be so supportive about it but he was anyway. And the same went for Paul. The arrangement wasn't going to suit either of them 100 per cent but they were both prepared to give it a go.

So that's how it started. From Chepstow in October until Sandown in April, Paul would have first call on me from Monday to Wednesday and on Friday and Saturday. He didn't really have many summer horses, so I was free to ride at home from May to September. With a bit of give and take on all sides, we said we'd try it and see how we got on.

I didn't take a retainer. I didn't want one. I've never had one with Willie or Paul. I like my own freedom and I like having gentlemen's agreements with them both. A gentleman's agreement cuts down your options but a retainer reduces your options to one. You're retained. You go where you are sent and you ride what you're given. If I'd had a retainer with Willie from the start, then strictly speaking I couldn't have ridden Papillon in 2000. If I'd taken a retainer from Paul in the summer of 2002, I couldn't have ridden Hedgehunter in 2005.

There might have been ways around both situations but you'd be relying on goodwill above and beyond the call of duty if you were trying to go down that road. I never wanted to get to the point where I could be offered the ride on, say, Best Mate in the Gold Cup but would have to turn it down to ride a 33–1 shot. Not that it ever happened, but I liked having that option if it came to the crunch.

It was the one bit of the deal that suited everyone really. As Dad said, if I took a retainer from Paul, it would be tough to say no to moving to England. And it suited Paul as well because a retainer works both ways. If I was getting paid a retainer, then in theory there'd be nothing to stop me insisting on riding a particular horse, no matter what the owner's preference was. This way, nobody was obliged to use me. There would be no needless friction there.

From the beginning, I knew that it was going to take a fair bit of work. For one thing, I was going to have to put in an awful lot of hours to make it work. But I didn't mind that at all. Getting up early has never bothered me so the difference between getting up at six o'clock to make a flight from Dublin or getting up after seven to go down to Willie's to ride out wasn't going to be a big problem to me.

But beyond that, it was going to take a lot of diplomacy. I was going to have to make a fair few political decisions to keep the peace. Not getting paid a retainer was my choice but I knew I wouldn't get very far if I abused the privilege all over the place. I would have to try and live up to my responsibilities to both Paul and Willie as best I could. I was going to have to start reading situations well.

I couldn't just be going where I thought the winner was. Sometimes I would have to turn up to meetings where it mattered more that I was actually there even if there was going to be a better ride elsewhere. It occasionally happened that there'd be a meeting in, say, Clonmel on a Sunday, an ordinary enough meeting that wouldn't match up with whatever was going on in England. I would have to nail my colours to the mast on those days and make good on my promise to Willie. The same went vice-versa.

I couldn't be flitting from one horse to another at the drop of a hat. I couldn't be jumping from Billy to Jack just to suit Ruby. I was going to really have to work at suiting both of these men to the point where they both felt the whole rigmarole was worth their while. It was going to take a lot of planning and delegating. Jennifer's workload was going to double and sometimes she was going to have to read the situations even better than I could. She did and still does.

There has been plenty of times that I've flown to England and back for one ride and there'll be plenty of times again. It's no hardship at all. I'll happily go for one horse if there's a chance of it paying off down the line. My childhood dream was to ride the best horses in the biggest races and sometimes you have to play the long game to get those rides. I knew from growing up with horses that bad luck and injuries can ruin many a horse's season so I'm always prepared to travel to give myself options.

The way I look at it, in order to have half a dozen very good chances going to Cheltenham, you might need to give yourself a couple of hundred chances at the start of the season. The more horses you can lay claim to, the more chances you're going to have to find a superstar. That's what I wanted above all. I wanted to find a great horse to be associated with. If I was riding for both yards, I had more of a chance of doing that. So I was always going to put in the hours if it meant keeping everyone happy.

The way I worked with Paul was completely different from the way I worked with Willie. I'd worked full-time with Willie since I was seventeen but this was a new beginning and given all the travelling I'd be doing, it would suit me better if my day-to-day duties meant just turning up at the races and riding the horses. I would school whenever Paul needed me to but I wasn't going to be in Ditcheat as much as I would be in Closutton.

But more than that, I wanted this to be a professional relationship first and foremost. He would provide the horses and I would do everything I could to get them across the line in front. Beyond that, there was no need for us to get in each other's way. I know I can be prickly enough sometimes. I wasn't going to be there first thing every morning getting in Paul's way. The more you see of somebody, the better chance you have of falling out. Better to keep it strictly professional.

Paul had no problem with that sort of arrangement. He had enough staff around the yard to ride out for him, so he didn't need me for that. I think he liked the idea of having someone who he didn't have to worry about, who he didn't have to mind or be giving out to for being late to work or anything like that. Instead of being his responsibility, I was going to be someone who came in and did a job for him and hopefully did it well.

Over the years, of course, we've become closer. Nowadays, we'd ring each other to chat about anything and everything, be it football, where we're going on holidays, all that mundane carry-on. I'd never have done that in the early days. He's always been very approachable but the way I saw it, he was under a lot of pressure from owners with a lot of money invested in their horses and he didn't need me being any sort of complication to him. This was simpler all round.

He was running a huge operation at Ditcheat even then. It was fascinating to see how different he and Willie were in their approach to training horses, given the fairly similar amount of success they ended up having. They're polar opposites on first sight. Where Paul trains his horses up a hill, Willie trains his on a round gallop. But whatever way they skin their cats, they keep doing it and doing it year after year.

If there's a key to Paul's success, it's that he puts massive emphasis on schooling them and then getting his horses very fit. It sounds simple but if it was, then everybody would be doing it. He's a ruthless judge of what a horse is capable of. He knows how good his horses are, he gets what he can out of them and he's not afraid to replace them if he thinks he's taken them as far as they're going to go.

If he gets a horse that the handicapper has clearly caught up with, he won't be afraid to sell it on and get in a younger one that might win three or four novice races in the year it would take for the first horse's mark to come back down. When a horse gets to a mark above his ability, it becomes very hard to win with them. If Paul thinks a horse has reached its level, he won't hang on to it just on the off chance it might improve again. That way, he keeps the yard fresh and keeps the winners flowing through.

I loved it from the start over there. I remember one day early on finding myself at Plumpton on a Monday for three races. They weren't particularly good races and nobody at the track or in the weighing room was pretending there were any superstars in the parade ring. But I rode two winners for Paul on French Executive and Joyeux Royale that afternoon, reasonably useful handicappers that went on to win £30,000 or £40,000 apiece for their owners over their racing lives.

And I remember thinking to myself that a year ago, I'd have been watching it on television and instead, here I was riding two winners for the day. Plumpton on a Monday, Exeter on a Tuesday or Folkestone on a Wednesday might not have been glamorous but this was a marvellous life to be living as far as I was concerned. Even on the bad days when I won no race at all, riding four races beat riding four lots hands down.

The travel was a headache but no more than that. The actual physical act of going from A to B to C took nothing out of me at all. I can sleep on a plane or in the back of a car at the drop of a hat, no bother to me. No, the only hardship in it – and it wasn't so much a hardship as a complication in the beginning – was the sheer amount of logistics involved. Plotting a way through the airline timetables between here and England, organising lifts in the early days and hire cars later on.

It was around then that I decided I needed a driver. I had known Niall Almond for a few years – he's a brother of Ian Almond with whom we had played indoor soccer on Tuesday nights way back when. He hasn't been called Niall in years and I've always known him as Bubba. I've never called him anything else.

Anyway, this new arrangement with Paul was going to take a lot of organising and plenty of work and Bubba was around and available, so I asked him if he fancied doing a bit of driving for me. It has worked out very well between us. I'd say between then and now, he's driven me more miles in my life than I have myself. Up and down every road in Ireland, although he doesn't come to England with me.

It's been some help to have him. Just take trips to the airport, for example. If I had a half past six flight out of Dublin, Bubba would collect me at half-four and I'd be asleep in the car by twenty to five. He'd drop me to the airport and then come back and collect me that night or the following night. Or on the days I'm racing in Ireland, he picks me up and drives to the races while I'm going through the entries or organising things on the phone.

He's a good reliable fella too. Give him the keys of the car and tell him to meet you in Moscow and he'll be there. He'll look through my rides for the day in the morning and if he sees I'm doing light, he'll turn up half an hour earlier to give me time in the sauna. If I could only get him to quit listening to Joe Duffy, he'd be perfect.

So Bubba came on board. But as far as the logistics of going to England and back went, Jennifer came into her own, forever working out the smoothest route for me. Take Plumpton as a random example. For Plumpton, you fly to Gatwick. I'd always err on the side of caution going there, so that means you're up early and at the airport early. Always on the way home I'd cut it as fine as possible, but never on the way there. Once you land, find your transport. In that first year, I was still only twenty-two and the insurance if I wanted to hire a car at the airport was crazy. So I'd try to organise someone to give me a lift – it was usually Mick Fitzgerald, Seamus Durack, Timmy Murphy, A.P. McCoy or Carl Llewellyn. The lads in England were brilliant to me in those days.

If all else failed, Paul would send someone to pick me up. He was great like that. I could ring him any day of the week looking for a lift from an airport to a racecourse and he'd have somebody on it in a flash. But I didn't want to be a burden. I didn't want him thinking he had to provide me with a chauffeur service. So as soon as I turned twenty-three, I started hiring cars over there myself. You make arrangements as the years go by. Nowadays, I share with Barry Geraghty a lot. If I'm at Plumpton or Fontwell, I have a good friend called Brian Cassidy living in Hickstead who comes to pick me up.

After about six months of running around, I had the whole thing down to a tee. Name any racecourse in Britain now and I'll tell you the best airport, the best car company, the best road and the best services off the top of my head. If *Mastermind* ever come calling, I have a handy specialist subject ready.

The next thing was to learn a whole new way of racing and a whole new set of tracks. I felt like I was starting off as an amateur all over again. Whereas for those first years as a teenager I was following Willie Mullins, Philip Fenton and Tony Martin around Gowran, Tipperary and Wexford, now I was following A.P. McCoy, Richard Johnson and Mick Fitz around Warwick, Market Rasen and Chepstow. I did exactly the same sort of thing as I had before – worked out the form (I was better at that now than when I was seventeen), picked out the lads on fancied runners who were likely to have been given similar riding instructions as me and followed one of them. It was the best way to figure it all out.

On heavy ground, Andrew Thornton was always a good man to make sure you were on the same line as. There might have been jockeys around the scene who were easier on the eye to watch in the saddle but nobody figured out where the good ground was better than he did.

Bit by bit, I gradually worked out the various tracks. I'd been to Cheltenham a good bit obviously and the likes of Sandown a couple of times too. But most of the tracks were new to me. I thoroughly enjoyed working them out. I walked them all as much as I could, looking out for little details here and there.

I loved working out the best way to ride the figure of eight track in Fontwell, a unique track that takes you both left handed and right handed a couple of times. Or working out that the ground is always better out under the hedge in Plumpton early on in the season, until it gets too chopped up and you have to come back to the inside as the year wears on. Or that there's an old roadway down the back straight in Stratford to keep in mind. The bits and pieces that give you that little edge in a race.

I had to get used to a completely different racing culture over there as well. On good ground, racing is the same the world over. Most races are true-run and the best horse generally wins. But on winter ground, Ireland and England are worlds apart.

I'd watched English racing all my life but until I was in the middle of it, day after day, I never really got the difference between the two. Once the tapes go up in England, it's all go. You couldn't kick for home early enough in England. The jockeys would be winding up a finish from a good distance out, setting sail at the earliest opportunity. This was so different from back home. In Ireland, you were always encouraged to leave your run as late as possible.

There's a fundamental difference there and both sides are convinced they're right. I struggled back then – and I still do in all honesty – to set sail a long way from home. The only place you win is at the winning post, and the line is the only place you have to be in front. To me, the cardinal sin is going too fast and not getting home. If one thing kills me after a race, it's the thought of having done that.

We do a lot of our racing on soft ground and when you learn to read races, you'll work out that you need to ride conservatively on soft ground. You can make up a lot of ground late in the race. If you can finish faster than the others in the last half mile, you'll end up with a much better placing than your horse probably deserves.

Without getting too technical about it, basically it comes down to sectional times. James Willoughby wrote a brilliant article in the *Racing Post* about this a couple of years ago. If you can run the first half of the race on soft ground a second a furlong slower than the rest of the field, you will generally run the last half of the race around a second and a half a furlong quicker than them. It's no different in principle than if a human is running a marathon – bursting a gut for the first thirteen miles generally won't pay off over the second thirteen but a steady pace from the start will gradually allow you to build up a head of steam.

Take any two-mile race, hurdle or chase. If you're coming up the home straight in a two-mile race and your horse is slowing down in the last fifty yards, you've misjudged the pace. You've gone too fast too soon. If you've ridden your fractions properly and kept to your sectional times, your horse should be running when the post comes. A two-mile steeplechaser shouldn't be finishing tired if he's fit but the one sure way to make him weary late on is to set sail too soon.

I took a while to adapt to it over there, purely because of that instinct they have in England to start the finish earlier than at home. For one thing, you need to be fitter. I lost three pounds in the first couple of months over there just from race-riding. I went from ten stone five stripped to ten stone two, purely from riding seven days a week and being involved for four or five of those days in races where I was having to get motoring earlier than I was used to. I'd have horses off the bridle an age before I would have at home, working harder for longer from further out.

There's a huge difference there. Say you're riding a race at Leopardstown and your horse is off the bridle jumping the last ditch (which is five furlongs out), you'll be near enough pulling up coming to the last fence. But there are times when you'd be off the bridle at Chepstow with five to jump. And still win! That was the mad thing for me. You could still win most of your races riding in a way that went against the waiting instinct I'd grown up with.

There wasn't a snowball's chance of you winning a race in Ireland if you set sail with five to jump. Not a hope. If you were foolish enough to try it, you'd have three lads sitting up behind you on the bridle with smiles on their faces. But in England, those three lads would get involved and all four of you would take each other on in a mad dash for the line. It made for true-run races but it was alien to me for a good few months.

I had no real choice in the matter either. That's the culture of English racing and it's the way a lot of English trainers and owners want to see their horses ridden. It was all very well in the early days for me to be of the opinion that horses should be delivered late to win in the last furlong but when it didn't come off, I came back into the ring to find owners who were annoyed that I hadn't made more use of their horse. In the end, they pay the bills and their opinion has to be listened to.

That didn't always mean doing what I was told. They may stump up the money but they don't always know best. They can't. There were plenty of times when I'd chat to an owner before a race and he'd be telling me that I had to kick on at the fourth-last and I'd be thinking to myself, 'You have no chance of me doing that.' I can be fairly chippy sometimes and I occasionally wouldn't take kindly to being told what's what by some fella who's never ridden a horse, never ridden a race, never walked the back straight of the track we're at.

But look, I can think what I like but the owner is the most important part of the jigsaw. Smile, get on the horse, do what you think is best, take the bollocking if it doesn't work out. That's the job.

There were plenty of times it didn't work out in those early days with Paul and I'd say, hand on heart, it probably took me about two years to fully adapt to riding in England and Ireland at the same time. It happened a few times that I would come home from three days' racing in England to a meeting in Thurles on a Thursday and finish third in the first race because I'd hit the front way too soon. Switching from one mode to the other was definitely something I found difficult for a while.

I made plenty of mistakes and lost races I should have won but bit by bit I got used to it and seemed to keep most people happy.

On the first Saturday of October, I rode a treble for Paul at Chepstow, which was the best possible start I could have gotten off to. I was enjoying myself and handling the travelling and the hours pretty well.

But I was lucky too. There's every chance it could have gone wrong without the help of Gillian, Jennifer, Paul and Willie. Maybe the luckiest break I got, though, came from someone who would become both a close friend and a fierce rival over the years. He goes by plenty of names and a lot of people just use his surname when they're talking about him, which is a sure sign of a legend. I call him A.P.

In early December 2001, Henrietta Knight asked me to come to England to ride a few races and school some horses at her yard in Wantage, Oxfordshire. Jim Culloty had broken his arm in a fall at Taunton the week before the Hennessy and since I was going to be in England to ride Commanche Court in that race on the Saturday, I'd filled in on a horse of hers called Southern Star at Newbury on the Friday. It was the first time I'd ridden for her and she asked me over for a few days about a fortnight later.

It was to be a straightforward enough job. Head over on the Wednesday, do some schooling in the mornings, go racing in Ludlow on the Thursday and Cheltenham on the Friday and then home again in time for Navan on the Saturday. My only problem was that I had nowhere to stay for the two nights. I didn't know anybody in that part of England, or at least I didn't think so. So I rang James Nash. He'd know if I did or not.

'Who lives near Wantage that we know?' I asked.

'McCoy only lives up the road,' he said. 'Ring A.P., he'll sort you out.'

'Jesus,' I said. 'I don't really know him that well. Is there nobody else?'

'Just ring him. It'll be grand.'

I wasn't too sure about this at all. I wasn't on much more than nodding terms with Tony McCoy at that point. I'd say the most interaction we'd ever had was that April when we ran back up the course at Aintree and remounted Papillon and Blowing Wind in the Grand National. Beyond that, we'd say hello if we ran into each other but that was about the height of it. Now I was ringing him looking to stay in his house.

But I needn't have worried. He couldn't have been more sound about it. He gave me directions, said to come on round, that the spare room was mine if I wanted it. I stayed those two nights and before I went home on the Friday, he told me that any time I was over again just to give him a shout and there'd be a bed there waiting for me. So I did and there was and there has been ever since. I nearly have squatter's rights by now.

When it came about then a year later that I was going to have my new arrangement with Paul Nicholls, the use of A.P.'s spare room was great. To have a familiar face to sit down with after a day's racing, to have somewhere comfortable, welcoming and homely to spend the evenings was a big help.

Because there's no doubt about it – all the travelling and running around in a solitary sport like racing can be fairly wearing on the soul if you let it. I was leaving Ireland every week on a Monday morning, going racing at, say, Fontwell on Monday, Chepstow on Tuesday and Ludlow on Wednesday and flying home that night. It wouldn't have been very good for the spirits to be staying in a hotel or in digs. I could just see myself sitting in some Travelodge on a Monday night after a blank card that afternoon thinking I'd rather be at home with Gillian. There's every chance that could have worn me down bit by bit.

I'm not sure it would have been as easy for me to last in England without that spare room and the welcome I got from A.P. and his then girlfriend and now wife, Chanelle. I know I would have done a couple of years going over and back and would have stuck it out just to give it a chance, but if I'd been living with strangers in a guesthouse in the evenings or been stuck with the four walls of a hotel room, it could have ground me down. This way, although I didn't know A.P. very well in the beginning, we at least had common ground for conversations.

In fairness, we got on very well from the start. I wouldn't be the most needy house guest you ever came across. I have no special dietary requirements (none more special than his anyway) and I'm reasonably neat and tidy. He's never taken a penny in rent from me but I would always have tried to pay my way in some shape or form. I'd often offer to drive if it was needed.

I found him great company. It didn't matter to me that he'd been champion jockey six years in a row when I started with Paul. Well, it did but not on a person to person level. I was in awe of him as a rider. I always have been and I still am today. But that would never have made me feel self-conscious or make me worry that I couldn't slag him or talk to him.

Growing up, I was never allowed to be stroppy at home. If the racing went bad in the afternoon neither Mam, when I was a teenager, nor Gillian, as I got older, would ever put up with me taking it home that night. If you had a bad day, you left it in the car. So I guess I just had that same instinct when A.P. and myself would be driving home from the races. If he was after having a bad day and was in a bit of a strop, the only thing I knew to do in that situation would be to slag him, the same as David Casey or James Nash would have done with me.

Mick Fitzgerald was the same with A.P. 'Fitzy' would slag the arse off him every day of the week and twice as bad on Saturdays.

Seamus Durack too. Everybody would. We all treated him as just another jockey, just another fella in the weighing room. And I've always got on great with him as a result.

I made a good friend along the way, which was something I wasn't expecting at all. I'm not the friendliest guy in the world and most of my close friends are the lads I knew as a teenager. I can count the friends I've made as an adult. I can be cold when someone meets me for the first time. I'd always be polite but I wouldn't always go out of my way to be the life and soul.

I have a terrible habit of giving the smart-arsed answer. If I think somebody's asked me a stupid question or even if they've just got me at the wrong time when I've something on my mind, my first instinct a lot of the time is to come out with the sharp reply. So people come away thinking, 'Jaysus, that Ruby Walsh is rude.' And I'm the one who ends up kicking myself and thinking I'm an awful eejit.

My problem half the time is that I find it hard to just let things slide and do like everybody else does. For example, every jockey who ever rode a horse in a race gets stopped and asked for tips. It happens. It has always happened and it always will. You might be walking through an airport or coming back to the weighing room from walking the track and there's nothing surer than you'll get asked if you fancy anything that day.

I got advice when I was about seventeen that all I ever have to do when that happens is give the name of a horse. Pick a horse, any horse. All the punter wants is a name. All they want is to go back to their friends and say, 'I ran into yer man Ruby Walsh, he fancies Such-And-Such in the novice hurdle.' Give them a name and if it wins, it makes their day and they'll raise a glass to you afterwards. If it doesn't, sure that's racing and we go again.

But I still struggle to just blurt one out, even all these years later.

I know what I should do but I still find myself sometimes going, 'Well, I don't really fancy anything today,' and I don't like tipping losers. And it'd always be because I'd genuinely have doubts. But that's missing the point. The point is, it's only good manners to give them a horse. By saying nothing, I'm only bringing needless bad feeling on myself. At best, the punter watches me walk away into the weighing room thinking that I know well what's going to win and just won't tell him. At worst, two of my horses go and win and the punter thinks I put him off a nice double.

I guess it's because of the nature of the sport. People are always looking for winners from you. Everybody you meet wants to think they have the inside track, a tip for a horse that nobody else has. And I understand that, I do. But it can get fairly tiresome all the same, especially if I have something on my mind or if I'm busy.

Take the Leopardstown gallops that are traditionally held after racing on the Sunday a week before the start of Cheltenham. A lot of Irish trainers use this as the last serious piece of work before heading off to the festival. Obviously, as it's a race day, a lot of the punters stay on to watch. They get given a bit of a guide as to who's riding which horses by looking at the different coloured caps we're wearing but nobody is in traditional racing colours. So it can be hard to follow for the punters who stay on to watch, which means they'll often ask as you trot by what the name of your horse is.

And I can't help it. Part of me just instinctively bristles at being asked. I want to say to the fella, 'Look, it's really none of your business what the name of the horse is. I'm here to do a job. I'm here to school this horse, to think about what's going on, what he needs, what might happen to him at Cheltenham. I'm not here to multi-task so that I can help you out. This is work.' But that would take too long. So I usually don't answer.

I don't think I'm cocky or arrogant but I have no doubt that I can come across like that sometimes. The thing is, it's hard to maintain an even composure sometimes. You'd be amazed at some of the people you meet who want to tell you how to ride a horse. I'll listen to Dad, I'll listen to Willie, and I'll listen to Paul. I'll listen to other trainers and jockeys even if I disagree with them because at least they're coming from a place of knowledge and expertise. I'll listen to owners as well because they pay the bills and a good bit of the time they have a fair idea of what they're talking about.

But you wouldn't believe how often I'll be sitting beside some fella on a flight back from Birmingham, Bristol or Heathrow and he'll be asking me did I not think of maybe making a bit more use of this horse or that horse. Or over the years when we'd be out in Dublin after the Hennessy meeting in Leopardstown and some big lump would be telling me I went too soon on one that got beaten. And I'll be sitting there thinking, 'Are you for real? You never sat on a horse in your life.' I won't say it but my demeanour will give me away. That sort of chap will very likely go away thinking that Ruby Walsh is a terrible cocky fella who thinks he's better than everyone.

It's not true. Not true at all. But it's very hard sometimes just to smile and nod. I remember when I was about nineteen being at the races at Tralee and some fella was giving me loads across the railing after a race. In my naivety, I started giving him loads back until after a few seconds, I felt somebody at my elbow. It was Richard Dunwoody, pushing me away and telling me to trot on. 'Shut up,' he said. 'You'll get nowhere answering them.'

And he was 100 per cent right. Dad and Willie would say the same. Smile. Nod. Turn your back. Tell them they're probably right. No point getting into it. But sometimes I can't resist a comeback. It's just in my nature.

That's one of the main reasons myself and A.P. hit it off. Neither of us would take any offence at the smart-arsed answer. Most of the time, the usual response to each other would be to find something equally smart to say in reply. He understands only too well the difference between your public and private face anyway – look at the amount of people who thought he's this depressed, obsessive grump with no sense of humour! He's not, never has been in my company anyway. We all have bad days. That's part of life.

The fact that we've been competing against each other ever since I started working for Paul never made the least bit of difference to either of us. When I rode a treble for Paul at Chepstow on that first big Saturday in October 2002, he won two of the other four races on the card. Even though the relationship between our bosses might have got a bit spicy at times – check out Paul's book *Lucky Break* for the inside track – there was never anything between me and A.P. We just got on with our races and tried to beat each other on the track every time we could.

A fortnight after that treble, I was starting getting into a rhythm with Paul. I went over and rode two in Hereford on a Friday and then went to Market Rasen the next day to ride another couple for Paul and a few spares for other trainers. All those rides and I only had one winner all weekend. But what a winner.

Azertyuiop was a bit different to any horse I'd ever ridden before. Alexander Banquet was a classy horse. Florida Pearl was top, top-class, even if he and I had no luck together. Commanche Court and Papillon were great too but none of them was anything like Azertyuiop. Put it this way – Papillon was the best two-mile steeplechaser I'd ridden up to that point and he turned out to be a Grand National horse.

This day in Market Rasen, I could not get Azertyuiop to settle. It was a novice chase over two miles one furlong and he just ran away with me. He bucked out and pulled so hard that I was a complete passenger all the way around. He went flat out from fence to fence and didn't give a damn who or what was up on his back. Not until we got to the last fence did I have any sort of control over him beyond pointing him in the right direction. By then, we were the length of the straight clear of the rest of the field.

I was blown away that day. I'd never got that sort of feel off any horse in my life. Usually if you're on a horse that pulled as hard as he did and went the gallop he did, you wouldn't have a hope of winning but this horse won by a distance. I couldn't believe that he was still so full of running all the way to the line. When I got off him in the parade ring, Paul had a big smile on his face. 'Well, what did you think of that?' he said. I was nearly lost for words.

If I'd had any doubts about giving it a go in England, they disappeared with Azertyuiop. I just hadn't ever ridden this sort of horse in Ireland. Azertyuiop was one of the new batch of French-bred superstars that were becoming the big trend in England, followed in the next few years by Kauto Star, Master Minded, Big Buck's and loads more. Horses like that were the best reason for splitting my time between Ireland and England. It's very rare that you can get down off a horse in the middle of October and be convinced you've just ridden the next winner of the Arkle but that was the case with Azertyuiop.

The big Saturday races were what Paul was after and we won our first Tingle Creek together that winter with Cenkos. The two favourites that day, Flagship Uberalles and Moscow Flyer, had a coming together in the middle of the race that ended up with Barry Geraghty on the ground and opened the race up for the rest of us. Cenkos did it well though and won by fourteen lengths.

Paul had a string of serious horses with which he picked off good races. Young Devereaux won a nice pot in Sandown just before Christmas and another in Kempton in January, beating the good Pipe horse Seebald both times. See More Business was still on the go at the age of thirteen and he won a decent Gold Cup trial that February in Wincanton. Shotgun Willy won the big Grand National trial at Haydock in early March to give Paul some hope for a race in which he was starting to get tired of having a poor record.

But Azertyuiop was the big hope going to Cheltenham 2003. He'd had two runs since that first novice chase in Market Rasen and you could hardly count the distances he won by. I think it was something like sixteen lengths in Cheltenham in November and twenty-five in Wincanton in February. We went to Cheltenham full of confidence in him and rightly so. He bolted in and won by ten lengths. Nobody had come close to him all season and he was by far the easiest Cheltenham Festival winner I had to my name by then.

Thank God for him, too, because I had no luck with any of my other rides that week. None of Willie's really fired and our best result of the week together was a third place for Macs Gildoran in the Cathcart Chase. I had a couple of thirds as well for Paul, on Cenkos in the Champion Chase and Ad Hoc in the William Hill. But like all the other jockeys that week, I was living in Barry Geraghty's world. He could do no wrong and rode five winners. Commanche Court ran in the Gold Cup but finished well down the field as Best Mate won his second in a row.

By the time the summer came around, I was happy enough with how the new arrangement had worked out. I ended up with seventy-six winners in England and seventy-eight at home, including some big races at the end of the season. Paul brought Sporazene and Le Roi Miguel over to win two Grade Ones at Punchestown and Ad Hoc won another Whitbread (or Attheraces Gold Cup as it was known then) in Sandown. I'll take that sort of return from any season.

But that summer was a desperately sad time for all of us in Irish racing. We lost two jockeys within a couple of months, the first racecourse deaths since Jim Lombard died after a fall in a banks race at Punchestown in the mid 1980s. Kieran Kelly and Seán Cleary were the same generation as me, doing the same job, taking the same risks and both of them died in random racecourse accidents that year. It was heartbreaking.

I didn't know Seán all that well. He was a flat jockey working in Jim Bolger's yard and we'd seldom have crossed paths. Any time there's a mixed card, they tend to keep the flat jockeys at one end of the weighing room and the jump jockeys at the other just for space reasons so we'd have known each other by sight but that was it. He died in a freak accident in Galway that November, when a horse he was riding clipped the heels of the one in front of him and he fell. He was on life support for almost a week before he died. I was in Melbourne with Davy Condon who was a good friend of Seán's. While we were all upset, Davy was heartbroken.

I knew Kieran Kelly very well though. We had started out at more or less the same time and had ridden against each other all the way up along from back as far as 1995. He'd started off in Mickey Flynn's yard then moved to work for Dessie Hughes where he'd been getting on great, winning good races on the likes of Colonel Braxton, Timbera and Mutineer. But his biggest days had come on Hardy Eustace. He'd won the Royal Bond at Fairyhouse and a good novice hurdle at Leopardstown over Christmas already that season, before the biggest win of his career in the Royal and Sun Alliance Hurdle at Cheltenham.

We got on well together. His spot in the weighing room in Kilbeggan was right beside mine and he was a great guy to have next to you, full of banter and good humour. I wasn't riding in the race he fell in that evening but I was in the one that came after it. You could tell straight away there was something seriously wrong because the fence was still dolled off for the next race and as we went down to the start, you could see why. Some of the medical equipment had been left on the track in the rush to get Kieran away to the hospital.

That evening, everybody was ringing around to see if there was any news. The Dublin Horse Show was on that week so after racing Gillian and I and a few friends went up to it. Paul Carberry was there as well. I got a phone call from Dad at one stage to say that the word wasn't good. In the back of our heads we were going, 'Ah, he'll pull through, at least it's not the worst news.' But it was only delaying the worst news. Kilbeggan was on a Friday night; he died the following Tuesday.

We were racing in Gowran Park that evening when the news came through. It knocked the stuffing out of every one of us. It was just sickening to hear. Norman Williamson was one of the older lads in the weighing room and he took it upon himself to tell fellas one by one as they were coming off the track. I liked the way he did that – no big announcement, no histrionics. Just a quiet word in each man's ear so they could take a little time with it.

You have to understand what a weighing room is like for us. A weighing room is more than a changing room. It's more like a community. It's a friendly place where we all find our little spot and settle into our little routines. From the first day you get a ride at a racecourse until the day you retire, the weighing room is where you make good friends and have great fun. It's where you celebrate your wins and lick your wounds after a defeat.

How many sports can you think of where the competitors get changed side by side, go out and try as hard as possible to beat each other and then come back to the same room and change back in the same spot? Golf and tennis maybe, but that's about it. We live each other's lives, organise lifts among ourselves, book hotel rooms together, turn up at each other's birthdays and stag parties and weddings. And that all starts in the weighing room.

Being in that room makes us all very protective of each other. Jockeys will back jockeys ninety-nine times out of 100. We argue amongst ourselves, of course we do. We're athletes filled with adrenaline in a sport that can get fairly hairy at times. But I can count the punch-ups I've seen on one hand. And they're never actual punch-ups anyway. Not proper ones. If two fellas start, there's half a dozen pulling them apart within seconds.

But we don't let things fester. There's too much slagging to let things fester. Carry a grudge and you'll get it slagged out of you. You have to have a thick skin and I've seen plenty of shy young fellas who go into the weighing room at seventeen and don't say a word for two years but who grow into men then and learn to dish it out. I was one myself.

A weighing room is a great place that you never get tired of. I see it in the fellas who've retired, how they revel in dropping by the odd time to say hello to everyone. They might not miss the sauna or the wasting or the big fences but they miss the weighing room.

Bring death into that weighing room and everybody stops. It's often a lively place where you struggle to hear yourself think but that day in Gowran, there was just silence. Some of Kieran Kelly's best friends were in that room. We were all just numb.

It's too easy to say that we were all sitting there thinking, 'Jesus, that could have been me.' We weren't. We were all sitting there in shock at the thought of Kieran dying. But in the days that followed, it probably hit a few of us. This had never happened before while any of us were in the weighing room but we all know the chance we take when we get on a horse. It's part of the life you choose.

Fellas get injured. Some get very badly hurt like Shane Broderick, who was paralysed after a fall in Fairyhouse or Jimmy Mansell, who had a bad fall in Ballinrobe and had to retire. On extremely rare occasions, something horrific happens and there's a death. It's desperately sad and we all feel it to our bones. But it didn't make me question what I do for a living or anything like that.

When the news came through in Gowran that evening, I took off my colours and said I was going home. There were two races left on the card but I didn't care about them just at that moment. There were a few of the lads who were based in the Curragh who really knew Kieran well, the likes of Alan Crowe and Garrett Cotter and more and they had no interest in riding in the last two either. So myself and Norman went to the stewards.

I'll never forget the stewards in Gowran that evening and I still can't believe the stance they took. They could have had a bit of human decency and made life a lot easier for us, but we nearly had to beg them to call off the last two races. Norman and I went into them and said, 'Look, don't know if you've heard but Kieran Kelly has passed away in the last hour or so. Now, we're not refusing to ride in the last two races but there are a lot of lads in the weighing room who don't want to ride and we'd prefer it if you called the last two races off as a mark of respect.'

I expected them to just say, 'Yeah, Jesus, of course we will. Sure it's only right.' But instead, the chairman of the stewards said, 'Let's get this straight – ye're not refusing to ride. So if we decide to race, ye'll ride?' And I said, 'Well, yeah but we're asking as a mark of respect that ye don't do that.'

'OK,' he said. 'But if we decide to keep racing, ye'll ride.' I was getting annoyed now, thinking to myself that this wasn't right. So we left the stewards' room while they deliberated. When we were called back, they asked for a representative of the amateur jockeys to join us so Denis Cullen came as well. They wanted to know whether if we didn't ride, would the amateurs take the rides in the professional race. But Denis said no, that if the professionals weren't going to ride as a mark of respect, neither were the amateurs.

In the end they called the two races off but they weren't happy about doing it. They were worried about what they'd tell the public. I told them to show me where the microphone was and I'd make the announcement myself. So I did. I told them that Kieran Kelly had passed away in the afternoon. That he was a proper jockey and even more so, a proper man. And that as a mark of respect, his friends and colleagues in the weighing room have asked that the last two races on the card be cancelled. The public are decent people and not one of them said a bad word to us as we left.

That was the worst day I ever had in racing. Probably the worst day any of us ever had. Any time I think I've had a bad day,

I remember Kieran and snap myself out of it. Losing a race or breaking a bone doesn't compare to that feeling when the news came through. It took a while for everyone to move on. But Kieran Kelly will never be forgotten.

CHAPTER 9

Ruby, meet Kauto

Injured again. You get used to it after a while. If you're going to spend your life on the back of a live animal going at thirty miles an hour, you're going to fall sometimes. The average is around once in every eight or nine rides. After the vast majority of them you hop right back on your feet and if it's sore at all, the pain has more or less passed by the time you reach the weighing room. Anything else, you try to shake off before the next race.

It's just an instinct that's bred into jockeys. Your first thought is the next race. Can I ride? How long will I be out? When can I get back? It can lead to comical scenes sometimes.

When I was nineteen, I was brought down in a beginners' chase in Fairyhouse on a horse of Willie's called Kings Return. I came back into the weighing room, passed everybody who was asking if I was all right and put on a set of Seamus Ross's colours. Seamus has had horses with Dad for years and Royal Signature was his runner that day. Dad came to the door of the weighing room and saw me with the colours on.

'What are you doing?'

'I'm riding Royal Signature in the next for you.'

'What are you talking about? No you're not.'

'I am of course.'

'You're not. You rode him earlier. He finished second!'

'Did I?'

'Yes! Get changed, you're not riding again today.'

So I stood myself down for the day by telling the doctor I had a sore knee after the fall. I didn't want him to think I had concussion because then he'd stand me down, probably only forty-eight hours, but there was a chance it might be more. As it was, I was back for the weekend and only missed one meeting. Mind you, I couldn't find my car when I went out to the car park.

It was the height of stupidity, of course. You shouldn't take risks with your head like that. I'm pretty sure that's the only time I've managed to get away with trying to fool a doctor into thinking I had all my wits about me.

In Listowel in September 2003, I had no problem with concussion but I did have another hip injury. It annoyed the hell out of me. Whereas the fall in 2001 had been a bad one, this one was just unlucky. I was on a horse of Joe Crowley's called Caishill, racing on the new track when he hit the top of the third fence past the stands. It was a bad mistake and he felt like he was going to fall so I slipped the reins a little to let his head go.

But fair play to the horse, he found a leg out of somewhere and managed to stand up. Since I had let out the reins though, this meant that I was going backwards with nothing to stop me. Gravity took over eventually, just as we were crossing the road where the traffic comes in and out, about fifteen strides past the fence. So when I hit the ground, I landed on road rather than grass.

This one hurt. Not as bad as the time before in Listowel when I'd dislocated the hip, but pretty bad all the same. I was fit to stand up and tried to walk over to the ambulance but I knew it wasn't good. I went to Tralee Hospital to get it x-rayed and it turned out that I'd fractured the hip right on the ball of the joint. The doctor said he was going to put a pin in it.

This set off alarm bells. I don't mind getting a cast put on by a doctor I don't know but a pin is a different story. I wouldn't want a pin put in at all if I could help it but definitely not without Bill Quinlan seeing it first. So I signed myself out of the hospital and Dad drove back to Kill.

By the next morning Bill had seen me in St Vincent's. He sent me for an MRI scan which showed that the ball at the head of the joint had a crack in it that went three-quarters of the way through. He said as long as I rested it and didn't put any weight on it, the crack would close up naturally in about six to eight weeks. No pin necessary.

Just like two years before, I said to hell with this and booked a holiday. It was a trip of a lifetime. I started in New Jersey with the jump Breeders' Cup with Dad and Jennifer and Gerry Hogan before heading to Santa Anita in California for the flat Breeders' Cup, where I met Gillian. And then we headed on to the one city in the world any Irish sports fan wanted to be that month. Melbourne. The International Rules series was on between Australia and Ireland, the Rugby World Cup was on and Willie even had a runner in the Melbourne Cup. It was great for me but when you consider that Gillian went from Dublin to Los Angeles to Melbourne without catching her breath, she was well in need of a holiday by the time we landed in Australia.

The Breeders' Cup was a great night. Mick Kinane and Aidan O'Brien had another winner, this time with High Chaparral who dead-heated with Johar in the Breeders' Cup Turf. In Melbourne we watched the International Rules at the Melbourne Cricket Ground (the famous MCG) on the Friday night. As far as I could see, they should have renamed it No Rules Whatsoever rather than International Rules because I couldn't tell you what was going on.

On Saturday night, we went to see Australia beat Ireland in the Telstra Dome in the Rugby World Cup. We had some great nights out and met plenty of friends. Everybody seemed to be in the Crowne Plaza which, once you found your way into, you couldn't find your way out of. It was some weekend to be Irish in Melbourne. Everywhere you went you ran into somebody you knew from home.

The Melbourne Cup was mindboggling. The magnitude of it is just incredible. I thought Cheltenham was a big deal. I thought the Grand National was a big deal. I thought the Breeders' Cup was a big deal. But they're all chicken feed compared to the Melbourne Cup. The size of the crowds blew me away. When they say it's the race that stops the nation, they're not joking.

It was a great holiday from start to finish. I was at the point now where I could enjoy an extended break like that. There was a huge difference between then and when I broke my leg as a nineteen-year-old because the mental toll taken by the time off wasn't nearly as great. Obviously, I would have still preferred to have been able to ride but at least now I wasn't fretting every day about the rides I was missing and what sort of future I'd be coming back to. At least not to the same extent.

That was one of the main things that changed as I got older. It still kills me to watch a horse I'd have ridden win a big race with me in an armchair and crutches leaning against the wall of the sitting room. But I know from past injuries that it's possible to get back to the same level of fitness that I had before and that if I work hard enough there's a good chance of getting the rides back. So if I'm watching a horse win that I would have been on,

I think of its potential and what we might win together in the future. That's what I try and convince myself of anyway.

I wasn't long back in action before the big Saturday races started coming thick and fast. I love that stretch from late October to Christmas, when every weekend brings serious racing in England that Paul is mad to win and has laid out his horses for. On the last Saturday in November, Strong Flow won the Hennessy. He was only a novice that year and Paul was having doubts over whether or not to run him but he needn't have worried. He hacked up.

The very next week, I was back on Azertyuiop to take on Moscow Flyer in the Tingle Creek at Sandown. He'd galloped straight into the first fence at Exeter a few weeks earlier and unseated Mick Fitzgerald so this was effectively his first run of the season and he was short the match practice he would have needed to compete with as good a horse as Moscow. But getting back on him was exciting because straight away I could feel the difference between him and most other horses I'd ridden.

He was a championship horse, no doubt about it. He jumped his fences so quickly and so economically. He never bent his back over a fence, always just lifted his shoulders and cleared the jump. Then when he hit the ground on the other side, he was always running. We were disappointed that day in Sandown but not heartbroken. He was going to be our Champion Chase horse for the season and if you thought one thing, it was that Paul would get him to Cheltenham ready for action.

Azertyuiop came on a ton for that run and although he got beaten again next time out in the Victor Chandler at Ascot in January, it was only by a neck in the end and he was giving Isio nearly a stone and a half in weight. We were delighted with the run and knew he'd make amends next time out in the Game Spirit. He did too, by twelve lengths.

That set the scene for the Champion Chase. All season, people had been saying it was a two-horse race between Azertyuiop and Moscow Flyer. Moscow was a great champion, unbeaten over fences any time he finished his race. He'd won an Arkle, he'd won a Tingle Creek, he'd won a Champion Chase and every good two-mile chase there was to win in Ireland as well. But he some-times had issues getting round. Every few races, he either fell or sent Barry flying. He'd done it in the Tingle Creek that Cenkos had won and again at Punchestown the following year.

And lo and behold, he did it again in the Champion Chase at Cheltenham. You know the way jockeys hate getting unseated? Well, this was one of the times that deserved an asterisk to go with it to let you know that the jockey hadn't a hope of staying on. Unless Barry had been tied to the horse that day, he wasn't going to survive the mistake at the fourth-last.

With Moscow gone, Azertyuiop bolted in. We went a length clear three out, three lengths clear at the second-last and had seven lengths on the field jumping the final fence. He won every bit as easily as he'd won the Arkle the previous year.

I was leading rider at the festival for the first time that year. On top of Azertyuiop, St Pirran won the Grand Annual and Spora-zene won the County Hurdle. When Earthmover won the Fox-hunters, it meant that Paul was leading trainer at the festival for the first time since 1999 with four winners. Since Earthmover beat Dad's horse Never Compromise in that race, I was happy for Paul but I wished his fourth winner had come some other way.

He and I were a good team by this stage. We rarely disagreed over the best way to ride a particular horse and most of the time his instructions were just to go and do what I thought was best. I think he probably came to realise that's what I'd do anyway. I took instructions on board for every race if they were given to me but once I was out there, I was going to ride how I was going to ride. I was a lot more comfortable backing myself by that stage, no matter who the trainer was. I was nearly twenty-five, old enough and experienced enough to know that once the tapes went up, I was the one in charge.

It got me in trouble later that year when I got a fairly public dressing-down from John Hales, the owner of Azertyuiop, after the Tingle Creek. By the time we got to Sandown this time around, people were excited at the thought of a clash between Azertyuiop and Moscow Flyer. They'd only met twice before then, with Azertyuiop not up to his best on one occasion and Moscow sending Barry into the clouds on the other. This time, nobody wanted to hear any excuses. It was a showdown, plain and simple. We had the Arkle winner Well Chief in the race as well, but as far as everyone was concerned he was a horse with potential whereas the other two were superstars.

Paul entered Cenkos in the race and he made the running with Barry following on Moscow Flyer. Although Azertyuiop was keen enough from the start, Barry was outside me and in front of me all the way. No sign of a jumping error either. We went a right gallop and when we came away from the three railway fences down the back, Barry was a couple of lengths in front of me as we turned for the pond fence.

He took a peep around to see where he was. I was happy enough with where I was at that point. I gave Azertyuiop a little squeeze just to mosey up on to Moscow's tail but the problem came when we got to the pond fence. Moscow pinged it, Azertyuiop didn't. Moscow landed running, Azertyuiop landed in a heap. By the time we'd gathered ourselves, Barry was gone. To this day, I think he won with a fair bit in hand. We got to within a couple of lengths but still only beat Well Chief by a short head or so.

John wasn't happy. In fact, he was pretty annoyed with me. He said I should have gone upsides Barry going down the back and taken him on at the railway fences. When a few reporters asked him what he thought, he said the same to them. So there were a few headlines criticising the way I rode the race. I said nothing, just stood there and took it. John was absolutely entitled to his opinion and as the man who paid the bills for the horse he was absolutely entitled to air them.

That doesn't mean I agreed with him about the way the horse should have been ridden. I didn't then and I don't now. Paul said to me a few days later that I should have gone to challenge Moscow earlier and we had to agree to disagree in the end. Even now, I still don't think I did anything wrong that day. The reality of it is that I don't think Azertyuiop would have won whatever way I rode him. Moscow was the better horse on the day. He never did anything in front and if I'd gone to challenge him, I think there's a fair chance that he might have won further and my lad could have finished third.

But the key is that I don't know that for sure. I might think it – and, as the jockey in the race, I'd say I have as valid a view on it as anyone else – but I don't know. The only thing I know for certain is that the way I rode him didn't work out. I've thought about it a few times since on that basis and wondered whether or not I should have just done as I was told. We might not have won that way either but at least then there would have been no hassle afterwards.

That's a dishonest way of doing things though. I wouldn't have been true to myself if I'd just gone with the flow. Nor, for that matter, would I have been true to John Hales if I'd done it his way, as odd as that sounds. I'm paid to ride the best race I can and get the best result. If I'd done as I was told and Azertyuiop had lost, I'd have been kicking myself for not doing what I thought was right. This way, I have no regrets. Even now, knowing how the race panned out and what the result in the books says, I'm fairly sure I'd ride him the same way again. If Azertyuiop pings the pond fence and lands running the same as Moscow, you never know what might happen from there.

There was never any bad feeling between John and me in the aftermath. He loves his horses and he wears his heart on his sleeve. He wanted 'x' done and I did 'y', simple as that. Three weeks later, Azertyuiop was entered in the King George and I actually ended up annoying another of Paul's owners, Andy Stewart, by taking the ride after previously committing to ride Le Roi Miguel in the race.

This was one of those situations where I couldn't be sending Jennifer out to bat for me. I had to be the one to make the phone call. I'd ridden Le Roi Miguel to win the Peterborough Chase at Huntingdon a few weeks before the Tingle Creek. He was a very good horse and we'd won those Grade Ones together at Aintree and Punchestown the previous year. But he was no Azertyuiop, who by now was a higher-rated steeplechaser than even Best Mate who'd won the last three Gold Cups. If Paul wanted to step Azertyuiop up to three miles around Kempton, then I wanted to be on him.

Paul was in an awkward position because John and Andy were two of the biggest owners in his yard. I was in Portarlington the day he rang to say he was entering Azertyuiop in the King George. He suggested that I let Paul Carberry take the ride since I'd already told Andy I'd ride his horse in the race.

My first instinct was to say fair enough. But no more than a minute later, I rang Paul back and said I couldn't do it. Azertyuiop was the better horse, simple as that. The furthest he'd ever raced over was two miles four furlongs in the Aintree Hurdle two and a half years previously. This was going to be a big step up and I wasn't going to miss out on it.

I rang Andy up and said: 'Look, I'm very sorry but Azertyuiop is going to run in the King George and I'm going to ride him.' He wasn't best pleased, obviously. By me doing this, I was demoting his horse and basically saying Le Roi Miguel was an also-ran. That's how Andy would have seen it anyway.

But I knew that if I was lining up at Kempton in the same race as Azertyuiop, all I'd have been doing was looking over at Paul Carberry wondering what sort of feel he was getting, wondering how well Azertyuiop was going. What would have been the point of me riding Le Roi Miguel? I would have struggled to give him an honest ride in those circumstances.

In the end, it didn't matter. Azertyuiop finished third that day without threatening Kicking King. And to be honest about it, I don't think he ever really got over going the three miles. Although he scrambled a win against Well Chief in Newbury the next time out, he ran a stinker in the Champion Chase.

He was a different horse by then. Whereas in the Tingle Creek I had been trying to settle him going down the back straight, I was having to squeeze him to stay in touch in the Champion Chase only three months later. He got injured in Sandown when second to Well Chief that April and never ran again, retired when he was only eight years old. It was a sad way for a brilliant horse to finish his career.

As for Le Roi Miguel, I rode him again in Aintree that year to finish second in the Melling Chase, again to the great Moscow Flyer. Just like with John Hales, I was keen to make sure there was no bad feeling between myself and Andy. We actually had a treble together five days later at Cheltenham and thankfully that was only the beginning of the good days for us. The likes of Big Buck's and Celestial Halo have come along since and brought his family a lot of success.

I've always known there's no point falling out with owners. Racing is a small world and one thing we all know for sure is that everybody will meet again down the road. I've made mistakes that have cost owners prize money. I know I have. But I've never done it deliberately in my life. And if I make an error of judgement, I'm the first to say it as soon as I get off the horse. I never try to pull the wool over owners' eyes. I'll always be honest and straight and if an owner still wants to have a go, then fair enough. He pays the bills, he can have his go.

The King George was on a Sunday that year, and after a treble on the Tuesday at Chepstow that included the Welsh National on Silver Birch, I went to Newbury on the Wednesday to ride a four-year-old novice steeplechaser for Paul. I had to do ten stone seven on him and Paul said he thought he might turn out to be a decent enough sort. He was another of Paul's French imports and this was going to be his first run in England. I'd never sat on him nor even seen him before until I walked out into the parade ring. Paul said just to drop him in third or fourth and see how I got on. That was how I met Kauto Star.

Pronounced 'Auto' with a K in front of it, by the way – even though I've always struggled to get 'Kayto' out of my head. I really should get it right because I always hate it when people pronounce my surname as 'Welsh' rather than 'Walsh'.

I wasn't expecting a whole lot that day. No matter how much Paul thought of him, this looked like a hot enough novice chase. You had Locksmith, who looked to me to be a decent Pipe horse and you had Foreman, who'd won the AIG Champion Hurdle at Leopardstown the previous season. As far as I was concerned, it might not have been the Arkle but it was an Arkle-like race in terms of quality.

Granted, they never turned out to be superstars afterwards but those horses had big reputations going to Newbury. I actually remember thinking that if Paul thought so much of this new French horse, maybe he shouldn't be running in a tough race like this first time out in England. That's why he's the trainer and I'm the jockey.

So I dropped him in third or fourth and he travelled like a dream and jumped like a stag. Halfway down the back straight he was doing a half-speed in front and after he jumped the last on his own he sprinted all the way to the line. I just thought to myself, 'Jesus, this is an aeroplane.' I couldn't believe how easily he'd won. These were horses with serious reputations and he'd just galloped them into the ground.

Just like we had with Azertyuiop a couple of years earlier, we were full sure we had the Arkle winner on our hands. He was made favourite for the race that day. Paul wanted to get another run into him before Cheltenham so he went to Exeter at the end of January. But Kauto had been such a good winner at Newbury that nobody fancied taking him on so it was only a three-horse race in the end up. He went off the 2–11 favourite.

It was the same story again most of the way around. We went a decent gallop and once we'd jumped the last ditch five out, I said I'd let him roll along. There wasn't a bother on him until he got a bit tight at the second-last and turned over. By the time he and I had jumped to our feet, there was still nothing gone by us. He'd been that far ahead. It was only as I grabbed his reins that Andrew Thornton went by on Mistral De La Cour, going about two miles an hour as he headed up to the last fence.

I didn't think twice. I hopped back up on Kauto to give chase.

The only problem was that Kauto was wearing a bar bit and when he fell the reins had gone over the top of the bar on the right-hand side which meant I only had the use of the left rein. The reins were basically of no use to me at all. So I was going down to the last not only with no stirrups but with no reins either. It meant I was loose on his back as he jumped the last.

He jumped it well enough in the circumstances but the lack of reins cost us the race. If I'd had reins, I'd have had a hold of him coming to the fence and he'd have been a lot quicker over it. As soon as we landed, I hit him a few flicks and he took off. He sprinted to the line from there and if the winning post had been another stride further on, he'd have got up. As it was, we lost by a short head.

I got back in to the parade ring and we all had mixed feelings about it. Clive Smith, his owner, and Paul were there and we were all disappointed that he'd fallen and that he'd just failed to get up to win. But we were delighted with the way he tore after Andrew's horse once he got back on his feet. He was obviously a really exciting prospect.

We were racing in Taunton the next day so I stayed at A.P.'s place that night. First thing the next morning, I got a phone call from Paul. There was a problem with Kauto Star. He was lame on one of his hind legs. Once they x-rayed him, they found there was a hairline fracture in his hock and that put him out for the season.

World War Three broke out. I got plenty of stick for remounting. People put two and two together and decided they knew for certain they had four. Henrietta Knight had a go, the RSPCA had a go, and plenty of people had a go. I was lambasted for this terrible act of cruelty to the horse.

It was all rubbish. It never once crossed my mind that I might have done anything to injure the horse. Until Paul rang me to tell me he was lame, I hadn't given the race a second thought other than to maybe say to A.P. that I thought Kauto was a machine. Remounting wasn't an issue at all.

It wasn't. I had been remounting horses all my life. Ever since I was a kid riding ponies, if you fell off you got right back on. But you always did it for a reason. If Ted, Katie and I had were out hacking across the fields as youngsters and one of us had a fall, we got back on our pony because it was a good walk back to the house. If I'm schooling a racehorse and we take a fall, I get up and catch him before we go again so that the horse can get his confidence back. If you're hunting and you fall off, you have to get back on to go and catch up because the hunt will go on without you. It was second nature to me. It's all I'd ever done.

If I fall in a race and we're a mile from the finish, I'll always hop back on and canter home. The only reason you'd rarely ever remount and keep going in the race is that 999 times out of 1000, the rest of the field is a furlong away by the time you and the horse are ready to go again. When I remounted Papillon in the Grand National, it was because A.P. and I knew there were only two horses left standing and there was a good reason to go again, because we could finish third or fourth. If there'd been six horses left up ahead of us, we wouldn't have bothered.

The same applied with Kauto at Exeter. This was a three-horse race that had already been reduced to a two-horse race after Tom Scudamore's horse Goldbrook had pulled up before the third-last. If there'd been six horses in the race, there'd have been no reason to remount. But by the time Kauto and I were both back on our feet, nothing had gone past us. So when Andrew went by at a snail's pace, straight away I made a snap judgement that the race was there to be won. It turned out I was wrong by a few inches so it wasn't such a bad guess.

I know it looked bad that Kauto missed the Arkle because of the injury but nobody knows one way or the other when or where the fracture to the hock happened. Nobody knows if it happened in the fall or if it was caused on the way to the line. Nobody knows that he didn't just crack it off something in his box. There's a fair likelihood that it happened in the fall but nobody knows. And yet the way people went on, you'd swear this was definitive proof that remounting is cruel on racehorses.

It took a few years but the BHA eventually banned remounting in 2009. In my opinion, it's not a good rule at all and I find it pretty insulting to me as a jockey. It's basically saying that we can't be trusted to look after a horse, that we're too greedy to worry about the safety of these animals. It's saying that we're not capable of making that decision and that really, we're just there to kick them, slap them and use them for whatever gain we can get out of them. It's a completely unfair perception if it exists and it must exist somewhere along the line within the authorities for this decision to be arrived at.

Maybe they did it for public relations reasons. But I think they'd be better off educating the public about what it means to remount a horse rather than just to ban it outright. Because if you're going to start with the remounting, where do you stop? Do you stop horses running if they sweat up in the ring beforehand because that signifies that they're agitated and nervous? Do you cancel racing in the rain because horses aren't all that keen about running when it's pouring down? The whole thing is ridiculous.

But it's a battle that's lost now and I just hope the Turf Club don't go the same way in Ireland. Actually, it was never even a

The final fence in the 2007 Gold Cup. It wasn't tidy but Kauto and I got there in the end.

Me and A.P. McCoy walking back after we both came down in the Arkle in 2007, me on Twist Magic and him on future Grand National winner Don't Push It.

At Punchestown with David Casey. I wonder what we were looking at.

Left Master Minded's first Champion Chase win in 2008.

Opposite page Andreas gives me my 200th winner of the 2008–09 season.

Me, Paul Nicholls and Clive Smith after Master Minded's first Champion Chase win in 2008.

Winning the Irish Champion Hurdle at Leopardstown on Brave Inca in 2008.

Posing for the Injured Jockeys' Fund Calendar in 2008, schooling at the Curragh.

Kauto Star winning his fourth King George in a row in 2009.

Neptune Collonges winning the Irish Hennessy in 2009.

Above Denman's second Hennessy win in 2009.

Below Meeting Gillian in the winners' enclosure after Kauto's second Gold Cup in 2009. The man with the red tie is Paul Nicholls' father, Brian.

Paul Nicholls, Clive Smith and me celebrating Kauto Star's second Gold Cup win in 2009.

Twist Magic winning the 2009 Tingle Creek.

battle. The BHA wanted it done and the majority of the press seemed to go along with it. When the decision was announced in October 2009, the *Racing Post* rang four jockeys in England to get a comment and not one newspaper rang me to ask what I thought. But what picture did they most of them use with their articles? Me on Kauto Star in January 2005.

In the end, I didn't lose too much sleep over it. Paul Nicholls never said a cross word to me about remounting Kauto Star and, more to the point, neither did Clive Smith. They both knew I hadn't done anything wrong and that I'd tried to get the best possible result for both of them. He ended up lame and missed the Arkle. In time, it might have been for the best anyway.

I don't think many people would argue it did much lasting damage, that's for sure.

CHAPTER 10

Hedgehunter

I always felt lucky to have won the Grand National with Papillon so early on but to be honest I didn't actually realise just how lucky I'd been. As the years went by, I realised that the race is only the half of it – you need a crazy amount of luck to even get a horse to the start. You need everything to go right for months in advance, sometimes up to a year and a half in advance. That's a lot of time, energy, money and patience to put into one horse for one race.

Yet every year in October, the owners and trainers of anything up to about 200 horses will think about entering. And when the entries come out in February, there'll be well over 100 horses in the race. After the final forfeit stage five days before the race, there'll still be sixty-five horses left in. Declarations are made two days before when the top forty in the weights are allowed to run. To find yourself riding one of those and be in with a chance going out on to the second circuit on the day takes huge amounts of luck.

If you want to try to win the Grand National, you have to play the system. You have to find a horse that you have a different opinion about to the handicapper. That's all handicapping is. It's an opinion. It's the one job in the BHA or the Turf Club where somebody gets paid for their opinion. At every other level, in every other job, you're met with rules that you have to follow. If you think a rule is wrong, there's usually nothing you can do about it only roll your eyes and get on with it. You can moan and whinge but generally you'll get nowhere.

But with an opinion, there's a grey area. Because an opinion can be wrong. And it's when you think the handicapper's opinion of a horse is too low that you move in and exploit it. That's how you play the system. If you think you've got a decent steeplechaser at the start of the season and the handicapper gives him a mark that makes you think he's missing something, you ask yourself if he'll stay four and a half miles. If the answer is yes, then you protect that mark for the winter.

When Hedgehunter fell at the last in the 2004 National, I'd say Willie Mullins was straight away thinking of the following year. He ran a bit free that day with David Casey and nobody could be sure just how well he'd have seen out the trip if he'd stayed on his feet. I was watching from the weighing room, having broken my wrist in a novice chase the day before, and to me he looked like he probably would have finished third. Willie would have decided pretty quickly that this horse's official rating would have to be protected once he came back after the summer.

Hedgehunter was a horse that had been a fixture in Willie's yard for nearly as far back as any of us could remember. He was definitely there as a three-year-old so that would mean he was about the place from 1999 or so onwards. He was owned initially by a man in Canada and he took an age starting off to get a win under his belt. Poor James Nash rode him in umpteen bumpers and was always second – in fact, he came second in nine of his first dozen races. By the time he eventually won a maiden hurdle in Clonmel in 2002 he was six. For a horse that turned out to be of such high quality, that's fairly old.

But he came alive when Willie sent him chasing the following season. By God, he could jump. He was by Montelimar, the sire of Monty's Pass who won a Grand National for Jimmy Mangan and Barry Geraghty. Willie ran him at Punchestown one day in February 2003 in the three-and-a-half-mile Grand National trial with Sam Curling claiming seven pounds off him. I was on a horse of Frances Crowley's called Golden Storm in that race and Hedgehunter had us beaten from early on. He jumped out in front and was never seen again. In a fourteen-runner race, half the field had pulled up by the end and the rest of us were strung out like the washing.

It was some performance and it was no surprise when Trevor Hemmings bought him that summer as a Grand National horse. He ran in the four-miler at Cheltenham that year but made a terrible mistake at the notorious second-last when travelling like a winner for Jamie Codd, and David Casey was fourth on him in the Hennessy that Strong Flow won in November. It was a combination of that race, the Welsh National, where he ran well but faded into third behind Bindaree, and the run at Aintree a few months later that made me think that maybe he just lacked that bit of stamina needed to win in 2005. But in between he also won the Thyestes at Gowran in 2004 with David on his back, which is usually a good pointer for the National.

Never underestimate Willie Mullins's ability to point a horse at a particular race and to get him there jumping out of his skin. From that fall in the 2004 National until the following spring, Hedgehunter didn't jump a fence in public. He ran over hurdles in Thurles, Clonmel, Fairyhouse, Leopardstown and Punchestown and only came back running over fences in the Bobbyjo Chase in

February. Willie had successfully managed to keep his chase mark at 144 so that when the weights came out, he was given eleven stone one pounds to carry. Usually, the rule of thumb is that horses carrying over eleven stone struggle to win the National but as far as I was concerned, Hedgehunter was well capable of being an exception.

I had another good Cheltenham that year. By now, I knew where to set the bar with the festival. If you can walk away from the week with one winner and no broken bones you've had a good Cheltenham. You may not be over the moon, you may think you should have had more but it's just too competitive to expect anything better than that.

This time around, I had two winners. Not enough to be leading rider again but pretty enjoyable all the same since one was for Paul – Thisthatandtother in the *Daily Telegraph* Chase (later known as the Ryanair) – and the other was Missed That in the Champion Bumper for Willie. I hadn't ridden a winner for Willie at Cheltenham in seven years, since Alexander Banquet all the way back in 1998. It was nice to get another one on the board for him.

All the while, we had Hedgehunter in the back of our minds. When Willie had asked me if I'd ride him in the National, I didn't think twice about it. I looked through the weights a couple of times and thought he had an outstanding chance. He was a really good traveller and had only ever fallen that one time at Aintree the year before. My worry was that it had been a tired fall and that maybe the trip might catch him out. He didn't do an awful lot off the bridle but that wasn't reason enough to look elsewhere.

When the day came, Willie had him in unbelievable nick. He was sweating in the parade ring beforehand but that was just Hedgehunter for you. He sweated so much more than any other horse I've ever known. Any paddock punters who looked at him in the parade ring would have to have been put off when they saw the amount of sweat that would roll off him, but it didn't mean a thing. The really weird thing was that when we'd go out on to the track and start racing, he wouldn't have a bead of sweat on him. The further he raced, the drier he got and he'd be bone dry jumping the last. But as soon as you pulled him up, straight away he'd be drenched in sweat again.

If it was any other horse, you'd be worried. All horses are different and there are plenty who you like to see with a little bit of sweat up their neck before a race. Kauto Star is like that and you could see it with Sea The Stars on the flat too. It means they're getting revved up. But with other horses, you hate to see it. You'd be very worried if you saw a horse like Big Buck's sweating up beforehand, for instance.

But Hedgehunter was a waterfall before a race, especially in his early days. He got very worked up as a young horse when you were riding him. When you went up to the gallops at Willie's, he'd be caked in sweat. And because he'd get so tense, he'd always be quite free once a race started. The reason he had so many second places early in his career was that he just ran too keen. The older he got, the more used to it he got and the quicker he settled. Still, when Willie and I talked about the National, we both agreed that the key would be to get him to switch off as quickly as possible.

Some jockeys hate Grand National day. They hate all the fuss and bother, the fact that there's a build-up of fifty minutes before the race, all that stuff. Mostly, they hate the lottery aspect to it and they hate it more and more every year until they retire having had no luck in the race. Either that, or they hate it until the day their number comes up and then they describe it as the best day of their lives. See A.P. McCoy for details.

Where I sat in the old weighing room at Aintree, I had Barry on one side and Paul Carberry on the other. We love Grand National day. I heard Barry describe it to the BBC one year as the best craic you'd have all season. Paul and I would say the same. But then we've all had the luck to win it.

The build-up can definitely be daunting the first time you go through it. Every year there are a few young lads riding in the race for the first time and they'll be just like I was in 2000. Quiet, nervous, wound up. No laughing or joking. Mad for it all to get started.

It takes ages though. We go out for a group photo first of all, like a bunch of kamikaze pilots. Thankfully, we all plan to come back. Then it's into the parade ring to find your connections. But you'd nearly need satellite navigation for the job because it's bedlam out there. There are forty horses with forty sets of connections and every last one of them seem to be able to find five more friends and family for the day. Everyone's buzzing, everyone's excited. No point trying to have any sort of proper tactical conversation with the owner or trainer. You'd have that done beforehand. It's best of luck everybody and away we go.

Then they have to organise the parade. That means getting all forty horses in order. That's forty horses, forty grooms and forty jockeys all trying to get themselves organised to walk up past the stands in their position according to race number. You canter then from the bottom of the parade which is at the furlong pole, past the winning post and down to the first fence which is another two furlongs away. You canter all the way down and all the way back. By the time you make it to where we all circle at the start, twenty-five minutes have passed since we left the weighing room.

On a normal day in Leopardstown or Kempton, it wouldn't take more than ten.

And that's all before we try to get the thing started. Every year, something different happens at the start and every year, you find people giving out about it and saying there has to be a better, more efficient way to start the race. My only response to that is that the Grand National has been run for over 170 years. If there was an easier way to start it, somebody would have thought of it by now.

Jockeys seem to get the blame more often than not. They say we don't do enough to control the horses, we don't behave ourselves and are too interested in fighting our way into a good starting position. We even had one starter a few years ago blaming the Irish jockeys specifically, which was very unfair.

It's all rubbish. First of all, with the exception of the one year the race was voided after the false start, there's never any more than a ten-minute delay. It's the biggest race of the year so ten minutes isn't going to kill anybody. Secondly, if there wasn't such a long build-up to race time, the horses and jockeys wouldn't be so anxious to get on with it. The build-up is a massive part of the Grand National with all the crowds, music, noise and razzmatazz but you can't forget these are animals at the same time. They're going to do their own thing.

But the main point for me is that the start is important in the Grand National. People wonder what difference it could possibly make where you are at the start of a four-and-a-half-mile race. Well, it makes a massive difference, especially when the ground is on the good side. Your position when you get to the first at Aintree is vital on good ground. The lad on your inner might be a neck up on you because you didn't get away quick enough at the start and if he jumps to his right going over the first, you could be goosed. You can't take the chance. You have to be where you want to be.

When you're preparing for the Grand National, you can only plan for the first fence and after that you have to improvise. Imagine how it is with forty jockeys all having that plan for that first fence. Do you think that some of those plans might be similar? Imagine the determination of everyone down at that start to get themselves into the right place, to be ready when the tape goes up.

Miss the jump in the Grand National on good ground and you may as well turn around and head back to the unsaddling enclosure. You're going to the first behind a wall of horses and you have no idea what's lying on the other side when you get there. Or even if it's soft ground, you still want to be in a certain place starting off. You've spent two days looking through the card in quiet moments and you've picked out at least ten horses that you think are dodgy jumpers, so you want to be as far away from them as possible.

Now, there's nothing surer but that you'll get stuck beside or behind at least one or two of them but you'll jostle and bustle right up until the starter shouts 'Come on!' to try and get a better spot. Again, a lot of the race comes down to luck and you have to try to take as much of the luck out of it as you can. The race is unpredictable enough without giving yourself the handicap of having to follow a sketchy jumper. It's the Grand National, there's half a million quid for the winner and you're not going to give an inch anywhere.

I like to head down the middle to inside, but I'm hardly unique in that. I'd say there are twenty jockeys in every National looking to head down the same part of the track but there's only room for about five or six. Basically, I'd always try and have it so that by the time we're crossing the Melling Road on the way down to the first, there's nothing directly in front of me. I might only jump the fence in eighth place but ideally with more outside me than inside me.

In that respect, Hedgehunter was a great horse for the Grand National because of that instinct he had to be keen early on. Whereas that would usually be a drawback, at least at Aintree it meant that he could get himself a clear run to the first fence. Once we were over the first couple, I managed to get him to settle down and hunt him round. I couldn't be certain he was going to get the trip so I was trying to hang on to him and tried to save as much of his energy as possible.

There'd sometimes be a bit of chat on the way round. It depends who's around you. You'd all be keeping an eye out for loose horses and that kind of thing and you might have a bit of banter early on but not too much and not for too long. If anything, the only interaction you'd have with the other riders would be to warn them to move out a bit, say when you're coming to Becher's and the Canal Turn.

Hedgehunter gave me some spin over those fences. Apart from getting in a bit close to the first ditch, his jumping was spectacular. It was nearly too good actually, because after a while I realised that he was jumping so well and travelling so easily that I was a good bit closer to the pace than I wanted to be. He was brilliant at the Chair and popped the water jump without a thought, so that by the time we started out on the second circuit we were nearly upsides with the leaders.

I didn't want to be so close that early. There was still two and a quarter miles left and I didn't want to be the one doing all the work up front. So I kept having to take a pull on Hedgehunter and easing back. I was getting a good run towards the inside and just kept taking him back until A.P. went past on Clan Royal on my outside. This was ideal for me because Clan Royal had an obvious chance in the race having finished second the year before. So I would have a good horse to follow and then aim for when I decided to make my challenge near the end.

Unfortunately for them, a couple of loose horse ran amok at Becher's and ended up causing Clan Royal to refuse. Fortunately, they were just about far enough ahead of us for me to avoid them. I was able to ease out a little and jump the fence unhindered but with Clan Royal gone, I was now disputing the lead with Robert 'Choc' Thornton on Innox and David Dunsdon on Joly Bey. And because I was on the inside of the lads and we were turning left from Becher's over Foinavon, I found myself a couple of lengths clear at the Canal Turn.

That was not the plan. All I could think of was that I didn't know if this lad was going to stay the trip and that he never found much off the bridle. I basically needed to hold him up to save as much energy as possible for the finish. The thoughts of getting to the elbow, asking him for a last effort and getting nothing out of him worried me.

These are the things you think about, especially out at that end of the racecourse. People wouldn't know it unless they'd been involved in the race but when you reach the four fences after the Canal Turn, there is complete silence. It's almost eerie. You've spent your whole day in the middle of this unbelievable buzz of excitement and then all of a sudden you find yourself with literally about a minute's peace. There are about 55,000 people at the racecourse but for all you can hear out at that end of the track, you may as well be on the gallops at home. Especially if you're in front like Hedgehunter was. Once you come to the Melling Road, you start to hear the crowd again and you know the race is getting serious.

We got to the second-last and I still hadn't moved a muscle on him. I had been able to slow him down all the way from Valentine's to here. I was in front about a mile too soon but I could tell, too, that everyone around me was starting to get to work. Meanwhile I was sitting still. That's never bad.

When I took a quick look around after the second-last, I saw I had a couple of lengths on Royal Auclair and Christian Williams who was flat to the boards. I'd ridden Royal Auclair four times that winter for Paul and while he was a decent enough sort, I knew he was carrying over half a stone more than Hedgehunter. But still I didn't risk kicking on and pressing home the advantage I had.

When you jump the last at Aintree, there's a big screen on your left about twenty yards past the fence. I looked up as we went past and because of the slight delay in the television pictures, it showed us jumping the fence. I could see we were three or four lengths in front and I was still holding on to him. I was actually smiling heading to the elbow.

When we got there, I couldn't resist any longer. I changed hands on him and opened him up. He just sprinted to the line. We were five lengths clear at the elbow and fourteen clear by the time we crossed the finish, without me having to get over serious on him. I've joked with Willie since that, if I'd been using my head, I'd have just niggled him home from the elbow. That way, he'd have got half the penalty and we would have a better chance of winning again the following year. But I couldn't do that, not when it had just taken every last bit of restraint to stop myself pushing the button after jumping the last and putting such a huge race to bed.

This was a totally different experience to the first time around. Nothing could ever top the win with Papillon because it had all just been so unexpected. To win it at my first attempt, to win it with Dad, to do it all as a family thing was an experience that couldn't ever be bettered. There was so much emotion involved with that day, especially after coming back from the broken leg. It was the greatest day I've ever had or will ever have in racing.

The win with Hedgehunter was incredibly special in its own way though because it was for Willie and I was old enough to appreciate it more. I'd been riding for him for ten years and he had been very good to me. He'd taught me so much, he'd given me every chance to make it in the sport. Another trainer might have dug his heels in or fallen out with me when I wanted to combine working in Ireland and England but all he was ever interested in was making it work. He'd always been very good about it, even though he didn't have to be.

When we met in the winners' enclosure, we didn't say very much. There wasn't much to say. You just end up smiling and laughing through an experience like that and enjoying it for what it is. A special day, the best we've had together.

CHAPTER 11

Crushed

If there's one thing that would surprise the man in the street about my life as a jockey, it's the amount of fast food I end up having to eat. I never eat before I ride so I'm always starving when I'm finished. There's an image of jockeys out there that has us down as a gang of pale stick-figures who can barely stand up with the hunger half the time. If we eat at all, it's celery sticks and steamed chicken all the way. But it's not true. Not completely true anyway.

Absolutely, there are plenty of times when you have to 'do light' and those times aren't easy. Sometimes, if I'm trying to do really light, you'll see me buy a sandwich in an airport, eat the filling and throw the bread away. Not fun. And yeah, there are jockeys who have to do it more often than others, just as there are lads who have bigger frames thanks to mother nature and who have to suffer more to get rid of the last horrible pounds to make the weight. But as a group of sports persons on the road, junk food is often all there is.

Especially in the summer months when race meetings aren't finished until eight or nine o'clock. Ask most Irish jockeys and they'll be able to tell you where the best Burger Kings, Subways and McDonalds are within an hour's drive of any Irish racecourse.

Not only that, but they'll be able to tell you that a McDonald's burger takes less time to work off than a Burger King. They'll tell you which garages do the best rolls, which ones do the cheapest coffee, where to go for something quick and tasty and bad for you in Longford, Athlone, Mountrath, wherever. I know it seems an odd thing for a jockey to be expert in but that's the life we lead.

There's a simple enough reason for it too. The plain truth is that the food served in well over half of the weighing rooms in Ireland just isn't worth eating. Some places have been good for years – you always got well looked after in Tramore, Punchestown and Galway, for example – and others like Ballinrobe, Wexford, Thurles and Leopardstown have started to catch up. But that's seven out of twenty-six. We've got promises from a few more that things will change but by and large the facilities for jockeys in Ireland are a disgrace.

And not just with regard to food either. I remember being in the weighing room in Thurles one time when water came pouring down from the seam in the roof on to our clothes. John Cullen and Ken Whelan got their stuff drenched but I managed to move mine because I wasn't riding a race at the time. It turned out that there was plumbing trouble in the ladies' toilet and the leak eventually came through the ceiling and down into the weighing room. Thurles has improved since, thanks to the Moloney family who own it, and it's a track National Hunt racing in Ireland needs more than any other.

Other things too. We've got used to showers running cold over the years and nobody minds too much because we know it can happen. But sometimes you go in and there's not even cold water coming out. No shower after a race! It wouldn't happen anywhere else but Ireland.

From speaking to my sister Katie, the lady jockeys' facilities are even worse in most places. They make a nice effort in Tramore and it's good in Punchestown too. But if you asked her if there are many racecourses in Ireland with separate female sauna facilities, she'd give you some look.

The Association of Irish Racecourses is the ones who look after that side of things and I've always felt that jockeys were nearly a hindrance to them more than anything. We're an annoyance, a pain in the arse, always looking for something. But all we ever look for from them is the basic, normal things that any racecourse should have.

Myself and Barry Geraghty were sitting in Kempton one day in the jockeys' lounge. It has three or four couches, a few televisions, a pool table, and a little kitchenette in the corner. Barry and I were talking about it, knowing a place like that is unthinkable at an Irish racecourse. It would be seen as a completely unreasonable idea if we brought it up. We'd be told there's no money.

We know there's no money. Of course there's no money now. But Irish racing never saw as much money in its history as it did during the boom and all they did with it from the jockeys' point of view was the bare minimum. They built a new weighing room in Kilbeggan only because they had to – the old one was disgusting. There are new weighing rooms in several places but some still don't have saunas. That's terrible. A sauna is a basic requirement of a jockey's working life but we're made to feel like it's a luxury.

At Leopardstown on the Sunday week before Cheltenham one year, we told them that if there was no sauna installed by the time we came back for the Christmas meeting, there'd be no jockeys riding. The sauna was put in, but imagine having to go to those lengths to get basic facilities on a Grade One track?

It comes down to something I've always felt. There's an attitude in racing that jockeys are pretty far down the food chain. If you're a jockey, you're thought of as the boy in the room. And why would anyone want to listen to what the boy has to say when there are men around?

Take the new weighing rooms that were built during the good times. The weighing room is where we spend our lives. It's our changing room, our wash room, our waiting room, our home away from home wherever we go. You would think, in that case, that when it came to building these new ones, they'd put a lot of emphasis on whatever suggestions the jockeys or valets had. But no matter what we said, the weighing rooms still ended up being too small.

That's just the attitude towards jockeys in Ireland. We're made to feel as if we should count ourselves lucky to be doing this for a living at all. And we are. And we know we are. But that's no reason not to treat us like professional sports people.

Some tracks put up an ample supply of water for us but very few have isotonic drinks. I've gone into the man behind the counter in the canteen in Limerick to ask for a bottle of water just in my breeches and body protector and he's sent me back to the weighing room to get the price of it. Could you imagine that happening to Ronan O'Gara in Thomond Park? Or to Colm Cooper in Croke Park?

Things aren't perfect in England either but at least over there they're treated as professionals. Any time you get a fall in England, they have a physiotherapist on site ready to work on you. The physios are there all day and there'll be one wherever you're racing the next day if you need a rub before you ride. I can count the amount of times I've seen a physio on one hand at an Irish racecourse, and although the Turf Club will pick up your physio bill once you've been injured, you have to physically go and find the physio yourself and bring back the receipt. It's a small thing and it probably sounds like a petty thing but it's the difference between being treated like an amateur and a professional.

But amateur, professional, none of it matters. Maybe it's just me – and I know I'm well able to have a go – but some people in authority never miss a chance to put you in your box. An example: a group of us were fined by the stewards in 2006 at Galway when we all walked at the start of a race because nobody wanted to make the running. It made a bit of a splash in the papers but we still came out being made to feel like bold schoolboys. Myself, Barry, Paul Carberry, Andrew McNamara, Davy Russell, Denis O'Regan, Paddy Flood, Adrian Lane, Shay Barry and Robert Power – each of us got fined €200 apiece for 'acting in a manner prejudicial to the good image of Irish racing'. That's what the charge was.

There were ten of us in the race and we all had instructions from the trainers to try to hold our horses up. Nobody wanted to make the running. So we walked. And we walked. For about forty-five seconds until Andy Mac finally set off in front.

To me, the start of that race was what race riding is all about. Everybody thought they had the quickest horse so nobody cared how slow we went. We weren't doing it for the craic. Nobody was laughing or joking around. It was deadly serious because we knew that somebody was going to have to go eventually. Who was going to crack? Who was prepared to wait the longest? In a way, who had the most nerve?

People said it was a farcical way to start a race. It wasn't at all. It's race-riding. It's tactics. It's a mental battle to see who can think it out the best and who can make the right call under the pressure of a race situation. When we got under way, it turned into a cracking race, with four of us jumping the last in a line. Barry's horse won by a length and a half.

But it didn't suit the stewards that day and so we all got done for it. It wasn't the amount of the fine, just this notion that we had prejudiced the good image of Irish racing. If any one of us had stopped a horse, we'd have accepted the charge because then we would have prejudiced the good image of Irish racing. But this was actually the exact opposite of that. We had all done exactly what we thought was in the best interest of our horse winning the race.

Apparently, it looked bad. Well, first of all, that's a matter of opinion. To me, it would look worse if every horse went flat out from flag fall and only two finished. That's not race-riding. Race-riding involves tactics and thinking, not leaving your brain in the weighing room and going as fast as you can.

Second of all, who cares what it looks like? People said we didn't give the punters value but what more value do you expect as a punter than the horse being ridden to obtain its best possible finishing position? And anyway, punters aren't our primary responsibility. We owe the owner and trainer first and foremost, and every jockey in that race was trying to do his best for his connections. We appealed but got nowhere. I thought it was an absolutely farcical call, a complete disgrace.

Prejudicial to the good image of Irish racing? Says who? There were no complaints from any of the owners or trainers. The racing public are never slow to let you know if they think they've been short changed but not one said a word to me or any of the rest of the lads. The media didn't even give out about it. There was a discussion on RTE the following Sunday between Robert Hall, Donn McClean and Ger Lyons and they came down 2–1 in our favour.

In racing, there are rules we have to abide by that cover how you should behave and ride the start of a race, how you should ride the race itself, how you should behave in the finish of a race. We didn't break any of those rules. They had to get us on this catch-all rule that was vague enough to suit a situation where they took the hump with how we started the race.

There were ten jockeys in that race and every one of us has done his bit for the good name of Irish racing. We all went out with our trainers' instructions and there's nobody who can say that the likes of Jessica Harrington, Willie Mullins, Noel Meade and Enda Bolger haven't done wonders for the good image of Irish racing. There was no public outcry about the race. No bookmakers complained. The assistant handicapper Andrew Shaw actually came with us to the appeal and said that, from a handicapping point of view, the race was perfect. Each horse ran on its merits.

And yet, we were still put in our place good and proper. We were basically taken in hand and shown that if we thought we were the smart fellas, we were wrong. We were humiliated even though in my opinion we had not broken a rule. It was ridiculous.

But life goes on. You learn to live with it. Away from stupid rows like that, I still headed into the 2005 to 2006 season on a real high. I was champion jockey again for the first time in four years and things were going to plan with both Willie and Paul. Kauto Star was back on the scene and we were delighted with him when he was second in the Haldon Gold Cup at Exeter in November. Then he won the Tingle Creek for the first time in December with Mick Fitz on his back, since I was out with a dislocated shoulder.

It happened in a fall at Navan from a horse of Tony Mullins's called McGruders Cross. It was annoying and painful and it put me out for four weeks. Those are the ones you really hate – a fall at the last ditch when a race is up for grabs and then a four-week break coming up to Christmas. Not that absolute worst timing possible but not far off it.

Gillian and I got engaged on Christmas Eve. We'd known each other for around ten years by then so it was probably past time. When we started going out, I wasn't Ruby Walsh the jockey. I was Ruby Walsh, the amateur who worked in Willie's yard. She was there through all the good days and bad days from Pardubice to Aintree to Cheltenham and it was hard to imagine life without her. So I popped the question and thankfully she said yes.

We had a lovely Christmas. We were racing, naturally enough. I won on my first couple of rides back on St Stephen's Day at Sandown. The King George meeting had been moved there because Kempton was closed and I won the novice chase on Hoo La Baloo and the Christmas Hurdle on Feathered Lady for Colm Murphy. I had a couple of winners at Chepstow the following day and then came back and went to Leopardstown where I won a good novice chase for Dad on the Wednesday on Southern Vic.

At the end of the week, it was back to England again to ride at the New Year's Day meeting at Cheltenham and have my first encounter with Denman, in the rearranged Challow Hurdle. He had won a couple of times in Wincanton for Christian Williams and I'd watched those races thinking that this was a big, awkward, quirky yoke. He ran left and right and looked like the kind of horse that was going to take a lot of manoeuvring by whoever was going to be riding him. Just from the outside looking in, he looked like a real handful. This was the first time I sat on him. I knew nothing about him other than what I'd seen on television.

He popped out and ran free as the wind before I eventually let him stride along. But he was such an awkward so-and-so – as we came past the stand for the first time, he wanted to go up the finishing chute and it took a big tug from me to get him on the right course. But I managed to get him to turn left and go up and around the bend. We went down the back, tanking along, turned down the hill on the new track at Cheltenham and I took a peep after we jumped the second-last.

But a peep was no good to me because as far as I could make out, there were no horses behind me. I actually had to turn around and have a proper look to see where they were. Denman had just galloped them into the ground. They were strung out a mile behind us and he was still pulling away from them. He bolted in and I came back to the ring on him thinking this was one serious horse.

He really surprised me by how easily he won. The thing with horses that are carting you along like that and running free is that you don't know how fast you're going. They're covering more ground than you're accounting for in your head. The lads behind me thought it was a much better race than I did.

That was an eventful day all round. I rode a winner in the first, got awarded the second in the stewards' room on Pirate Flagship, got unseated from Le Duc in the third and took a bad fall from Sporazene in the fourth. And that was just the start of it.

Other falls have hurt more but this one from Sporazene was probably the scariest ever. I landed straight down on my head and felt like I was suffocating. I was lying at the back of the hurdle and I just couldn't get a breath. It was the first time that I ever was frightened by a fall. It felt like being winded, but I'd been winded plenty of times before and just rolled over and gradually got my breath back. That wasn't happening this time. No matter what I did, I couldn't get a breath for ages. I felt like I was choking.

They strapped me into the ambulance and took me back to the medical room where I was thoroughly examined and it was about an hour before I was felt halfway right. Because I'd been so short of breath for so long they sent me down to Cheltenham Hospital where they x-rayed my lungs but found nothing wrong. I was very sore and decided I was going home there and then and not to Exeter the next day.

Have you ever tried to book a flight on New Year's Day for New Year's Day? I wouldn't recommend it. I was sore and cranky and I wanted to go home but Jennifer couldn't get anybody in Ryanair or Aer Lingus to pick up a phone. I knew there were flights to Dublin from Birmingham and Bristol but I needed to find out which of them had an available seat.

Dad decided to ring Michael O'Leary, Ryanair's chief executive, who he trains horses for. Michael went off to check and rang back five minutes later to say there was a ticket waiting for me at Bristol Airport. I'm not big into pulling strings like that but there wasn't much choice that day. All I wanted was to get home. I was in agony by now. When we landed back in Dublin, the plane parked up at the 'A' gates and it took me forty minutes to walk from there to the front door. I was literally struggling to put one foot in front of the other. Thank God pier 'D' wasn't open yet. It's so far from the front that the 'D' might as well stand for Drogheda.

I thought it must have been my ribs or something because the pain was coming right out through my sternum, a pounding pain through the front of my chest. Any bit of movement hurt it. When I got home to Gillian, it was killing me to either sit down on the couch or get up out of it. So I lay down on the floor, which was a little better.

This went on all through that night and the next day. I was too sore to move and too uncomfortable to sleep. By about three o'clock the next morning, I couldn't take much more of it so I asked Gillian to take me to Naas Hospital. They checked everything out – my heart, my lungs, my ribs, everything. They x-rayed me, took blood and asked question after question to try to find out what was wrong. I eventually snapped at one of them and said, 'Look. Imagine you're standing on the bonnet of a car going along at thirty miles an hour and all of a sudden you fall off and you land on your head. That's what happened to me. What do you think is wrong?'

But they could find nothing. Eventually, they said that I had acid in my stomach and that I was getting reflux from it. That sounded a small enough thing to me but whatever. I went home thinking to myself that I had been to two hospitals and neither of them thought there was anything wrong with me, so maybe I should just get on with it. Maybe I was going soft. Right enough, the pain eased a bit over the next couple of days and I went back to work.

I had a decent couple of weeks too, including a five-timer at Wincanton on a Saturday when Paul very nearly went through the card. The following Thursday was the Thyestes meeting in Gowran Park. I rode Livingstonebramble in the big one but finished nowhere and then took a fall off Frances Crowley's horse Riverboatman a couple of races later.

I can safely say that for as long as I'm riding horses, this was the gentlest fall I've ever had or will ever have. People have had worse falls out of bed. Riverboatman stumbled, then he sat down, before he eventually lay down. I fell off him at zero miles an hour, just rolled off to the side as he came down. I would say the total distance of the fall was maybe six inches.

But by Jesus, it hurt. I could barely move, I was in that much pain. I got up and walked to the ambulance room, which was the golfers' changing room, where Gillian was waiting. John Downey was the doctor on duty and he suggested we go to Kilkenny

Hospital where I told them I had this same pain in my chest that I'd had for three and a half weeks since the fall in Cheltenham. Just out of desperation really, Gillian asked if they could x-ray my back as well as my chest. So they did.

A little while later, one of the nurses met Gillian in the corridor and just quietly said to her, 'Best of luck, now.' Whatever it was about the way she said it, Gillian knew something was up. Next thing we knew, the curtains flew back and five nurses came charging into my cubicle. They told me not to move, strapped me to a backboard, stuck me in a neck brace and put me in an ambulance. They were telling me it looked like I'd crushed a vertebra and that I was being transferred to Waterford straight away. I was trying to tell them that this had happened on New Year's Eve and that I'd been riding with it ever since but nobody was listening. I didn't think there was a need for all the drama.

When I got to Waterford, the hospital there was bedlam. The place was jammed, with people lying on trolleys in the corridors everywhere you looked. They eventually managed to get me into a ladies' ward thanks to Gillian's uncle, Dr Paul Walsh. He's a local GP and he told them I was his nephew. The surgeon in Waterford was Tadgh O'Sullivan and once he looked at me the next morning, he discharged me in a back brace and told me I would be out for six weeks, right up until just before Cheltenham.

Denman won again while I was out, this time at Bangor in February. He went off at something like 1–12 and won the length of the straight for Christian but looking in from the outside, I didn't think he was as impressive this time around.

He went off the 11–10 favourite in the Sun Alliance Hurdle and I didn't make half enough use of him. I didn't know him well enough and didn't trust him enough to do his own thing. I tried instead to settle him in. He was keen and free but I kept fighting him. In my head, I was thinking that it's all very well running away to your heart's content when you're 1–12 at Bangor but this is the Cheltenham Festival and you'll get found out doing that around here.

My mistake. Basically, I should have thrown the reins at him and let him at it. Knowing him as I came to know him, Denman would have slowed down in front anyway. But I didn't and even though I led off the home turn, Nicanor passed us after the last and beat us by a couple of lengths. I kicked myself afterwards for not making enough use of him. He definitely had the speed to beat that field but because I'd been trying to settle him in, he'd been fighting me all the way. I should have left him off. He got beaten because he'd taken too much out of himself on the way round.

I was leading rider for the second time at that Cheltenham. Tony Martin rang me on the Sunday before the festival started to say that Paul Carberry looked like he might be claimed by Noel Meade on Tuesday and asked if I would fancy the ride on Dun Doire in the William Hill Trophy. I jumped at the chance and he won well. Add to that the first and last races of the meeting on Noland and Desert Quest for Paul and it was a very successful week.

But we came very close to making it an incredible one. I had three options in the Gold Cup – Royal Auclair, Cornish Rebel and Hedgehunter. I came down on Hedgehunter's side but to be honest I couldn't really see any of them winning. Willie fancied Hedgehunter but by now I considered him a Grand National horse.

Shows what I know. Willie sees things in horses that nobody else does. That's what sets him apart. He runs horses in races that nobody else would consider running them in. Nobody only Willie would have brought Tourist Attraction to Cheltenham in 1995 but Willie did and won the Supreme Novices at 25–1. The same goes for Ebaziyan and Joe Cullen. Nobody would have imagined Joe Cullen was the best bumper horse in training in 2000 because his one win had been the previous June and he hadn't run for nine months. But Willie knew what he was doing and he won the Champion Bumper for Charlie Swan at 20–1.

Bit by bit over the years, I have worked out when to question him and when to shut up for fear of looking like a fool. When I was twenty or twenty-one I had no problem making a comment on a horse that he was sending to some race that I thought he hadn't a hope of winning. I'd tell him I thought he was mad. Then I'd end up looking like a gobshite when he won. The older I got, the more I learned to stay quiet and just ride what I was asked to.

It was a very fast run Gold Cup from the flag fall. They went a proper gallop and I was happy enough to drop Hedgehunter in a long way off the pace. If they were going to go that fast, they weren't all going to get home. One thing you could be sure of with Hedgehunter – he was going to be staying on when a lot of them were fading.

As usual, he was jumping like a stag and had gotten into a lovely rhythm. As we were heading down the back straight, he was making ground on the rest of them with every jump and we were creeping through the field. I started thinking we had a chance around then because nothing was jumping as well as we were and nothing was going to keep going as long as we would.

Ask Conor O'Dwyer and he'll tell you that War Of Attrition jumped super all the way but I'm certain that we were making up ground on him at every fence. We jumped the fourth-last in fifth or sixth place but unfortunately, as we ran down the hill, the third-last was being omitted because Timmy Murphy was getting seen to by the medical staff after a fall from Celestial Gold on the first circuit.

This didn't suit me at all. I needed every jump there could possibly be and a couple more besides because that's where Hedgehunter had the advantage. Barry Geraghty was in front on Forget The Past but Conor was coming on his outside and I was tracking him, travelling away and delighted with where I was. I even thought of Commanche Court in 2002 as we swung down the hill and warned myself not to make my challenge too soon. We jumped the second-last a length down and I switched out to make my run. I genuinely thought for a few seconds as he started to pick up that we were going to win the Gold Cup.

But it wasn't to be. War Of Attrition landed running at the back of the last and found that bit more up the run-in. He was a classy horse on his day and deserved his win. We were delighted with Hedgehunter, who had run a cracker and was surely now well in at the weights going to Aintree. He would still be top weight but he was still giving the rest of the field less weight than would have been the case if they'd framed the weights after the Gold Cup instead of before it. I wasn't getting off him anyway, that was for sure.

I was actually fairly confident going there. I knew he'd jump, I knew he'd travel, I knew he'd stay. But again, you need all the luck in the world and when I heard rain tapping on the window in Liverpool on the Friday night, I knew our luck was out. Carrying top weight for four and a half miles at Aintree is hard enough. Doing it after a night's rain has softened up the course and changed the going from Good to Good To Soft was going to make it even harder. The older Hedgehunter got, the faster he liked the ground. This wasn't going to suit him as well as the previous year had.

Still, he ran his heart out and I did think we had a chance for most of the way. I thought 'Slippers' Madden was a threat on Numbersixvalverde but in my head I was thinking that I'd ridden that horse a few times before and he's always liable to make a bad mistake somewhere along the way. He'd stay forever but there was always a chance he could hit one and it would be game over. But fair play to Slippers, he sat tight the one time Numbersix clouted a fence and although we were still in contention going to the last, he pulled away and won it well.

We had no complaints. How could you have, with a horse like Hedgehunter? He was so brave and such a great jumper, the kind of horse you'd always feel it was an honour to be involved with. He was never as good again, even though I rode him in two more Grand Nationals just on the off chance that he might come up trumps. But he didn't need to. He'd done his bit.

CHAPTER 12

Finding gold

Gillian and I got married that summer. Just about. For most weddings, it's the bride who's under pressure to turn up in time but I guess I had to be different. It wasn't my fault, not completely. But I was lucky to make it in the end. For a while there, you wouldn't have backed me in-running.

It happened like this. We were getting married on Monday, 3 July, the day after the Irish Derby. Once we looked through the racing calendar, it was more or less the only day of the year for us to get married. It suited most of our friends anyway. But the day before it was the English Summer National at Uttoxeter.

Gillian describes that race as the bane of her life. Ever since I started riding for Paul, the English Summer National has messed up more holiday plans than she can count. A couple of times I'd said to her in early June that Paul had nothing for Uttoxeter and we could go away somewhere, only to get to the week before and find I had to go to her and say sorry, I'm riding in the Summer National. She even came along one year. She didn't come a second year.

Anyway, it's a good race with a nice pot by the standards of summer racing – nearly a £50,000 first prize – and Paul doesn't ever ask a whole lot of me during the summer months, so I like to go. So I sorted it out, booked a nice early half past seven flight home from Birmingham that night and everything was sorted. I got to Uttoxeter, all ready and togged out but next thing you knew, a fire broke out just before the start of the first race.

A generator attached to one of the Betfair vans had overheated and the whole thing had gone up in flames. That was bad enough but it was right beside the main stand and was threatening to set it on fire as well. The whole stand was evacuated and the crowd were sent out on to the middle of the racecourse to get away from it. There was a big thick cloud of black smoke over the betting ring. Thankfully, nobody was injured.

Now, obviously this was bad news for Uttoxeter. And it was worse news for Betfair. But we're selfish creatures at the back of it all and I took one look at what was happening and decided this was very good news for the soon to be Mr and Mrs Walsh. I rang Gillian straight away and said, 'Look, there's a fire at Uttoxeter. Racing will be called off. I'm going to get an earlier flight home.' She was delighted and so was I.

They were evacuating the weighing room too but as everybody was leaving, I had a brainwave. I'd heard enough stories about the time Aintree was evacuated before the 1997 Grand National because of a bomb scare, about how it was chaos trying to leave the racecourse and how jockeys had to leave all their stuff behind. 'To hell with that,' I thought and I got changed back into my street clothes and was the last one out of the weighing room. I went out to the car and sat there waiting for the announcement to come. I was determined that as soon as they said racing was abandoned, I was on the road.

The fire started at two o'clock. By half past two there was no announcement. By three o'clock, still nothing. At a quarter past three, the public address system came on: 'Racing will go ahead as planned. The first race will be run at three-fifty . . .'

That meant that the Summer National, which was supposed to be off at four twenty-five, wouldn't start now until five past six. Meanwhile, my flight was leaving at seven-thirty. It was going to be tight but I thought it was just about doable. A.P. and Chanelle were on the same flight. We'd be cutting it fine but we lived in hope.

The horse, Sweet Diversion finished fourth. He was bang there coming to the second-last but didn't see out the trip. I was out of there like a flash and away down the A515 to Birmingham, raced into the airport late, looked up at the board – flight delayed. Excellent.

Rang Gillian. Good news. The flight's delayed. I'm going to make it. That was half-seven. Half-eight came and went. Half-nine came and went. A massive thunderstorm over the Irish Sea – the kind that comes along once every couple of years maybe – was keeping planes out of the sky between Ireland and England.

Finally, we boarded at around eleven o'clock. We were sitting there ready to go when a voice came over the intercom to say there was something wrong with the air conditioning on the plane. They couldn't run air through the jets to get them started or something. Whatever it was, we were stuck on the tarmac for another hour. We finally took off after midnight and it was about two-thirty in the morning by the time I got home.

It's safe to say I'd missed the rehearsal dinner. Thanks to Gillian, her family and my family, everything was sorted and they'd all gone to bed. She'd been very patient about it all but I'm sure she was sick of people reassuring her that I'd make it: 'Sure if the worst comes to the worst, he can get the boat, can't he?' It isn't really the kind of thing a bride wants to be hearing the night before her wedding. But when she woke up the next morning, everything was hunky-dory. I was there in plenty of time. Bolted up. Gillian's parents Noel and Angela hosted the wedding at their house and we had a fabulous day.

Heading into that season, we all thought Kauto Star was a proper horse. I thought it, Paul thought it, everyone in Ditcheat thought it. But an outsider looking in at his first couple of seasons in England would have needed convincing, and he had plenty of doubters. Understandably so. In two campaigns, he only had five races to show for himself and in three of those he either fell or finished second (or both, in the case of the infamous run at Exeter). Two wins from five races was hardly champion form in the book and when you threw in two injury lay-offs you came up with a lot of frustration.

And yet every time we went to the races with him, we were full of hope. It was more than hope even. It was excitement. I thought he had potential that for one reason and another he just wasn't showing. After he won the Tingle Creek with Mick Fitz on his back in December 2005, it was full steam ahead to the Champion Chase. But the weather messed us around that winter big time. Between the hopping and trotting, there was no good two-mile race around Christmas for him and then the Game Spirit was lost to frost in February.

All the same, we still went to Cheltenham certain that he had a huge chance in the Champion Chase. I schooled him at Exeter upsides Joe Tizzard on Cenkos about a fortnight before Cheltenham and he was flying. He was very fresh and quite brave over his fences, throwing in some spectacular leaps. He worked like the horse we all knew him to be. When I got off him and spoke to Paul and Clive Smith, I told them I thought he was back to his best.

But the Champion Chase turned out to be a disaster. Kauto raced away from the start and ran too keen early on. He only made it to the third fence. We galloped down to it and he stood miles off it and jumped like he thought he had wings. He hadn't. He landed right in the middle of the fence and turned over.

I was in doormat territory for a few seconds. Moscow Flyer came galloping past and clambered over me rather than going round me which left me bruised and stiff as a poker for the rest of the week. Something kicked Kauto on the way by and cracked his hock – a different one to the one that had been cracked in Exeter the previous year. Same result, though. Kauto was out for the rest of the season.

Everybody was frustrated with him because he wasn't doing himself justice on the racecourse. We all wanted him to show the world how good he was but he wasn't doing it consistently. Paul decided over the summer that maybe we should step him up in trip. It wasn't that he wasn't fast enough to win over two miles – the Tingle Creek win disproved that idea. It was more that he was getting older and he just thought he'd be well up to getting further.

So it was in the two months between the end of October and the King George that Kauto Star properly arrived. He went from being a very promising, occasionally frustrating steeplechaser to being the most talked about horse in training. First he went to Aintree for the Old Roan Chase over two and a half miles. He had top weight but it didn't matter in the least. He won by twenty-one lengths without coming off the bridle. It was just effortless. This was more like it.

So we knew he got two and a half miles. Now we had to find

out if he could stay three. Paul sent him to Haydock for the Betfair Chase four weeks later. Betfair were putting up £1million for any horse that could win this race, the King George and the Gold Cup in the same season, so the field was pretty useful. You had Beef Or Salmon in there who, although he never managed to show his true form in England, won Grade One after Grade One at home. You had L'Ami and Ollie Magern and Kingscliff too, who'd all won serious pots in their time.

But Kauto Star just blew them all away that day. We went there worried about whether he'd stay or not – Paul had been so uptight that he didn't even watch the race. He couldn't. I suppose when you realise that something special might be about to happen, your biggest fear is that it won't. But he needn't have worried. We came away thinking that anything was possible now. This was a Grade One race and I had time to take my goggles off and pat him down his neck all the way from the last fence to the line and still win by seventeen lengths.

Any doubts I had melted away after we jumped the second-last. He was tucked in behind Ollie Magern and got in a bit deep to the fence but when he landed, I gave him a squeeze and he just came alive. That's when I knew, right at that moment. One squeeze and he was away. It was all over then and once he pinged the last he just took off like a sprinter. I came back into the winners' enclosure smiling from ear to ear.

It was around this time Denman went novice chasing. He'd had one defeat over hurdles – a defeat that had been my fault, not his – but one look at him told you what his future held. A steeplechaser was all he was ever destined to be because of his size. Hurdles were only ever going to get in his way. Saying that, he was actually a brilliant jumper of hurdles for a horse his size. He got off the ground very athletically and never kicked them out of the ground. But you knew just to look at him taking a hurdle that if he got up over his fences that powerfully, he was going to be a monster.

He went to Exeter for his first run over fences and he won by ten lengths. Choc Thornton was riding Penzance, the main opposition in the race, and although we went a serious gallop Denman couldn't get away. We came to the third-last fence in the lead, but not by much, and Denman just walked into it. He gave it a real, solid clout. But he stood up, not a bother on him.

Looking back, I don't think he made another mistake like it at a fence for a couple of years. I never worry about a novice making a blunder in an early race as long as they stand up because you'll very often find that they learn from it down the line. That was definitely the case with Denman, who jumped the last two without a problem and won well. That was October 2006 and he didn't lose a race from then until February 2009.

Kauto was on the up as well. I was on my way to Folkestone nine days after the Betfair Chase win when I got a phone call from Paul asking what I thought of the idea of running him in the Tingle Creek that Saturday. My instinctive reaction was that it was a mad idea. That we were trying to get him to settle and relax for three-mile races already so what would be the point of dropping him back to two miles?

I put down the phone and all it took was about a minute and a half before I remembered what the point was. This was a horse who had already won the race, who hadn't very many miles on the clock because of all the injuries he'd had over the past two seasons and who very obviously loved to race. Why run? Because he'd probably win the race and everyone would enjoy it. Simple as.

I rang Paul back. 'I was wrong,' I said. 'Put him in the race.

Sure he could be dead by Christmas. He won't come off the bridle anyway.' And he didn't. He beat them all going away, including Voy Por Ustedes who had won the Arkle earlier in the year and would go on to win a Champion Chase.

Classy as he was, that day showed us he was a battler too. When we crossed the winning line and had just about come to a stop, Carl Llewellyn's horse Dempsey came galloping up on our inside. He was loose, after falling and sending Andrew Tinkler flying at the sixth-last fence. As he came to us, Kauto heard him coming and took off with him. I had to pull him up and calm him down, to let him know his work was done for the day.

He made one little mistake at the second-last but it was my fault more than his. I got a bit carried away and wound him up for it like we were a length behind rather than five in front. Kauto got me out of a hole with that one by shortening himself and finding his way to the other side. He'd worked it out by himself with no help from me. If anyone brought it up afterwards, I knew who was to blame so I wasn't worried.

By now, I was getting to know what the thrill of being attached to a potential superstar was like. Kauto had won over two miles, two and a half miles and three miles all within the space of six weeks. He had annihilated the best steeplechasers in England over every trip. There hadn't been a horse that could do this in my lifetime. Every jockey would love to have a horse that people automatically think of when they hear his name and I knew that Kauto Star had it in him to be for me what Best Mate was for Jim Culloty or what Istabraq was for Charlie Swan.

Our only concern, heading to the King George, was that his tendency to jump to his left a bit might count against him on a fast, right-handed track like Kempton. He was going to take a bit of placing through the race. There's a school of thought that says if a horse jumps to his left on a right-handed track you should place him on the inside so that he has horses outside him to keep him straight. I don't agree with that at all. I think you only make a horse nervous if you do that because you're basically taking away their freedom to jump the fence in their own natural rhythm. You have to allow them to shorten naturally into a fence. So I always go down the centre with a horse like that, just to allow it one stride left or right coming into the fence. That way, it's easier to keep the horse balanced.

It worked perfectly in the King George, for most of the way around. Kauto jumped and travelled super. Not so much as a hair out of place until we came to the fourth-last which he absolutely clattered, and I don't know how he stood up at it. He came to the fence, went to take off, put his feet right down on the take-off board and somehow got to the other side. I don't know what he did or how he got to the back of it but he kept going.

He had Exotic Dancer and Racing Demon for company but he stretched away from them between the third-last and second-last and was well clear by the time he got to the last. And then we went and made a complete mess of it as well. For some reason, he just jumped right in on top of it, slap into the middle of the fence. He frightened the life out of me but again, he found his feet and ran on to win easily enough. But all anyone could talk about afterwards were these mistakes.

I couldn't understand where they were coming from or how they were happening. He had been so spectacular over his fences in the Betfair and had gotten me out of trouble at the second-last in the Tingle Creek. I couldn't figure out why he'd kicked not one but two fences out of the ground under no massive pressure at Kempton. It was so unlike him.

What I did know was that he found a way to keep going

both times, which was a real tribute to his jumping. The secret to him staying upright was how low he kept his hind end. If his style of jumping threw his arse away up in the air, he'd have pitched over on his head and sent me flying at least once that winter and probably more. But his natural way of jumping kept it very low.

You often see some horses arc themselves over a fence, making a very round shape, but in that situation, once they hit the fence hard the momentum of their hind end carries it in a loop. With Kauto Star, there was no arc and the momentum carried him more forward than up. It was because of that action that he got away with paddling through the odd one. If that arc wasn't so flat, he would have tipped up a couple of times and I'd have known all about it.

But he didn't. That was the main thing as far as I was concerned. The papers were full of doubts about him and if I heard one fella say that Kauto wouldn't get away with those mistakes around Cheltenham, I heard fifty of them. But as far as I could see, they were all talking about what might happen. I was more interested in what had happened. Kauto had run four races and had posted four wins. He'd done so at the three different trips and by enormous distances. People could focus on the negatives if they wanted but I thought it was doing the horse a disservice to ignore the positives. He was in line to pick up a £1 million bonus if he won the Gold Cup and yet there was all this talk about him being unproven yet.

It was the same story after the Aon Chase at Newbury in February. Granted, he wasn't very easy on the eye that day. He was way too keen and pulled the arms off me all the way around, I couldn't get him to settle and we only just beat L'Ami by a head. And, of course, he had to step into the middle of the last to frighten me again and give his doubters more reason to reinforce their views going into Cheltenham.

Denman ran that day at Newbury as well and, just to complicate matters, we had a different kind of worry with him. He's such a wilful, quirky horse that you couldn't but have worries about him. Myself, A.P. McCoy and Timmy Murphy lined up for a three-horse novice chase and with just a few seconds to go until the off, Denman decided he didn't want to go anywhere. Because of his tendency to run a bit free when he gets going, he's not the sort of horse you want to be giving a smack at the start because that might only send him off even faster than normal. I eventually got him interested just in time for the tapes to go up and he ended up winning by a distance but it was nervy for a few seconds.

He's a funny one. You couldn't but love him. They've always been wary at Ditcheat that some day he'll just refuse to move. I wouldn't put it past him either. Some day he'll take a notion and decide that all these nice people can just go on about their day, thanks very much. And he'll stand and look around him and decide he isn't interested. So Paul's assistant, Dan Skelton, always goes down to the start to lead him around and keep him moving. It's a huge help to have someone who knows what they're at on the ground with you when you're dealing with a horse like Denman.

The build-up to that Cheltenham was as tense a time as I've ever known. There was a lot of money riding on the race, a lot of hype around it too. Everywhere I turned there was speculation over both Kauto's jumping and the fact that he'd never been beyond three miles before. Would he get round? Would he stay? At times in the weeks running up to the festival, it sometimes felt like the only people who actually thought he was going to win were those closest to him.

But there was more to it than that as well. This was the first time I'd ever gone to the Gold Cup riding the favourite. Commanche Court had been a 25–1 shot, Rince Ri had been 20–1, Hedgehunter had been any price you liked. Kauto was the favourite from Christmas on.

It was an edgy time. I try not to get too wound up for big races because it's not fair on the people around me. But this was new to me. I kept saying to people that if you just thought of the race as a three-and-a-quarter-mile Gold Cup trial rather than the Gold Cup itself, then given his form and that of the opposition, Kauto was an odds-on shot. I kept letting on as if it was just any other race. And I genuinely felt that at the time, or at least I convinced myself I did.

But it was obviously more than that. I wouldn't have wound myself up so much for a three-and-a-quarter-mile Gold Cup trial. I wouldn't have been constantly thinking about it or spending as much time wondering about the best way to approach it. It got to the point where on the Sunday twelve days before the race, I was lying awake at six o'clock in the morning thinking about it. This was no good – I couldn't sleep now. I had to sort it out.

So I got up out of bed and got in the car and just drove and drove. Up and down and in and out the roads of County Kildare. No radio, nothing but silence for me to think about the Gold Cup and how it might pan out. I went through every horse and every jockey and every plan they might go out into the race with.

I rode the race fifty different ways in my head. Like, did I ride the race to cover my own arse or should I be brave on him? The easy thing to do would be to position him on the outside, keep close to the pace all the way, not take any risks and if he's good enough to win, then so be it. And if he isn't, then it wasn't his day.

I could do that and nobody would have a bad word to say about me.

But the other way of playing it would be to do what's best for the horse. Be brave with him, keep him on the inner because he jumped a little to the left, let him use his speed in the last quarter of the race. I knew that with Evan Williams's horse State Of Play in the race, there'd be someone for me to park myself behind going down the inner. I knew his jockey Paul Maloney had been handy and had hugged the rail in his wins in the Hennessy earlier in the season and at Aintree the previous year. If I tracked him for the first couple of miles, I knew I'd be on the better horse when it came to the business end of the race.

So I decided the best way to do it was like I'd done with Commanche Court and Hedgehunter. Drop him in, creep away round, be close enough to the pace three out. I'd ridden in six Gold Cups by now and none of them had ever been anything less than a real good gallop from the off. I came back home that day after a couple of hours in a much better mood. I had no problem sleeping that night or any night afterwards.

The way that Cheltenham started for me didn't bode well. On another day and with a bit of luck, I could have had three winners by the end of the first day. Definitely, if you'd told me that morning that Granit Jack would get beaten by Ebaziyan in the Supreme Novices' and that Brave Inca would follow Sublimity home in the Champion Hurdle, I'd have laughed at you. And to this day, I maintain that Twist Magic would have taken all the beating in the Arkle if he hadn't fallen in the second-last upsides Don't Push It, who fell as well. He was absolutely tanking underneath me.

Denman finally got his due on the Wednesday in the Royal and Sun Alliance Chase. I made sure I'd learned my lesson from the previous year. If Denman wanted to go faster, I wasn't going slow him down. He got a willing partner that day too in Aces Four, a Ferdy Murphy horse that Graham Lee was riding. The pair of us had pulled away from the pack by about seven or eight lengths coming down the hill to the third-last and I was actually a little worried that we were going maybe just a bit too quick.

Because he had such a long stride, it was sometimes hard to gauge just how fast Denman was going when you were up on his back. This has happened to me a few times with different horses. Sometimes they make it look and feel so easy that I'm not actually sure whether it was as good a performance as it looked. But then I'll ask Barry or A.P. or one of the other lads in the race how their lad found it and they'll say they were beaten three out. That's the sort of horse Denman is when he's on form.

One way or the other, he was going too fast coming down the hill at Cheltenham for Aces Four. Graham did well to stay on after his horse did the splits at the third-last while Denman threw in a mighty leap. We won going away from there, easy enough in the end. It was an incredible performance. I was delighted for him and for Paul and the owners Paul Barber and Harry Findlay. Denman was the sort of horse that people could dismiss as being too quirky to be top class until he went and won something big. Now he had.

I got a nice surprise when Taranis won the Ryanair on the Thursday – my best hope for him had been that he'd run into a place. He jumped super but I got to the front too soon on him and he pricked his ears on the run-in. Our Vic almost chased him down but he just held on.

Then it all came down to Kauto in the Gold Cup. By the time the race came, I was just mad to get on with it. We lined up for the race and I realised after going 100 yards that nobody wanted to go a good gallop. So much for my big plans based on the fact that every Gold Cup is a true-run race. I couldn't believe it. I kept saying to myself that surely somebody was going to quicken it up but they didn't. It wasn't that we were walking around but we weren't going fast either.

I was happy enough with that. It let me switch Kauto off and get him settled. It just seemed odd to me. I would have thought the others would have tried to test his stamina and test his jumping. But no – we went at such a steady pace that as we turned left down the hill with three to jump, there were ten horses ahead of me. I eased him out after the third-last and between there and the second-last, it was like he'd been fired from a slingshot. He just flew off the bend and passed them all. I knew A.P. would be coming behind me on Exotic Dancer so I shut the door by coming in and taking the inside rail and once Kauto pinged the second-last the job was just about done.

People asked me afterwards was I worried coming down to the last fence. I think everybody else was because he'd made such a habit of demolishing fences late on in his races all through that winter. That was understandable enough; I can see why people would have been holding their breath as we came to it. But I can honestly say it never entered my head.

I just didn't have the time. Going from the second-last and the last at Cheltenham in the Gold Cup takes around eight seconds. Count that in your head. Now imagine spending those eight seconds landing the far side of the second-last, changing your hands, seeing the last, getting there, looking for a stride, getting in the air. Eight seconds watching from the stands or on television pass in what feels like 0.8 seconds for me in those circumstances.

I looked for a stride but couldn't find one coming to the last and he hit it halfway up. Burst it out of the ground. But again, there wasn't a hint of a thought that he might fall. Not for a second was I worried. Kauto got to the back of it, got running and sprinted away up for the line. Kauto Star, Gold Cup winner 2007.

That was a fabulous day. Everything was vindicated then. All the faith that Paul and Clive had shown in the horse, all the different chances they'd given him to show what he could do over the various trips, they all paid off that day. This was it now. Kauto Star was as good as there was anywhere. Nobody could doubt him now.

I was on top of the world. I'd handled the pressure of the build-up and had ridden the race I wanted to ride and it had paid off. After finishing second twice in the Gold Cup, I had ridden the winner now. It meant that I didn't have to spend my life regretting going too soon on Commanche Court in 2002. I would still love to have that race back but at least now I wasn't going to grow old thinking I'd blown my only chance at the one race I always wanted to win. People respect a Grand National winner but they know there's so much luck involved. The Gold Cup is the championship race.

Paul and the team at Ditcheat had done a great job with the horse, bringing him back from the fall in the Champion Chase to win six races out of six culminating in the Gold Cup. He had left the tactics up to me and when I told him what my plan was, he said that if that's what I wanted to do, that's what I should. That was how much we had learned to trust each other since I had started to work with him in 2002.

CHAPTER 13

Head to head

A jockey's fitness is different to the fitness needed in just about every other sport. You never hear of a jockey with a pulled hamstring or a strained quad – the only way you'd hurt a quad muscle is if you fell and got a kick on it from a passing horse. If you watch football players, rugby players or basically nearly any other sports people get ready for action, they'll be doing loads of stretching because for them to be explosive, it's all about the expansion of their muscles. Not us. The last time I did any serious stretching that wasn't injury-related, I was getting ready to play under-age rugby for Naas.

We're different. For us, it's all about muscle compaction. When you're riding a horse, the key is not to move. Everything is compressed. You're trying to achieve a stillness on a horse's back so that you can manipulate him the way you want. It comes back to the fact that the simple laws of physics won't allow a ten-and-a-half-stone man force a half-ton horse to do what he wants by brute force. You have to do it subtly; you have to get the knack of holding them and settling them and trying not to give mixed signals. To do this over an average of, say, ten to twelve miles per race meeting takes a lot of strength and fitness, just not the kind of strength and fitness most sports people would be used to.

I remember watching Steve Collins, the boxer, ride in a charity race. This was in the late 1990s when he wasn't long after beating Chris Eubank so he was a seriously fit man. It was over a mile and six furlongs at Fairyhouse and when he came in afterwards, he was a beaten man. The horse had taken a bit of a hold and by the time he got over the line he was wrecked.

It's just a totally different kind of fitness. I could ride ten horses in a day and be grand, Steve Collins couldn't ride one. I wouldn't last a round in a boxing ring though. Nor would I be fit enough to play a full football match. But I could walk as far as you like.

Because of the peculiar type of fitness needed, I've found that really the only way to get racing fit is by race-riding. It's such a specialised activity that you can only prepare for it by doing it. If I was out injured for any length of time, I'd always do a bit on the exercise bike all right but that's just to keep the weight in line. You can't train for it. Riding out is a help but not a substitute.

I got another taste of the sidelines in the run-up to Christmas 2007. The fall this time was at the Paddy Power meeting at Cheltenham in November when a horse of Paul's called Willy-anwoody came down at the third-last. That was a terrible day for Paul because he lost both Willyanwoody and Granit Jack in the same afternoon, but although I had sympathy for him I was just in too much pain with the shoulder I'd just dislocated.

It was unbelievably sore. Usually when you dislocate a shoulder it comes out at the front, but this one had been pushed back at force and taken out of the socket, taking a load of ligaments, muscles and nerve endings out with it. They put it back in when I got to the ambulance room at Cheltenham but the pain didn't ease that much. X-rays later found that there were two cracks in the humerus head into the bargain.

On top of everything, that was definitely the worst timing of any injury I'd had up to then. The Paddy Power meeting was on 17 November. The following Saturday, Kauto Star went to Haydock for the Betfair Chase. He'd been lifeless when I'd ridden him in his first run back the previous month, the day Monet's Garden beat him. We never worked out why and I was mad to get back on him and see what was wrong. Instead, I was watching on television as Sam Thomas rode him to beat Exotic Dancer.

Seven days later, Denman reappeared and won his first Hennessy. By now, I was having regular cryotherapy sessions in White's Hotel in Wexford to try to speed up the healing process and I was due another day of it that Saturday. Basically, cryotherapy is where they put you in a chamber where the temperature is taken down to below –110 degrees Celsius and your body reacts by redirecting your blood to the centre of your body to conserve heat. Once you step out of the chamber, the blood is pumped around your body more vigorously than before and this helps the healing. You go into the chamber four times over the course of a day, with a couple of hours in between each one. It's pure torture at those temperatures but you'll do anything to get back.

David Cox had introduced me to this torture about a week before but on this day, Ted drove me down. He knew I was going to go to Wexford and he suggested he'd come with me. He knew Denman was running in the Hennessy and that there was a fair chance he'd win. He wanted to be a brother and not have me stand somewhere on my own watching it. That's the kind of brother he's always been. Always around at the right time to say the right thing and, just as important, knowing when to say nothing.

We watched the Hennessy in a betting shop in Wexford town. As they went down the back straight for the second time, the pair of us just turned and looked at each other. We didn't say anything but we knew what was about to happen.

I wasn't surprised in the least. Denman got huge plaudits for the win, and rightly so, but I did think he'd win beforehand. I knew it was a lot of weight to carry but I was fairly sure he'd be up to it. Paul rang me that morning and sounded nervous on the phone but as far as I could see, this was a race made for him. Off a mark of 161, he was a good thing in my eyes and that's how it turned out.

Still, it was no fun watching the race. I was fit to puke up on the counter, in all honesty. They had all backed him in the shop. I'll never forget it – the whole place had backed him and the whole place knew I should have been riding him. I stood there and watched him bound up the home straight, happy but pissed off at the same time.

I turned and walked out the door. Not one of the punters cracked a joke, not one of them jeered and not one of them even said a word. They all just went about their business. As I walked out the door I said to Ted, 'Well, they were sound enough anyway.' I remember thinking to myself that any one of them could have started slagging me or come out with a smart remark. I was expecting one of them to say something. But they didn't and I respected them for it. There's nothing worse than having your face rubbed in it. I thought to myself, 'Fair fecking play to ye, lads.'

Because that was a hard one to take. I was happy for Sam, Paul and the owners but it was a rough one to have to watch. I'll never forget the lads that were in that betting shop in Wexford town. I went straight back into the cryotherapy chamber for more. I was supposed to do three minutes but I did four and a half. Whatever

I had to do, I was getting back for the King George and the Lexus Chase at Leopardstown.

The torture wasn't over though, physical or mental. The following Saturday is the Tingle Creek and I thought that Paul's runner, Twist Magic, would go to Sandown with a real chance to keep Paul's record in the race going. Myself and Gillian decided to take a holiday so we went out to Hong Kong. Pat Smullen was riding in Sha Tin on the Sunday and we went and had a great week with him and his wife Frances Crowley, who I'd ridden countless horses for down the years. I didn't let the Tingle Creek spoil it but I still drew plenty of strange looks as Gillian and I stood in the foyer of the hotel at ten on the Saturday night, listening to it on loudspeaker on my phone. Pat was standing behind me saying he wouldn't be able to cope with having to do that. I'm not sure how I was coping either.

Those four weeks were a bitch, no two ways about it. The dislocated shoulder was bad enough and sore enough on its own but to be sitting helpless while these horses won these races was a killer. I had got used to it over the years but only up to a point. I didn't need reminding that good horses are going to win, no matter who's on their backs, but I was getting it week after week. I wouldn't have been human if it didn't hurt.

These were prestige races and I wanted to be a part of them, to be on these horses' backs. I was talking to Sam quite a bit, answering any questions he had about best way to ride the races and when they came off I was happy that they did. But I wouldn't be a sportsman if I didn't want to be looking out between their ears, getting that adrenaline rush, crossing the line in front. Instead I was on the couch in Calverstown, in a betting shop in Wexford and in a hotel lobby in Hong Kong. Everywhere but where I wanted to be.

Come hell or high water, I was coming back for Christmas. Kauto was going for a second King George and Denman was heading to Leopardstown for the Lexus. The shoulder was probably only about ninety per cent right but I had done all I could for it and the only way forward was to race-ride.

Missing those races in November and December had consequences down the line, no doubt about it. It was always Paul's intention to keep Kauto and Denman apart right up until the Gold Cup and he was leaving it to me to decide which of them I would like to ride. If I had ridden Denman in the Hennessy, things might have been different, come Cheltenham. I would definitely have had a different opinion anyway. Whether or not it would have been enough to get me off Kauto, I'll never know. But since all I was doing when he was in Newbury was standing in the bookie's in Wexford, I only had the judgement of what I could see on the television.

And as far as I was concerned, the Hennessy was a moderate race. Yes, it was a great weight-carrying performance and yes, it was awesome to look at but I was convinced it was no more than he should have been capable of off a mark of 161. I looked through the field and asked myself, who had he actually beaten? Dream Alliance and Character Building were in second and third and they were a fair distance back. Did anyone really think that Kauto couldn't have done the same to them off a rating of 161?

If they did, then they would have changed their minds after the King George. Kauto absolutely trounced the field. I was having to take him back after the fifth-last so that he didn't find himself on his own and while I was doing that, A.P. McCoy was flat to the boards on Exotic Dancer. And there was no sign of a mistake at any of his fences either.

I had gone back over the races from the previous season

countless times to try to work out what was causing the blunders. I'd talked it over with Paul and with Dad to see if it was something I was doing rather than him. Paul said that switching him between trips had possibly confused him a little but I reckoned there had to be more to it. He was so athletic, such a good jumper when he jumped, so sure of what he was doing. If it was the case that he was untidy over all his jumps then we could have found something to fix. But it was the fact that the mistakes were random that made me think it could be my fault more than his.

The best theory I could come up with was that maybe I was being a bit too careful with him at times, late in races where we were out in front on our own. I was sometimes just looking for him to pop the fences instead of sending him for the spectacular jump. I was going, 'Whoa, boy' as we were coming to these fences to make sure we were ultra-safe over them instead of giving him a 'Go on!' and sending him at it. Maybe that was confusing him.

I decided that what I should be doing with him is using his cleverness and trusting him to make up his own mind. I had been telling anyone who'd listen that the one constant through it all was that he always stood up so I decided to listen to my own preaching. If he thinks he can make the jump, he'll go for it. And if he changes his mind, his knack of finding a way to the other side will keep him upright. I tried it out in the King George and I've never stopped sending him at his fences since. That theory worked until Gold Cup day 2010 anyway.

Two days later, I rode Denman in the Lexus and he won with plenty of authority. I've always been a believer in just doing enough to win. Beef Or Salmon's best days were behind him at that stage but The Listener had won the race the previous year and Mossbank was an up-and-coming horse for Michael Hourigan so it was a decent field. Even so, I thought Denman was a better horse than everything else in the race, a quicker horse and a stronger horse. There was no need to gallop them into the ground that day to win. More to the point, if he was going to try to win the Gold Cup in March what was the point in making him bust a gut in December?

All he had to do was get around to win, the same as Kauto had in the King George. In hindsight, what that meant for me personally is that I didn't get a feel for what he was capable of doing off a strong gallop at that stage in his career. The last time I'd ridden him was nine months previously in the Royal and Sun Alliance Chase in Cheltenham so I didn't know for sure how much he had come on. I would have suspected he had improved a lot but I couldn't have been certain. I would have found out if I'd looked to gallop everything else into the ground in Leop-ardstown but I just didn't see the point.

It wouldn't have been fair on the horse to make him do more than he needed to, just in order to settle my own curiosity. I would have been looking after my own interests instead of looking after Denman, Paul Barber, Harry Findlay and Paul Nicholls. I wouldn't have been a team player. Knowing what I know now, knowing everything that's happened since, I would still ride the race the same. You do what's needed in each specific race to win that race. Denman won that day, and won handy without me ever putting him to the pin of his collar. Job done.

What it meant in the long run, though, was that when it came to decision time, there's no doubt that I underestimated Denman. Not riding him in the Hennessy meant that my last experience of him when he was going all out was at the previous year's Chel-tenham and while he had been good that day, I thought Kauto Star had been better in the Gold Cup. And having just ridden him to hose up in the King George, I figured his improvement since March was to a better level than Denman could have improved to.

It was a tough choice. Apart from choosing which horse to ride, I was going to let down an owner as well. Myself and Clive Smith had been through a great couple of years together with Kauto but I'd known Paul Barber since I was a kid and he was a friend of the family. In the end, Paul and Harry wanted an answer before the Aon at Newbury at the start of February, which was only fair. I decided I couldn't get off Kauto.

I rode Regal Height in the Aon for Donald McCain and Sam rode Denman. I actually had a doubt after that race as to how straightforward the Gold Cup was going to be. A full two years after I'd ridden him for the first time, I think that was the first day I got a real appreciation for just what a powerful animal Denman is. I tried to follow on Regal Height and just got nowhere near him. I came away from Newbury going, 'Jesus, Rubes, this isn't as black and white as you thought.' Maybe I was in trouble. Maybe I'd got this wrong.

The build-up to the Gold Cup was relentless. It was totally different to the year before when although I was under pressure, at least I could sort of be left alone to deal with it in my own way. This time around, because it was a straight head-to-head duel between Denman and Kauto, the papers and television were looking to hype up the whole thing. Hype isn't really my style.

I knew racing had to take advantage of the match and promote itself to the wider sporting world and all that, but it all felt a bit artificial to me. I've never minded doing interviews and I know there are certain events you have to do to keep the sponsors happy and keep the money rolling in. But there were definitely times when I got a bit stroppy if people were asking me to turn up to shake hands and stand for photos. As far as I was concerned, my first commitments were to Willie Mullins and Paul Nicholls and whoever else I was riding for at the festival. Good luck to anyone else who wanted me to turn up places.

One thing I've made sure to put a lid on over the years is the amount of big race 'preview nights' I go to. When I was in my early twenties, I used to do anything up to a dozen of them a year. What I came to realise was that apart from the fact that they inevitably went on long into the night, by the end of a fortnight of them I was going to the festival with a thousand opinions in my head. I'd be lining up for the Supreme Novices on the Tuesday and in my head I'd be giving three-quarters of the field a chance to win. I'd have everyone's opinion but my own. Pure madness.

These days I only do two or sometimes three preview nights altogether. They can be great fun but you wouldn't want to place too much stock in them. I've said many times that opinions are what racing is built on, they're what frame the betting market and keep interest in the game going. But listen to too many of them and you'd end up going deaf, mad or both.

That was the year Cheltenham lost a day because of the high winds. I got a phone call at five past seven on the Wednesday morning from Alastair Down of Channel 4 saying it was looking like racing might be cancelled for the day so I hopped over the road to see what was going on. I called into the office of Simon Claisse, the clerk of the course, just as he called it off. I was hoping that they'd find a way to put all the races on and when Simon handed me the list for Thursday and Friday with ten races one day and nine the next, my eyes lit up. By Friday night, I was knackered and sore but it was a great couple of days' fun.

Master Minded in the Champion Chase was the single best performance of any horse I've ever been involved in. I didn't expect it; nobody expected it. I was even betwixt and between when it came to choosing either him or Twist Magic for the race at one point. But when he won the Game Spirit in February, I knew he was a serious horse. I just had no idea how serious. Say what you like about the horses he beat or what the form was like in the race – he was a five-year-old winning a Champion Chase by a distance. Some five-year-olds are still running in bumpers.

We knew Fiveforthree was a hell of a horse but Willie deliberated over whether to run him in the Ballymore or the Supreme Novices. When I was asked, my opinion was that he should go for the two mile five furlong race. He hadn't enough experience jumping to run in the two-mile race so Willie went for the Ballymore. Although he jumped a bit slow early on, he stuck his head out in the end to beat Venalmar. I got a couple of days' ban for the whip for my troubles.

Then Celestial Halo won the Triumph Hurdle. I'd gotten it wrong on him at Doncaster earlier in the season. I had tucked him in and he hadn't jumped well in behind horses and got outpaced by Sentry Duty. Mind you, Sentry Duty turned out to be a good horse for Nicky Henderson but I still felt that I could have done things differently on him. Once we got to Cheltenham, the instructions were to get him out of the gate and get him jumping. And he galloped Franchoek into the ground to finally get a win on the board for his owner Andy Stewart. For all the horses he'd had, this was his first ever Cheltenham winner.

But the Gold Cup was the race everyone had come to see. To this day, I don't think Kauto Star ran his race. People said it was the ground but I don't buy that at all. Whatever the ground conditions, Kauto is a horse that was able to travel well enough to win two Tingle Creeks when he was at his best. But on this day in the Gold Cup, he was struggling to travel well enough to keep up with Neptune Collonges. Neptune is a cracking good horse on which I've won some big prizes at Punchestown and Leopardstown but he'd been well behind Kauto in the previous year's Gold Cup.

Kauto didn't fire on the day. There was no gusto in him. He didn't travel like he does, he kept 'missing' at fences just because I couldn't get him into a rhythm. In saying that, he'd have wanted to be at his very best to beat Denman that day and I'm not even sure he would have. Denman put the gun to everybody's head and gave an awesome performance. Kauto didn't shine but Denman fairly kicked his arse for him.

We were struggling coming down the hill on the first circuit. I knew we were in trouble then. I was only just hanging on to Sam but Sam was hard on the bit, holding on to Denman. I was never holding on to Kauto that day. I was always clicking in his ear, trying to get him to go a stride faster, trying to get him on the bridle, trying to get him to jump. It was the first time he'd been like that underneath me since the day he couldn't beat Monet's Garden a few months earlier at Aintree.

Sam had a plan, kept to it and drove it home. They had us in their pocket from a long way out and they kept us there. As good as Denman's performance was, Sam's matched it. He won the race exactly the right way. Sense the weakness, go for it, finish it off.

Defeats don't come a lot harder to take than that one. I'd gotten it wrong. Not badly wrong, just wrong enough to finish second. But I was pretty down and disappointed in myself afterwards. I was disappointed that after having ridden Denman as a novice hurdler, as a novice steeplechaser and in the Lexus, I still hadn't fully realised what I was sitting on. I'd known from very early on with Kauto that this horse was something special. I had no excuse with Denman to get that call wrong. But I got it wrong.

To make matters just that little bit worse, I lost my temper on live television soon after the race. Derek Thompson of Channel 4 looked for me to come out of the weighing room and do a quick interview with him. My heart was in my boots but I didn't really mind doing it. You can't be a bad loser about these things – you have to front up and face them.

I went out and congratulated all involved with Denman and told Derek that although Kauto didn't travel, the better horse on the day won the race. That's racing. But when he asked me if I wished I had chosen to ride Denman I just snapped inside. That trigger in me that can't abide stupid questions from people who should know better just went off, and I couldn't swallow it in time.

'Tommo, that's probably the most ridiculous question I've ever been asked,' I said.

'It is. I know,' he said. 'But I had to ask it.'

'No, you didn't have to ask it,' I said. 'Look, you can only pick one. I picked the wrong one, but that's racing.'

Now, I have no problem with Derek Thompson at all. None whatsoever. But Christ almighty, I was only obliging Channel 4 by coming out to do the interview with him. I could have sat where I was in the weighing room and said no. I was just being sporting. Plus, I was standing waiting there for about five minutes while he got a cameraman to come over. Again, I didn't mind that too much but I would have thought I'd be cut a bit of slack in return. There was no need to try and get me to admit to millions watching on television that I'd made a balls of it.

We were ten minutes after the end of the Gold Cup. Of course I wished I'd chosen Denman! Was that not pretty self-evident? Would Tommo go up to somebody who had just missed a penalty in a World Cup final and ask if he regretted not putting it in the net? I did my usual – gave a smart answer, went away in a huff, felt like a twat afterwards.

The thing is, I've been asked silly questions a million times. I know that racing isn't the most easy sport in the world for outsiders to understand. I know there is a lot of jargon and rules and nuances that people wouldn't understand unless they've grown up with it, and that sometimes the ordinary Joe Soap would need a glossary to read the form book. So when a reporter comes to me and says, 'Look, I haven't a clue about racing at all so you might have to be patient with some of the questions ...' then of course I'll help them out. Once people are up front and honest and not trying to spoof you, then you do your best for them.

But Derek Thompson should have known better. Every man, woman and child watching knew that I had just chosen to ride the second horse in the Gold Cup when I could have chosen to ride the winner. What did he want me to say? 'No Tommo, I'm a born loser and finishing second is all I ever wanted ...'

I was leading rider at the festival again which made up for it a bit. But only a bit. I was pretty down for a little while afterwards. I spoke to Gillian about it that night and to Dad a few days later. But overall, it was something I had to deal with myself. I'd made the mistake, I'd picked the wrong one and I had to live with it.

That said, loyalty to a horse has always been me. I rode Hedgehunter in four Grand Nationals. I suppose deep down I was always going to ride Kauto in that Gold Cup. Maybe I was more disappointed in myself because I'd made an emotional call rather than a hard-nosed business call. But you are who you are.

I would go a bit quiet at times like that, retreat into myself for a spell. But it wouldn't be for long and there'd come a time when I'd shake myself and tell myself to get over it. And I think it's important to go through that. To think about it and work out in your mind where it went wrong. If you just throw your hands in the air and decide that shit happens, you're not going to improve. You might make that mistake again.

In picking horses, you'll often get it wrong. There's no need to beat yourself up over it too much. You get past it. That's racing. There's always another day, another race, another horse.

Coming out of Cheltenham that week, I was a dozen or so winners behind Davy Russell for the jockeys' championship. The weeks I had missed in November and December with the dislocated shoulder left me playing catch-up, so from there to the end of the season I chased down the title. Jennifer played a blinder over the closing weeks, pulling winners out of the fire for me at every turn. I had five winners at Punchestown – three for Willie, two for Paul, including Grade Ones for Twist Magic and Neptune Collonges. I finished with 131 winners, Davy had 126.

That Saturday was the last day of the season in England and I was at Sandown where I rode two winners – Poquelin and Andreas. They took my total number of winners for the English season up to sixty-nine which meant that for the first time in my career, I had ridden 200 winners in a season. The previous year I had ridden 198 and had been awarded two after other horses failed dope tests, but this was the first time I had physically ridden 200 winners.

I never thought for a second that Kauto Star was finished. He was only eight, rising nine, there was no way he was done. He'd been beaten by a nose at Aintree before the season was out but both Paul and I made a mess of that race and it wasn't the horse's fault at all. Paul wanted him ridden up with the pace and I went along with it, but instantly regretted it as he got involved in a battle with Our Vic from much too far out and then clouted the second-last as well. Paul gives the instructions but it's up to me to do the right thing. We wrote that day off as a bad experience rather than evidence that his best days were behind him.

Paul made a habit that year of bringing his horses over to chase good pots in Irish races. After Twist Magic and Neptune Collonges had won at Punchestown, Oslot won the Galway Plate – the first time I'd ridden the winner in the race since Moscow Express way back in 1999 – and Dear Villez won the Munster National. By the time he brought Kauto Star to Down Royal for the Grade One James Nicholson Chase in November, he was even third favourite for the Irish trainers' title behind Willie and Noel Meade.

Kauto didn't have to beat very much to win that day but I know Paul thought in time that the amount of travelling involved to get him from Ditcheat to Down Royal and back cost him the Betfair Chase in Haydock three weeks later. I'd have loved to have been able to agree or disagree but I couldn't. The curse of that Paddy Power meeting at Cheltenham had struck again.

I couldn't believe it. A year to the day since I'd dislocated my shoulder in Willyanwoody's fall, I was back in Cheltenham General yet again. Pride Of Dulcote was a talented novice in Paul's yard who'd won a maiden hurdle a few weeks earlier at Chepstow and who felt like he was going to win this one – a decent enough handicap hurdle with the likes of Fair Along and Powerstation in it – when he came down at the second-last. Powerstation flicked a hoof in my direction on the way past and gave me a good kick that left me lying on the ground in agony. A.P. McCoy was tailed off on his horse and as he went by asked if was OK. I could barely squeeze out a 'no'. Something was badly wrong.

What had happened was that a few weeks earlier I'd had a fall in Listowel from a horse called Quintana. I'd gone out over his head as he was falling but he found a leg and managed to stand up. However, the leg he found was placed right on my back and he tore the back protector right away from me. I had ridden away in Listowel but the bruising was wicked for about a week or ten days. Huge, wide, black bruising all around my chest and side. It turned out that the shoeing I'd gotten that day had caused a small tear in my spleen, not enough to be a massive problem but enough to weaken it. When Powerstation hit me a kick – and to be honest, I've been kicked harder plenty of times – it burst the whole thing open.

A.P. saw Gillian in the crowd as he went back in and told her something was up. He knew it wasn't just another fall. The pain was bad but I couldn't work out why. It was as if I'd broken a few ribs or something but the pain was in the soft tissue below my ribs rather than the bone. It eased a bit by the time we got to the ambulance room but it still wasn't great.

I had a bad pain in my left shoulder as well, the one I had dislocated, but I played it down when the doctors asked. I knew my body fairly well at this stage and I figured a night's rest would calm it down. But Gillian was standing beside the bed watching me talk to them and she thought there was more to it than that. She had asked Rabbit Slattery, the racecourse physio, why the doctors were enquiring about my shoulder. Rabbit told her that the nerves surrounding the spleen are connected to the shoulder and that a pain there could mean something was up with the spleen.

She waited until the doctors were talking amongst themselves before leaning in and whispering in my ear, 'If that shoulder is hurting you, you better tell them.' It was an order rather than friendly advice. So I told them. Straight away they transferred me to the Cheltenham General, where I went into accident and emergency.

The spleen had been ruptured, or as the doctor later put it, 'mangled'. Gradually the pain worsened and as I waited, I passed out. When I came round, Gillian was one side of the bed with the surgeon, Mr Bristol, and A.P. was the other. 'This is no good now,' I said. 'This thing will have to come out.'

Mr Bristol said, 'Well, not necessarily. It could heal by itself and we're thinking of keeping you in here and observing you for ten days or so to see if it sorts itself out.' I was about to pipe up and say ten days in hospital was out of the question when A.P. beat me to the punch. 'Ah no, that won't do,' he said. 'That's no good to him. I think you may take it out.'

The surgeon was dubious enough about this so he went off to ring Sue Smith, one of the doctors who works at the racecourse but also in the hospital. Sue basically told him that jockeys are a bit different to normal patients and that if I was saying it was sore, it was probably very bad. Her advice was to take it out so they did, and I woke up with an eight-inch scar to show for it.

I have to take medication every day but it's no hardship. I also have to get annual vaccinations and keep my prescriptions topped up. My local GP, Dr Brendan Doyle, is a great help in keeping on top of it. You'd be surprised at the amount of jockeys who are in the same boat. Paul Carberry has no spleen, Andy McNamara, Davy Condon don't have one either.

Thankfully, it only kept me out of action for twenty-seven days. I was in Cheltenham General for six days, at the end of which Mikael D'Haguenet's owner Rich Ricci very kindly flew me home from Staverton Airport. You're always grateful for small mercies like that.

Kauto unseated Sam in the Betfair Chase but he was back to his best again in the King George. Three King Georges in a row was some achievement for a horse that I think is better going the other way around but he was untouchable again that day. Albertas Run was second a good eight lengths down and Voy Por Ustedes was well beaten too. He was magnificent and it was a massive win for us because it reminded everyone that he hadn't gone away. Defeat in the Gold Cup and Aintree hadn't broken him and he looked as good as ever.

Paul was worried for a long time, though, about Denman. He had serious heart problems after coming back into training in the autumn and was out of sorts for a long time through the winter. His Gold Cup win was in March 2008 but it was February 2009 before he was back on a racecourse. I rode him that day at Kempton and I was shocked at the deterioration. He just wasn't the same horse at all – it was like riding an ordinary handicapper. It was beyond belief that this was a horse who had won the Gold Cup because he just never went a yard for me that day.

Still, we knew there was a great horse in there somewhere. I went down to school at Paul's about three weeks before the Gold Cup. I was on Kauto Star and Sam was on Denman. Paul Barber, Marianne Barber and Harry Findlay were there too. I was half a lap ahead of Sam so I was concentrating on what I was doing on Kauto. We always school with plenty of distance between us in the arena but all I could hear from behind was barrels being clattered and bars being hit and general untidiness from Denman.

When we came to a stop, there were just long faces all round. He was so lethargic and sloppy and the feeling was, 'Well, he can't go to the Gold Cup like that.' I said: 'No, that's right. He can't go off the run he had either. But how about you try something different with him? Send him up to the field and give him a school over the fences up there. It might wake him up, change his mind. You never know, something might spark in him.'

It was a long shot. But maybe the switch from the all-weather

Seven winners at Cheltenham, 2009

Quevega

Mikael D'Haguenet

Cooldine

Master Minded

American Trilogy

Big Buck's (left)

Kauto Star

Gillian, me, Isabelle and Elsa enjoying our first Christmas together in 2011.

The siblings at the 2010 National Hunt Awards in Adare. Ruby, Ted, Jennifer and Katie.

With Willie and Jackie Mullins the day before the start of the 2010
Cheltenham Festival.

Master Minded stays upright just about in the 2010 Game Spirit.

Cantering back after Kauto fell in the 2010 Gold Cup.

After breaking my arm at Aintree an hour before the 2010 Grand National.

Congratulating Katie after Thousand Stars' win at Cheltenham in 2010.

Sanctuaire's win at Cheltenham in 2010 took me past Pat Taaffe as the jockey with the most ever Festival winners.

Big Bucks doesn't disappoint as he wins his third World Hurdle in 2011.

Kauto Star greets his fans at Kempton after a fantastic fifth win in the King George in 2011.

schooling surface to actual grass would awaken something in him. Maybe the open space rather than the confines of the school might get him interested again. Sure enough, they did that the following week and he decided he was in the mood again.

I wasn't getting off Kauto Star though. Not a hope. I looked down through the card and as far as I could make out, the only dangers to Kauto were Denman and Neptune Collonges. The rest weren't in the picture at all. Kauto had beaten Exotic Dancer so many times and of the newcomers, Barbers Shop seemed to be all the rage, but I thought he'd have to improve at least a stone to get near Kauto.

That turned out to be an incredible Cheltenham for me. Paul and Willie had a lot of good runners and the way their best horses split couldn't have fallen into my lap any better. It actually started badly because Kempes nearly fell at the first in the first race, Tatenen fell at the third in the second and Celestial Halo got beaten by a short head in the third. But from there on, it turned into a glorious week.

Quevega appeared out of the dark in the last race on the first day and then I had a treble on the Wednesday. I had always thought from the first time I rode him work that Mikael D'Haguenet was something different. The pace he worked at and the stamina he showed was brilliant but his jumping ability set him apart as well. I thought he was as good a ride as I had at the meeting and so it proved. He actually ran a bit free and got tight into the second-last but I was able to straighten him up and power away to win.

Then Cooldine won the RSA Chase by fifteen lengths, near enough the easiest winner I rode all week. We were worried that he might jump to the right a bit too much but he kept it straight that day. And then Master Minded rocked up in the Champion

Chase with everyone expecting him to be as good as he was the year before, but that was unrealistic. I didn't mind if he won by a short head as long as he won. He did, and all of a sudden, I had four winners ridden. Then Thursday came and Big Buck's won the World Hurdle. I went into the race thinking that all I had to worry about was not being in front too soon and sure enough he picked up from the last and won well.

I was going into the Friday with five winners on the board. You're thinking that this can't keep going, that it has to stop somewhere. But it didn't. American Trilogy went into the County Hurdle with a better chance than his 20–1 odds suggested. I couldn't say I fancied him to win but I thought he'd go well. But to watch him win it, you wouldn't think it was a handicap at all.

And then Kauto rounded it all off. With Denman and Neptune Collonges in the race, I knew well that there'd be plenty of pace. Not that I was privy to the instructions Paul sent Christian Williams out with – I wasn't and would never be. But I knew enough about these horses to know exactly how they should be ridden. So I had it in my head all week that I would track Neptune down the hill and see who was around me after the third-last.

He jumped better that day than any other I can remember. Just floated over the fences and landed running each time. After he flew the fourth-last I was having to take him back because I didn't want to be there too soon. Sam came upsides on Denman and for a split second I started to get worried and thought they might have us again. Whatever way Denman caught my eye as Sam came rolling along, I thought he was going to give us a lot to do. I was full sure they were going a lot better than they actually were. I didn't know until I watched it back that Sam was working so hard just to keep up.

I decided there and then that I was going to set sail off the bend. Kauto pinged the third-last and when he got to the bend I gave him a squeeze and sent him on. If you ever watch the video, look for the acceleration just as we round the home turn. We were neck and neck turning in but Kauto was five lengths clear jumping the fence. That was the real Kauto Star. An extraordinary horse.

There was no drama to it this time. No problem with the last fence, nothing. Just sheer class. It was a better performance than 2007, better than anything he'd ever achieved up to then. The Gold Cup has been run since 1924 and this made Kauto Star the first horse ever to regain it after losing it. He was pure class that day. It seems amazing that a horse of his quality was always having to prove the doubters wrong, but he was well able for it.

And as for Denman, what could you say? It was an incredible performance from him and, by extension, an amazing training performance by Paul and everyone at Ditcheat. To see this horse in the middle of winter, you were worried would he ever go near a racecourse again, never mind finish second in a Gold Cup. I know Paul got nearly as big a buzz out of that as he did out of Kauto's win.

There was no way anyone could go to Cheltenham thinking seven winners was a possibility. No way in the world. I was just so lucky to have it happen to me. Willie's good horses were going in races that didn't clash with Paul; Paul had horses that he really fancied going in races that didn't clash with Willie. The one fifty-fifty decision I had to make was between Cooldine and What A Friend and it came off.

It was one of those weeks where it felt like everything I tried was coming off. I was like a golfer shooting a good round where every putt was dropping. I did nothing special on any of the seven horses that week, and didn't give any one of them in particular an outstanding ride. None of them needed it. Any jockey worth his salt would have won on them.

The big achievement for me was to get on the horses. It was the work all year to get to the point where the trainers want to put you on them. It's the one you might pull out of the fire on a Tuesday afternoon that keeps an owner or trainer happy that keeps you moving forward and gets you the big rides at the major festivals. That's what I'd be most proud of.

Punchestown rounded off a beano six weeks. I rode ten winners, nine for Willie and Master Minded for Paul. Willie trained twelve winners all week, an extraordinary performance. Hurricane Fly won one of the Grade One novice hurdles, Mikael D'Haguenet won the other one. Fiveforthree won the World Hurdle, another Grade One. Ballytrim, Equus Maximus, J'y Vole, Sesanta, Jayo and Jessies Dream were the others. That's some army of horses to have for the week. You have every chance with ammunition that good.

CHAPTER 14

Family fortune

Poor Commanche Court died at the end of May 2009. He got a bout of colic and had to be put down so that he didn't suffer for too long. He had meant an awful lot to our family over the years so although we were very sad about it when it happened, we made sure to remember the good days. He was fifteen when he died and he'd spent his years being looked after as well as any of us. It was terrible news to hear on the day itself, but you move on and you get past it, I guess. No point dwelling on it.

Much better to dwell on those big days we had with Commanche. The Triumph Hurdle, the Irish National, the Gold Cup that he nearly won, even if Dad thinks second was as good as he was ever going to be behind Best Mate. Most horses never get one of those days, never mind a career of them. And most families never get to enjoy anything like that thrill either. I still get a great kick out of riding a winner for Dad. I might only ride five or six of them a season these days because that's all Katie will let me ride! But there's still something that bit different about it.

October brought the greatest day of my life. Nothing that ever happened on a horse compares to the day Gillian had our little daughter Isabelle. That was on a completely different emotional level to anything that had gone before. The sense of responsibility, the sense of joy, the sense of awe – everything comes down on you at once. Bringing them both home healthy and happy and looking at what our future will be was a feeling like nothing I'd known.

I had to keep going with the day job, though. We went to Haydock with Kauto Star and I thought he got beaten. Definitely. Coming off the bend, I thought Paddy Brennan was going a bit better than me on Imperial Commander but the further down the straight we got, Kauto started to pick up and go by him. He was tired going to the last, though, and my instinct as we crossed the line was that Paddy had just chinned me. It's so hard to tell these things. I would always judge it by the body of the rider beside me and I was a fraction behind Paddy as we crossed the line. But Kauto got his neck out and his head down and we won by a nose. I thought we were lucky on the day.

Mind you, it looks like good form now that the season is over. Imperial Commander had, of course, won the previous year's Paddy Power Handicap Chase at Cheltenham in November and then the Ryanair Chase at the festival. So while it would have appeared on paper that he'd have to improve before the Gold Cup, the potential was obviously there.

The King George was incredible. Nacarat went a real good gallop but the further we went, the further Kauto was going to win that day. He was just brilliant. I wouldn't be a great man for showing off or playing to the gallery but on the way back in that day, I got a bit giddy. My gloves were old ones that were nearly done so I threw them into the crowd. And the British Horseracing Authority was bringing in new whips the following week so I threw it into the crowd as well. Maybe I got a bit carried away but if you couldn't do it after a performance like that, when could you?

To win four King Georges on the trot is an extraordinary achievement. Even Desert Orchid couldn't do it four years in a row. To come back for any Grade One race four years running, especially a three-mile chase, takes some amount of doing.

A day or two later, when I saw the time in which we had run the King George, it didn't look all that impressive on the bare numbers. So that put a slight doubt in my mind, enough to make me wonder, why wasn't it faster? Once I checked, I found that when you took ground conditions into account, the time was fine. But just for that one day, until I collected the stats together and compared like with like when it came to ground conditions from past King Georges, I had a small bit of doubt. I dismissed it then.

As for Denman, I went into the Hennessy with him honestly thinking we had no chance. I had ridden him work at Exeter ten days beforehand and to me he had worked badly, even by his standards. He gave me no feel whatsoever and running off a rating of 174, I thought he had no earthly hope. I didn't think it was possible to win a handicap off that high a mark. It would mean he'd be giving a horse of the calibre of What A Friend more than a stone and a half. Obviously the history books tell us that Arkle could give horses lumps of weight and that Desert Orchid could too. But in my riding career, I'd never seen a horse that was capable of it.

Even in the race itself, for the first half mile I thought we were at nothing. He was sluggish and slow and I couldn't get him into a rhythm. But he really is an awesome animal when he gets interested and gets going. He powered up the straight the first time and as we came round the bend, I could feel him thinking about it, almost tossing a coin in his mind to see whether this was worth the effort. As we turned into the back straight, I could feel him start to lengthen his stride and up his game and once he switched on then, nothing in the race stood a chance. He pinged the cross fence, got into the straight and did what he does best which is just gallop them into the ground.

He stuck his head down and just ground them all down. When he's right and he's going, he's such a perfect jumper. He makes mistakes when he empties out or if things aren't happening for him but when he's going forward and in a good mood, he's a magic jumper. For such a big horse, he's incredibly nimble with his feet.

For my money, this was a much better performance than his first Hennessy. It was just so heroic to go and do what he did after all the troubles he'd had and with all this weight on his back. Think of it this way: in 2007, he was the top novice steeplechaser of the previous season whereas in 2009 he was giving the top novices of the previous season over a stone in weight.

So in theory, I had a choice again in the New Year over what to ride in the Gold Cup. When you added up the Hennessy form, after Christmas especially, Denman looked to be back to his best. What A Friend winning the Lexus really made it look like a massive performance and obviously had me looking at Denman a second time. But realistically, I wasn't going to get off Kauto Star for the Gold Cup. Not after everything we'd been through together. When I didn't desert him the first time, I wasn't going to do it the second time. So I nailed my colours to the mast.

I'd have maybe liked to draw it out for as long as possible and maybe see what Denman did in the Aon but his owners wanted to use the same jockey in the Aon as would be riding him in the Gold Cup, which was fair enough. Anyway, even allowing for the fact that Paul always uses the Aon as a prep race and you can't go totally by what you see in it, I surely wouldn't have switched to Denman on what he did that day.

I was on Tricky Trickster and those mistakes looked even worse from behind than they did on television. The dust that flew up from the fourth-last when he hit it told me he really rooted it. And from where I was watching, I couldn't believe he stood up at the third-last. Considering where his hind end landed – right in the ditch – I'd have bet my life he was on the ground once he got to the other side. Instead, A.P. was unseated.

Niche Market had gone with Denman when they quickened up down the back straight and I couldn't go with them. Tricky just wasn't fast enough. But I had a feeling that Niche Market wouldn't be able to keep that sort of pace up all the way to the line. If he did, he was a much better horse than I'd ever given him credit for. So I figured that as the race came to a close, he'd tire. That's how it turned out, although I'd say I got a bit lucky to chin him on the line.

But in my own head, leaving the racecourse that day I thought I was on the right one for the Gold Cup. I was happy with Kauto Star. When Nacarat finished second in the *Racing Post* Chase, that cemented it. I know Razor Royale wouldn't be many people's idea of a horse to advertise the form but all I wanted to see out of that race was whether or not Nacarat kept going like he'd kept going in the King George. And he did, he ran all the way to the line in a race where they went a real good gallop. That was good enough for me. Sadly, it wasn't to be.

The Gold Cup actually started out perfectly for Kauto. I knew there wouldn't be much pace in the race – Carruthers was the only out and out front-runner and I knew Denman would need a mile to get going. Carruthers jumps a bit towards the right so I was happy enough to sit and follow him down the inner, which I did. He jumped lovely, settled great and all was going to plan. I even thought to myself, when we jumped the second ditch down the back, that if Mattie Batchelor didn't start going a bit quicker on Carruthers pretty soon, then I might go by him at the next fence and take it up myself. That's how well Kauto was going.

Then we came to the fence at the top of the hill and he just changed his mind right before it. His race should have finished there and then, but somehow he managed to stand up. Where his nose went, where his head went, his body should have followed. But it was the very same principle as when he was making those mistakes back in the winter of 2006 – his flat jumping action kept his momentum going forward instead of in a loop and it meant he could get a leg out underneath him in time. But he had hit the fence such a thump that I pretty much knew then our chance was gone.

I just sat tight on him then to try to ease him back into the race and to be fair to the horse he jumped the next two pretty well but not perfect. With a horse like Kauto that is such a good jumper normally, you'll nearly always find that if they hit a fence hard, they'll jump the next couple that bit cleaner than usual. He gave himself a bit of air over the next couple of fences because the memory of the previous one was in his head.

And while that's a good thing because it gets him that little bit more settled and brings him closer to getting back into a rhythm, the higher a horse jumps over a fence, the longer it takes for him to get back on the ground. We had a circuit and a half to go in the Gold Cup so there wasn't time to be giving away fractions at every jump. A.P. had seen me make the mistake so he drove Denman on and upped the tempo. He wasn't going to let me take a few fences to recover and let me get back into the race. I was going to need a miracle from there. I was playing the Lotto, crossing my fingers and hoping for the best.

With the pace upped, Kauto should have faded out of the race.

I think any other horse after a mistake like that and with a horse of the calibre of Denman stepping on the gas up front would have just drifted back in the field. I have massive respect for the way he kept in touch with the leaders from there, but I couldn't get him back on the bridle. I couldn't get him in my hands. I was having to squeeze him between jumps. I was having to fire him at his fences because he was losing ground the whole time.

Paul Townend had landed past me on Cooldine when I made the mistake and had taken the spot I wanted to be in so I had to switch Kauto out to get a position. But Paddy Brennan had also gone by on Imperial Commander so I had to switch again. No matter what I did, I couldn't get him balanced or on an even keel. If I'd been able to get him travelling, I could have maybe tried something, pulled him back off Imperial Commander's heels so that he could slot in behind him and track him. But I was having to push and cajole him, just to keep up with Paddy.

I tried everything. I switched him in, switched him out, got him to change legs. I was throwing every last bit of muck I had against the wall hoping that something would stick. But nothing did. We came to the fourth-last flat to the boards and he caught the top of it and turned over.

I thought that was it for him. Just as we went flying, I saw the way he was going to hit the ground and thought to myself, 'Oh, Christ no.' As he was disappearing, I was convinced it was a neck-breaker. The way the side of his head hit the ground, the way his body was going to follow together with the speed he was going as I went out over his ears, I didn't think he could survive it.

The ground was slippery and I got spun around on my front so that I was facing back towards the fence. I got up on my hands and knees about ten yards away from him. And then he stood up, thank God. That was the best sight.

I trotted him back in and met Clifford and Paul. Paul just looked at me and said, 'King George?' I smiled and said, 'King George. Why not?' Clive arrived then and was very magnanimous about it, just saying it's one of those things. They were both as relieved as I was that Kauto had got up right away.

Take nothing away from the winner at all. Paddy's horse jumped and travelled supremely well throughout the race. After Kauto made the mistake, he was the one I was trying to follow but he was just far too good for us on the day. Paddy gave him a wonderful ride and took everything A.P. threw at him from a mile out. They thoroughly deserved their day.

But I'll always wonder, what could I have done? Should I have gone by Carruthers earlier and forced the pace, giving Kauto something to think about instead of time to change his mind? Should I have settled further off Carruthers? You'll always wonder. You have to. I think if you don't do that, if you don't constantly examine what you might have done wrong, you aren't doing your job. You might never come up with the answer but you have to try.

Apart from Kauto, I had the usual mixed bag at Cheltenham. The winter had been good and I was going to Cheltenham with huge expectations. I always try and play it down and stick to the mantra of hoping to ride one winner and walk out in one piece. And I do believe that. But still, you can't help but want the big ones. So it was disappointing when Master Minded didn't show what he can do in the Champion Chase, for instance.

His problem was that he hated the ground, which was a good bit quicker this year. To walk it, you wouldn't know the difference really. But you knew it when you fell on it. I found out good and proper when I had the fall on Quel Esprit on the Wednesday. When I hit the ground my heels bounced in the air. That's when you know it's good ground – when you start to bounce.

The other fall I got that day was from Citizen Vic, and sadly it was a fatal one for the horse. His owner, Donal O'Connor, is a man who's been in racing a long, long time and Citizen Vic was probably as good a horse as he ever had. He was a Grade One winner and obviously had potential because as we came down to the second-last, he was in front in the RSA Chase. He jumped the second-last one of a line of four, all in with a shout when he fell and broke his neck. Such an unlucky fall too – most times a horse wouldn't break its neck in a fall like that but Citizen Vic just happened to flip over awkwardly.

I met Donal and his wife in the owners and trainers bar afterwards and I was dreading the conversation a little bit. What do you say? It's not like the loss of a human but it's a bad day for everyone involved. They've come to Cheltenham with high hopes and they're going home with nothing. Worse than nothing. But his reaction was simple. 'Look,' he said, 'it could be a lot worse. It's outside the back door.' That old Irish saying again. I thought the way he looked at it and dealt with it was commendable.

In the end, I had three winners. I thought Quevega was a good thing from a piece of work she'd done the week before and Sanctuaire was a horse I'd fancied since the day I had struggled to pull him up after the winning post in Taunton the previous month. Seriously, he ran away with me after winning and we were at the two mile three furlong start before I could get him pulled up. I came away thinking he was the best ride I had in the handicaps.

And of course Big Buck's did what Big Buck's does. He just sauntered around Cheltenham with his ears pricked and blew the rest of them away. He's a wonderful horse, one I love riding. You always have to be thinking when you're riding him, you always have to be judging the horse in front of you. You always want to give yourself a horse to aim at, be close enough but not too close.

You're alert the whole way round on Big Buck's because you know he'll do nothing in front. But at the same time, he's running in three-mile hurdle races because he's not quick, so you can't sit fifteen lengths off and expect him to zip upsides the leader between hurdles once you click in his ear. You have to judge it and time your run.

He never made a steeplechaser because he just took too long over his fences. He never made the big, bold leaps that Kauto Star and Denman would make. He likes to get in short at his jumps and he goes left as well. So by the time he gets in, gets up, gets over and repositions himself after going left, he's lost ground on the good jumpers. It's not that he can't do it, it's just that he takes too long to do it. But he has a magnificent engine and that's going to make him just about unbeatable as a staying hurdler.

He travelled so well this year. I couldn't believe that Sentry Duty or Karabak weren't behind me when I looked around. That's why I had to take a second look, just to make sure. I could see Tidal Bay in the corner of my eye and I knew he was in trouble but I was looking for the other two. They weren't there and he won easily.

Quevega meant I drew level with Pat Taaffe's all time Cheltenham Festival record of twenty-five winners, so when Sanctuaire won the Fred Winter, that gave me twenty-six. When I was growing up, all I ever wanted to do was be lucky enough to ride one winner at Cheltenham so to think now that, for the moment anyway, I'm the most winning rider there is something I'm hugely proud of. It isn't something I ever set out to do. I understand racing too well to know you couldn't ever think of it. But I also know that to ride that many winners at Cheltenham you have to work for the people who have the best horses. And there's no doubt that in having Willie Mullins and Paul Nicholls as employers, I'm in that position.

Cheltenham was great this year as well, obviously, because of Katie. I called into Kill on Mother's Day – two days before the festival – to drop flowers into Mam. I was heading away to Cheltenham that night. When I was there, the phone rang and it was Katie saying the Ferdy Murphy had rung her looking to see if she would ride one in a four-miler. It was funny just to watch the reactions. Mam was delighted, Dad wanted to know what the horse was. Mam and I burst out laughing at Dad. 'Sure does it matter what it is?' I said. 'Do you think she's going to say no?'

They lined up and I was in the weighing room, sitting on the table looking up at the television with Paul Carberry sitting right beside me on my left. Ken Whelan was sitting on the ground in front of me. A horse fell halfway down the back and I saw Katie switch inside on Poker De Sivola. When the camera cut to another shot, I could see her creeping closer to the leaders. 'Jeez,' I thought, 'she's moving up here. She's doing well enough.' But of course, at the front of the field Nina Carberry was travelling very well on Becauseicouldntsee.

By the time they came to the top of the hill, you could see there was a fair chance it was going to be between the two of them. The lads in the weighing room were laughing at us now because myself and Paul were roaring at the television and I was kicking the back off Ken Whelan on the floor in front of me. They jumped the last together but Katie's horse found that little bit more on the run-in. Wonderful, just wonderful.

It's hard to ride a winner at Cheltenham. Very hard. Harder still when you're an amateur and even harder again when you're a lady amateur. Then to go and ride a second winner was just amazing. But for me it was nearly even better. We were talking beforehand and she asked what I thought so I just said, 'Whatever you do, don't move running down the hill. It's a long way from the bend to the last hurdle so if you're going well enough try and time your challenge so you're upsides at the last.'

Tito Bustillo was nearly brought down at the second-last and any chance I had went there. So as the others were racing up to the last, I looked up and saw that most of the jockeys were hard at work on their horses, all except Katie and Paddy Brennan who was travelling well on Zanir. But after she jumped the last, I looked up on the big screen and she was away. Two winners at Cheltenham. Magic.

Aintree went well to begin with and looked like it was going to end up being a great weekend. Big Buck's won, What A Friend won, Tataniano won. Three Grade One winners and the Grand National to come. Big Fella Thanks had been laid out for the race and Paul and I thought he had a great chance. With a bit of luck on the way round, you'd never know what could happen.

But then Celestial Halo turned into the straight in the Aintree Hurdle, travelling well enough in front going to the second-last. As he got there, he was a bit too far off it to jump it so I went to let him shorten up at it. I wanted him to take three strides into it but he took two and took off. I knew as soon as he took off that he wasn't going to be getting there. He got far enough so that he didn't completely somersault but I got fired into the ground. I would actually have been OK as well, only for Won In The Dark coming behind me and standing on my shoulder. He drove my left arm into the ground and I knew I was in trouble.

I rolled over and sat up to find pins and needles in my hand and arm straight away. When I stood up and let it hang down, it flapped over and back like a pendulum under its own momentum.

I wasn't moving it – it was swinging by itself. The doctor arrived and I told him I thought I'd dislocated my elbow or my shoulder. I didn't know what it was but I knew it was bad, one way or the other. Dad arrived on the scene – he always has a habit of doing that somehow – and knew by taking one look at me that something was broken. Gillian met me on the way across the Melling Road and headed to Fazakerley Hospital in the ambulance.

The ambulance staff were great, the doctors too. The x-ray showed that the left humerus was broken in three places. They gave me the option of operating or leaving it so I could get operated on at home. While they were talking through all this and then putting the back slab on me, I was asking what the time was because I wanted to see the Grand National.

But there was no television. The best we could do was to sit beside a computer in the nurses' station where we listened to radio commentary coming from the internet. It must have been a local station or something. Let's put it this way, the chap commentating didn't sound like he did this as his regular Saturday afternoon job. He only named about half a dozen horses in the whole race and you could hardly follow him at all.

But the one horse he kept mentioning was Big Fella Thanks. Maybe he had him backed. He kept saying he was near the front, jumping this fence well or that fence well, still going very strong. He was getting very excited about him anyway. The further the race went and the better Big Fella Thanks was doing, the sorer and sorer I was getting in the nurses' station. That would have been some kick in the teeth.

So when I heard him say that Black Apalachi and Don't Push It were gone clear from the second-last, the pain started to ease a bit. And from there, I just wanted A.P. to win it. Which, of course, he did.

I knew it was something he always wanted to do. It's not that it really got to him that he hadn't won it, it was more that he got annoyed when people held it over him. The people who said that obviously didn't understand the amount of luck involved in winning the race but that didn't matter. They couldn't hold it over him now, anyway.

I met him back at the hotel we'd been staying at when I went to collect my stuff before heading to the airport. I was delighted for him. I'd never seen him as excited for as long as I've known him. Maybe he was that excited when he won the Gold Cup on Mr Mulligan in 1997 but I didn't know him back then. This was as thrilled as I'd ever seen him. It was brilliant and fully deserved.

I saw Bill Quinlan the next morning and as ever, he took care of me. He thought that maybe the arm wouldn't need an operation if it was plastered up the right way so that's what he did. I had it in plaster for four weeks and then in a brace for another four.

It meant I missed Punchestown though, which was as rough a week on the sidelines as I've ever had. Going back over all the other injuries, I missed big races here and there but I never missed a full festival. That was a long week. It was day after day of watching Willie's horses win race after race. I was working for RTE that week and putting a brave face on it but it was very hard to watch.

It doesn't get any easier to take. I could watch the races and be happy for Willie as he proved again what a good trainer he is, as if it needed proving. I could watch and be impressed again by Paul Townend as he showed how talented a rider he is. It was nice to see David Casey, Davy Condon, Patrick Mullins and Katie all ride good winners. But it wasn't a week I could enjoy.

I can't just sit back and smile when there are races out there to win and good horses out there to be ridden. Even when I know and admire the people involved. I have a good few years left in me yet before I retire, plenty of time to win plenty more races. I really don't want to have to endure too many more weeks like I had to at Punchestown.

I will probably be a trainer at some point in the future but that's a long way off yet. If and when I do, I'll do it having had the best schooling you could ever wish to have. Dad, Willie and Paul have taught me lots of stuff but they run yards that are team efforts. The things I've learned along the way from the likes of Paul Curran at Noel Meade's to Dinny Daly, Tracy Gilmore and Dick Dowling at Willie's to Clifford Baker in Paul's will stand to me for however long I'm in the sport. The side of racing nobody sees really is the travelling staff you meet at the racecourse and from Damien Byrne at Ballydoyle to Gail Carlisle in Closutton to Donna Blake in Ditcheat, you're forever coming across new ways of thinking about horses and new ways of trying to work them out.

But that's for a long way down the road and I'll hopefully be riding for at least another five or six years. I try not to get too far ahead of myself, just taking each day, each race and each horse as I find it. As I'm finishing this book, my left arm is in a sling. By the time you pick it up, my right arm might be. That's the unpredictability of racing for you.

But for now, the future is bright. I have a great life, a job I love, a wonderful family, a great wife and little daughter who is a new joy every day. I couldn't ask for better.

CHAPTER 15

Break time again

6 November 2010

A good day gone bad. We were racing at Down Royal and everything had gone to plan for most of the afternoon. Kauto Star had beaten Sizing Europe to win his first race back since falling in the Gold Cup and Paul Nicholls had sent The Nightingale over to win the other big chase of the day. We were going down to Dublin afterwards to watch Ireland play South Africa in the Aviva Stadium and Corrick Bridge was my last ride of the day. Gillian was actually standing down at the last fence so she could head on out to the car once the race ended and we could get on the road.

I'd ridden Corrick Bridge umpteen times before for Tony Martin without a bother. But this time he got the fifth fence all wrong, went through the top of it with his chest and turned a cartwheel. It all happened very quickly but I could tell on the way to the ground by the spot my leg was in and the way we were falling that he was going to land on it. I was falling off to the left-hand side of the horse and my right leg was still in the stirrup, so my leg was across the horse's back. As he somersaulted over, my leg was between his back and the ground and he just twisted it and snapped it.

I ended up with a spiral fracture from halfway down my right tibia to the ankle. The top of the fibula was broken too but that was kind of irrelevant in the scheme of things. Your fibula breaks in a reaction to the break of your tibia but since it's not a weight-bearing bone, it wasn't a big deal. You often hear of a fella breaking his leg in two places and it makes it sound like the whole thing is shattered to pieces. It's not always as serious as it sounds.

The broken tibia was serious, obviously, but it would heal. The ambulance took me to the Royal Victoria Hospital in Belfast, where they straightened the leg and put a cast on me overnight before operating on me in the morning. The type of break that it was, they couldn't really pin it and plate it. It was a displaced fracture so it had to be operated on but because of the extra callous bone that was in it from when I'd broken it before in the Czech Republic in 1999, they had to put a contraption on it called an Ilizarov frame.

The things you find yourself reading up on. Gavril Abramovich Ilizarov was a Russian orthopaedic surgeon in Siberia back in the 1950s, who developed a way of fixing a broken leg by using the spokes on a bicycle wheel. Basically, what I ended up having on my leg when I woke up from the operation were four stainless-steel rings with eight pins coming out of them going through the spiral fracture.

I'd say I was lucky in the sense that I broke my leg at Down Royal and not somewhere down the country. They don't use those frames very commonly in the south, not for common fractures anyway. They'd use them more for leg extensions and things like that. But the mess my leg was in, they decided to put the frame on me in the north.

I was OK with it in the end. Obviously with so many pin sites in the leg, there's a big chance of infection and if that had happened, I could have been out for longer. So we had to be very careful with it and I was never without an antibiotic the whole time I had it on me. But my very patient wife turned into Florence Nightingale. We checked it every day and thoroughly washed every pin site once a week – you had to keep them covered and change the swabs on them the whole time. At least I could wear it in the shower, though, which anyone who's had to wrap a plastic bag around a cast will tell you is a godsend.

It was an awkward yoke to have to carry around, all the same. One of the first things I had to do was go into Naas and buy two pairs of jeans and four pairs of trousers and then bring them round to the seamstress in Leighlinbridge and get her to sew the right legs of three of them onto the right legs of the other three so that they'd be double the width and would fit out over the frame.

But the worst of it had nothing to do with the awkwardness of the frame or anything like it. The worst of it was missing more or less a full winter's racing. I missed everything from the first week of November right up to a week or so before Cheltenham. Short of missing out on the festival itself, there's no worse time to get injured. For it to happen so soon after coming back from four months out with a broken arm was very hard to take.

It basically meant that from the day of the Grand National in 2010 to the week before the Cheltenham festival in 2011, the only real race riding I'd done was in August, September and October. That's no good to any jockey. I'd say I was the only man in Ireland all through that winter waking up every day praying for more snow, more ice, more racing to be called off so I didn't have to go downstairs and sit on the couch and watch it. I guarantee you I was the only person involved in racing who was delighted with the weather. It was selfish but it made everything easier on my mind.

The one big advantage of the Ilizarov frame was that as well as aiding the healing process in the leg, it allowed me to stay fit. It was very light so there was no hardship in carrying it around. I was walking on it by Christmas, a full two months away from getting it off. That wouldn't have happened if I'd had a cast on.

Ronan O'Gara introduced me to a guy called Brian Greene, who works with the Ireland rugby team. From the end of November all the way through the winter I met with him twice a week and we worked on a fitness routine that would have me ready for when the leg healed. In the beginning, it was as much a reason to have something to do as anything else. But over time, it was of huge benefit.

I'd always been diligent in trying to keep fit when I was out injured but this was different. This was a proper regime, starting with my core and going on from there. It was stuff I would never have done on my own because I would have needed somebody to push me.

I'll always do what I have to do but sometimes if I have any choice in the matter, I'll decide I don't have to do just as much as I originally thought. I was always like that, even if I ever had to go out for a run to keep fit as a schoolboy. I used to go running from our place out around the back road to Johnstown and home, a four-mile round trip that went in a circle. But if I'd had to run the two miles to the edge of Naas and the two miles back, I well know I wouldn't have bothered going the whole way in.

If someone is standing over my shoulder, I'll do twice as much as if I was in a room on my own. Brian pushed me and got more out of me and so by the end of it, I'd never felt as physically fit or strong. I knew that match practice was all I was short of when I got back riding.

Even though I'd spent eight of the previous eleven months on the sideline, it never entered my head that I might be any more injury-prone than any other jockey in the weighing room. It's just pure bad luck, that's all. When I broke my arm at Aintree, it wasn't because Celestial Halo fell – it was because the horse coming after him decided to use my shoulder as a landing board. The fall at Down Royal could have gone another way too but Corrick Bridge's momentum turned him over and my leg was just stuck where it was stuck. Just bad luck, that's all. I've had worse falls and walked away.

I made it back in time for Cheltenham. No danger I was going to miss it, obviously. I actually had a nasty enough fall at Naas the week before the festival when King Of The Refs came down at the last hurdle. I came away with a cut over the eye, which was handy in that it took attention away from what was actually the sorest part of the fall – I'd taken a bad rattle to my ribs which I didn't want anyone to know about. No way was I going to hospital a week before Cheltenham, not a hope. My ribs were damn sore but I wasn't going to miss Cheltenham because of them.

I went there with a good book of rides but I still didn't expect it to turn out as well as it did. Obviously, you'd be hoping that Quevega and Big Buck's would turn up the same as other years and, barring something going wrong, both of them would win. But it's still Cheltenham and you don't know what's going to happen. I never thought I'd be walking out of there on the first day after riding three winners.

A day like that makes you feel like you've answered a few questions. Without really listening to any of the chatter or reading any of the press, I knew that there were a lot of people who doubted whether I should even have been there. Whether I was fit enough, ready enough, strong enough. In one sense, it was great to justify the faith shown in me by Paul and Willie all through the long winter but in another it was great to be able to show the doubters they could go and jump.

Anyone looking at the Supreme Novices' would have said that Al Ferof had no chance at the top of the hill and even jumping the last he was a few lengths down. But his stamina told in the end and he battled up the hill to win.

It was great to get back on Hurricane Fly. I hadn't ridden him in a race in nearly two years but I knew him inside out. I'd never won the Champion Hurdle but then I'd never had a horse as good as Hurricane Fly to ride in it. People were wondering would he be able to travel but we had no doubt – he'd won in Auteuil over two miles and two furlongs. I was just happy he got to show what he could do.

He's an incredibly hard horse to train. He's very exuberant, always messing and bouncing and putting himself in danger. He doesn't just walk around in a straight line with his head down – he's always looking around him. He puts pressure on his legs by bouncing up and down and knocking himself off things so you always have to have an eye on him. The job Willie does in getting him to the starting line is a tribute to him. Paul Townend and Emmett Mullins ride him out and take a lot of care of him, which is what you have to do with a horse that's always play-acting.

Quevega won her third mares hurdle as easily as I'd hoped she would. She's an amazing mare, to turn up like that three years in a row and have no other horse fit to land a blow on her. I've heard people give out and say she should be tested against Big Buck's in the World Hurdle but to me, Willie's answer is perfect. This is Cheltenham – why would you leave a race behind that you're odds-on to win to take your chances against an odds-on horse in another race and maybe finish third? Cheltenham is all about winning.

As for Big Buck's, he was always going to face a more tactical race than he'd had there before. From the time Grands Crus won at Haydock and the Cleve Hurdle, you could see that we had a challenger who liked a bit of soft ground and who would keep galloping. Mourad and Fiveforthree were shaping well at home too for Willie so it wasn't a foregone conclusion.

I knew that the one thing they were going to do was sit behind me and follow Big Buck's round. If I was riding a horse to beat Big Buck's with his reputation at that stage, I'd do the exact same thing. There was no way any of the other jockeys were going to bounce out, give me a lead and set it up for me to go and win the race from the second last. They wanted to make Big Buck's do it himself. That might have worked in other years but as Big Buck's has matured and got more confidence and grown into himself, he's become a more professional horse.

Just as well he was too, because I lost my stick on the way to the last. I hit him on the hip and it bounced out of my hand about ten strides short of the hurdle. I wasn't even hitting him. I was just flicking him as he was extending his legs and trying to get him to extend them further. But since I hit in him on the hip, I caught bone instead of muscle and the thing bounced out of my hand and onto the ground.

I got a fright and for a second I got mixed up as to where the other horses were. Fiveforthree was coming up on my right but he's a grey too so for a split second I wasn't sure if he was actually Grands Crus. We jumped the last and I was using my legs now to get him to keep going forward, not knowing which horse was on my right and which was on my left until I caught sight of the Pipe bridle to my left. So I drifted over towards Grands Crus to give Big Buck's some company and he just picked up about four strides after the last and that was that.

He really is an amazing horse. I don't think people really realise how much ability he has. I have no doubt, for example, that he'd win an Ascot Gold Cup. Now, you wouldn't want him to do that because he's a big heavy jumping horse and this is a race in the middle of the summer. But in terms of pure ability, I'm certain he could win it. He's that good.

Final Approach gave me a fifth winner of the week but I needed a bit of luck. He should have gone at the first but he stood up somehow and when they got racing a long way from home, I was a fair bit back. But with four winners under my belt, confidence up and nothing to lose, I sent him on and took a chance that we'd get there. Won it by a nose. Great feeling, great week. Willie was leading trainer and I was leading jockey. All the work through the winter had been worth it just to get back for this.

Aintree was just as good with wins for Big Buck's, Master Minded and Zarkander. I thought The Midnight Club had a good shout in the Grand National but he hit the third fence a massive clout and it frightened the life out of him. We were losing ground with every jump from there to the end. If you take it that there were twenty-seven fences left after he nearly went, I can promise you we lost a length at each fence. That would at least have put him in the mix at the finish. I could have ridden Niche Market but I still think I was on the right horse. Maybe next time.

CHAPTER 16

Whipping up a storm

Our second daughter arrived on Easter Sunday. Gillian woke up early enough that morning and told me I was taking her to Mount Carmel before I went to Fairyhouse so off we went. Nothing more was going to happen for a while so I went racing. Had a winner in the first as well. Elsa arrived at 10.50 that night, the picture of health and wonder. She's a completely different child to her big sister. Isabelle is all go, full of chat and mischief. Elsa is quiet as a mouse, much more refined and not fussed about anything. Isabelle is mad about her and they get on great.

My big feeling after she was born was one of relief. Relief that she was well and that Gillian was fine. It doesn't get easier the second time around. You don't worry any less. You don't take anything more for granted. And it changes you as well. People who tell you it doesn't are lying. It changes your perspective on what's good and bad from day to day. It doesn't make you any less competitive but it totally changes how you feel when you lose.

You might have had a bad day at the track but it doesn't bring anything like the same sense of anxiety or panic as if there is something wrong with one of the girls. You get jocked off a horse or you get beaten on one you should have won on, you still worry.

You still beat yourself up and annoy yourself over how you're going to be better the next time. But it dissolves in an instant if there's something up with one of the girls.

It changes the way you see the world too. If I see a picture of the Children's Hospital in Crumlin in the paper now, I pick it up to read it whereas before it would have passed me by. Or if I hear about a kid being killed in an accident on a farm or getting knocked down in the street, it stops me in my tracks now. It just makes me feel lucky to have what I have and I find myself going home to hug them a bit tighter.

The summer came and went with another spell on the sidelines. We were racing in Killarney in July and I was on a horse of Michael Hourigan's called Friendly Society. We went off at a right gallop and the horse was running very free so I had a tight hold on the reins. At the first hurdle, the horse in front jumped across us and we clipped heels, which caused my lad's head to dip down between his legs. Because I had such a tight hold on the reins, I was pulled out head-first through his ears and right into the ground.

I flipped over and it felt like someone had plugged a 900-volt electrical wire into the middle of my back. From the bottom of my head, the sting went right down both my arms and out through my fingers. But the mad thing was, when it went out through my fingers, it felt like that was the end of it. I was fit to stand up, fit to walk around. I had a stiff neck right enough but I didn't think it was too bad.

I got into the ambulance knowing I was a bit stiff but knowing as well that we were two weeks away from Galway and I wasn't going to tell the doctor a whole lot. When he checked me out, I said I was grand. Gillian drove us back to the hotel and I couldn't turn my head but I figured a night's sleep would sort it out.

Wrong again. The next morning, my neck had gone from stiff to just completely locked in place. I couldn't move it to one side or the other. So it was down to Cork for a CT scan and they found that I had fractured the C7 and T1 vertebrae – the last in my neck and first in my back. It wasn't overly serious but it meant a couple of months out and six weeks in a neck brace. No Galway, no racing of any kind until the middle of September. It was no great hardship. As long as it wasn't in the winter and wasn't another leg injury or a bad back injury, I wasn't overly worried. It was an annoyance, no more than that.

Far more serious was the mess that the whole of English racing got itself in about a month after I got back riding. I was back in time for Listowel in mid-September but it was the middle of October when all the trouble over the new whip rules happened and all hell broke loose. The powers that be decided – just like that, without a trial period – to bring in a rule that you could only use your stick on a horse five times after the last fence or hurdle and eight times in total throughout the race.

They changed the rules for public perception, not for horse welfare. They were basically asking us to change the way we'd been riding our whole lives and they were asking us to do it overnight and for the wrong reasons. No wonder there was chaos. In my opinion, the rule was wrong then and it's still wrong now that they've had to amend it after all the trouble it caused. I never supported it right from the start.

Word came through in or around mid-August that there was something coming down the line. I remember were we talking about it at the Dublin Horse Show and even though we didn't know exactly what was going to be in the new rules, we had a feeling it wouldn't be good. Then, near the end of September, we got an email from the Professional Jockeys Association giving us the new guidelines and telling us they'd be coming into force from 10 October. So they were basically giving us a fortnight to change a lifetime's way of working.

That was one problem: the short notice. But the main problem was that the whole idea is flawed. They're trying to make a grey area black and white. They're hell-bent on doing it and all it has led to is ridiculous bans on jockeys who are only trying to do their best for the people who own the horses.

English racing has always been a flag-bearer when it comes to use of the whip. They always understood what it was for and how it should be used. They were the first ones to tighten up the rules and they drove whip technology so that it would still do the job required while at the same time causing minimal pain to the animal. But now they've made a farce of it.

Dominic Elsworth got a ban in December after a race at Sandown on a horse that would have been pulled up if he'd ridden to the guidelines. Instead, he got the horse to respond and it very nearly won, only just beaten by a neck. He got a seven-day ban for hitting his horse eleven times instead of eight. But the horse wasn't hurt, the viewing public got to see a thriller that went right to the line and the owners of Dominic's horse nearly got the biggest win of the horse's life. This was pure racing and yet the jockey ends up being banned for seven days and losing his share of the prize money.

If racing wants to go that way, then what they're saying is that they don't want true-run races. Our job as jockeys has always been first and foremost to achieve the best result possible. If Dominic's horse had pulled up after the eighth smack, how could he say that he had done his best to win? The rule is just wrong and it shows very little understanding of what horsemanship is.

I got done at Aintree on 22 October 2011 for something I had been doing my whole life, something that couldn't be more natural and has nothing to do with horse welfare. I was riding Edgardo Sol in the novice chase and I wanted him to change legs. If you've ever watched a horse running head-on, you'll have seen that they gallop diagonally and if you're on a left-handed track, you want them leading with their near fore. My lad was leading with his off fore and I had to get him to change.

Doing that is very simple – you just give the horse a flick down the shoulder and he knows to change. But here's where the rule is ridiculous. If you take your hand off the rein to give him the slap, it counts as one of the eight you're allowed. But your rein can be as long as you like so if you're riding with a longer rein and you keep it in your hand while you use the stick, it doesn't count. Whether you're holding the rein or not won't change how hard you hit the horse because all you're doing is giving it a backhand signal to change legs or concentrate.

That's what happened to me at Aintree. I got him to change legs but didn't count it as a smack. As far as I was concerned, I only hit the horse eight times in the race and the horse won by a nose. But the stewards brought me in and told me it was nine, including the smack down the shoulder. Bang – a five-day ban.

I was raging. Five days would mean missing out on good rides at Down Royal a fortnight later, where The Nightingale was going for the big Grade One and Kauto Stone would be running in the Grade Two race, not to mention good races in Cork the next day. And all for a small miscalculation that the horse would barely even have noticed. I lost my rag a bit and even asked the crowd near the weighing room if they thought there was anything wrong with my ride, seeing that public perception was apparently such a big deal.

There was a lot of fuss made in those couple of weeks that the big problem was the penalty structure. And yeah, the penalties were excessive but that didn't mean that everything was OK once they were changed. Because I still think the rule is fundamentally wrong. It's far too stringent. It lays down unnatural laws for a naturally unpredictable situation.

Unfortunately, common sense is not used. They say the rules are for the welfare of the horse. But what this has come to mean in practical terms is that there is now no such thing as the preventative use of the whip. If you take the scenario where I got banned at Aintree, what I was doing there was guarding against what might happen, i.e. that the horse might drift to the right because he was leading with his off fore instead of his near fore. So I was basically trying to predict the future and prevent my horse jumping to his right and into another horse if he got in tight at the last fence.

But by counting that as one of the smacks you're allowed for the whole race, you're left in a situation where you have to do without one of the ones to his hind quarters. These are the smacks that tell him to go forward. They're the signal that extra effort is needed from him if he has anything in the tank. My horse won that Aintree race by a nose – you can make up your own mind as to whether he would have if I'd hit him one time fewer.

But the point is that the one that sent me over the limit, the one I didn't count in my head, had nothing to do with horse welfare. Nobody in the BHA would argue that it had. Yet I got five days for it.

The whole situation is wrong. I've never been a whip-happy jockey and I've always hated seeing it used in the wrong way. I've always been a fan of whip rules and I've always spoken out about people using whips on horses that are out of contention.

But by making it so black and white, I feel as though they are saying that a jockey isn't capable of using his discretion over how to treat a horse. That's the bit that gets me. There's a lot of waffle talked, a lot of bullshit spoken. Like this idea of giving the horse time to respond – who can measure that outside of the horse and jockey in each specific case? Nobody can.

The only person who knows if a horse is responding is the jockey. It's a feeling, nothing more scientific than that. And responding doesn't mean going faster, by the way. Responding means not slowing down. If you're riding a horse at the end of a race and he's not slowing down when he should be tiring, that means he's responding to what the jockey is asking him to do. Yet there's this idea that you have to wait for a response, you have to give him three strides before you go again. It's nonsense, applying hard-and-fast rules to a situation that differs from race to race and from horse to horse.

I mean, how can it make any sense in the wide world that you are allowed seven uses of the whip in a five-furlong sprint race on the flat and only eight in four and a half miles around Aintree in the Grand National? I would love to have that explained to me. I would love for somebody who has experience of riding a racehorse to sit down and go through that one. It's madness.

To my mind, they're going the wrong way about it with the Grand National as well. Now, this is just my opinion and I totally accept that other people have different opinions to mine and that's fine. That's what makes the world go round. But for what it's worth, I think that the outcome they're trying to achieve with the Grand National – that is, fewer horses getting injured or not surviving the race – will not come about by making the fences smaller. If anything, they should be making them bigger.

This might sound strange but take it from somebody who's been riding in the race since he was twenty years old – the smaller the fences, the faster they jump them. The faster they jump them, the lower they get and the more horses will fall. All you are doing by making the fences smaller is speeding up the race and reducing the margin for error. I'm convinced it will do more harm than good.

Think of it this way. In a lot of towns and cities in Ireland over the past few years, there has been a move away from speedbumps that lead from one side of the street to the other and instead now you get two little bumps in the road, side by side with a gap in the middle. So now, instead of slowing down over these speedbumps, everybody just shifts to the side and points their wheels at the gaps without changing gear. Hardly anybody even slows down at them.

The same will happen with the smaller fences in the Grand National. Horses will get braver, jockeys will take advantage and take more risks. Hurdle races are faster than chases because the obstacles are smaller and if you keep lowering the size of the National fences, all you'll be doing is increasing the speed at which the horses run.

My idea is very simple. Lower the height of the stakes in the fences, fair enough. That reduces the risk of the horse hitting something solid high up in the fence and being turned over by it. So I have no problem with that. But I do think they should maintain the optical illusion of the height of the fence by piling more spruce on top. In the horse and jockey's mind, that fence will be something he has to be more careful at and so they will take more time over the jump.

Look, it's the Grand National. You will always get fallers. I don't give a damn what anybody says – people tune in for that reason. It's the most watched race of the year because people like to have a bet on it and half the fun is listening out to see if your lad is still standing or is he gone. The thrill of it and the attraction of it is the same every year – what's going to finish? What's going to fall? What number's mine? I'm not saying it's nice but that's the truth of it among the general public, the very general public that racing is trying to attract to the sport on a more regular basis.

As with the whip rules, I really think a lot more would be achieved if people were given more information on what racing is about and if they were better educated about the dangers and the likelihood of horses falling. I had often ridden both Dooney's Gate and Ornais, the two horses that died in the 2011 Grand National. I'd won on them both and they were two brilliant jumpers. Falls happen in racing and the faster they happen, the bigger chance there is that the result of the fall will be serious. That's why I just don't see the sense in making the fences smaller.

I appealed my five-day ban and went to a hearing in London but got nowhere. It was all very civil and straightforward. I presented my appeal, they questioned me. They accepted that I used the extra one for correction but I had still gone over the limit and the suspension was upheld.

In the end, I've changed the way I ride since then and so have plenty of the jockeys. Which I guess is what the rules were brought in for in the first place. But the effect it has had can't be the one they were looking for. I am definitely finding now that I'm finishing fourth or fifth on horses that would have finished third. I won't take the chance of picking up a ban just so the horse can win place money. Is that really what they want? Jockeys being OK with not finishing in their best possible position?

I can't get some horses to win races now that I could have got them close to before. I rode a horse at Newbury a few weeks before Christmas called Minella Stars. A big, lazy ex-point-to-pointer from Paul's yard who went off 12–5 favourite in a ten-runner novice chase. This lad would only go forward for a slap, nothing else.

He dawdled at the start of the race and just wasn't interested until I gave him a smack coming to the third fence. He definitely could have done with another five or six to get him into the race but if I used them to get him up to the leaders, I'd have used up my whole allocation and he wouldn't have won anyway. In the end, I left them to the end and he finished a remote third. He never had a chance to win that race – and not because he was beaten by better horses.

But that's the way of it. Different horses are going to win races now than would have won them before. It's just a fact of life, brought about by rules that don't tally with the actual experience of riding a horse to win a race. It's a real shame but I guess you just have to get on with it.

CHAPTER 17

Once a Star, always a Star

All through the summer, there were questions about whether or not Kauto Star would come back for another season. I guess you could see why. He hadn't performed at Punchestown in April, where I'd had to pull him up for the first time in his career. Long Run had beaten him convincingly in both the Gold Cup and the King George, the two races he was most famous for, the two he'd built every winter around going all the way back to 2006. So if people thought his time was up, they were entitled to their opinion.

Jockeys are the last people whose opinion matters in these situations. The owner, the trainer, the stable staff – they're the ones who know what's best for horses. They're the ones who take care of them, who see most of them, who know far better than the jockeys what the horses are feeling from day to day. Kauto and I have had some great days together but when you boil it down, I only ever see him at the racecourse or when I'm schooling him. That probably amounts to no more than eight or ten times a year. So whether he came back or not wasn't something I'd be getting involved in.

In the end, Paul Nicholls and Clive Smith decided he should

have another go. He'd won the Betfair Chase three times before and usually ran well around Haydock so that's where he was sent. He worked well at Exeter a week before the race along with Big Buck's and Mon Parrain but even so, I went to Haydock not expecting a whole lot from him. Certainly not expecting what I got.

How could I? He was running against Long Run who'd proven himself, who'd won the two big three-mile chases of the previous season and who'd beaten Kauto convincingly both days. Long Run was a young horse on the up, whereas no matter how good Kauto could be, he had obviously stopped improving by then.

At the same time, I knew Paul Nicholls wasn't going to bring him to Haydock for a day out. That isn't Paul's style. It isn't in his nature. He was obviously doing it because he thought Kauto would run a big race. He was in good nick and he'd worked well and if there was a chance that Long Run might be a bit rusty on his first run of the season, then Paul was going to try to take advantage. Being honest, I didn't think he'd win. But I knew he'd put it up to the younger horse.

And that's what he did. He went out and galloped and travelled, jumped from fence to fence and took the race to Long Run. We went to the front and kept the pressure on. A good gallop is what Kauto needs these days and a good gallop is what he set. When he was younger, it didn't matter if the pace was slow because he always had the speed to go and win it when it came to the finish. But nowadays, the faster they go, the better it is for him.

That's what top-class Grade One racing is anyway. It's like the 800 metres or the 1,500 metres at the Olympics when they go a serious pace right from the start and it becomes a test of who can live with that pace the longest. That's what happened at Haydock. We bucked out and set off at a decent clip and one by one the others dropped off and dropped off. Pure Faith went first and was pulled up. Time For Rupert went next and was beaten a long way out. Diamond Harry was off the bridle turning in. Weird Al was staying on and got close to Long Run after he had dropped off. But none of them could stick with the gallop that Kauto Star had set and he won by eight lengths in the end.

The feeling was different to before. In other years, we'd be going into the Betfair Chase just looking to get the season off to a good start. This time, we were going there hoping that this horse had just one more day in him. There was a huge crowd there and a lot of people came to see him because I guess they were hoping for one more day as well or maybe thinking that this might be the last one. But Paul had him spot on and nobody was talking about retiring him afterwards.

The one era that did come to an end soon after was Denman's, who was found with a tendon injury in the box next door to Kauto at Ditcheat. Funny, the one thing you would never have guessed would end Denman's career, certainly at his age, was a tendon injury. That's the kind of thing that happens to a young horse who maybe isn't fully developed yet. But Denman had been through a long career, running on every type of ground and in every type of race from point-to-points to Gold Cups. You could only say thanks be to God he got it as an eleven-year-old rather than as a seven-year-old.

People forget how delicate these animals are. Even a big old lump like Denman who's been around every block you can think of is still fragile and vulnerable to the smallest thing. So many horses don't get to fulfil their potential but he did and because of that, the day he was retired wasn't a sad day at all. He got to show the world what he could do. That's all a horse can ask for.

He was a wonderful horse to ride. Going all the way back to

his time as a novice, there was something different about him. He was the best jumper I ever sat on as a novice chaser – so sure over his jumps, never guessing, just getting from one side to the other like lightning. He had the power to stand off his fences and the technique to get in close. Either way was grand by him.

And as he got older, he just got better. He beat me in a Gold Cup with a performance I fully respect and his Hennessy win in 2009 was something I never thought was possible. For him to win like that giving a horse like What A Friend nearly two stone in weight was something I just didn't think any horse was capable of. I didn't think you could win a handicap with a rating of 174 but Denman proved me wrong. To me, that was incredible – the performance of a lifetime.

Christmas came and we went for the King George with Kauto Star. If I didn't think he'd win at Haydock, I definitely didn't think he'd win at Kempton. From conversations I'd had with Paul, I knew he'd run a very good race but whether it would be good enough to live with the improvement that Long Run was sure to produce, I couldn't be sure. I'd be lying if I said I thought he'd win.

No, in all honesty, I didn't think he would. I thought Long Run would improve – which he did. And I presumed, based on the previous year's performances, that improvement in a horse five years younger than Kauto Star would be enough to beat him. I don't think for one second that Long Run is a better horse than Kauto was in his prime – or what I thought was his prime between 2007 and 2009. But I did think coming into Christmas 2011 that the natural progression given the ages of the two horses would mean Long Run would have too much for us.

There was definitely less pressure on us. I guess pressure is what you make it but there's no doubt there was less focus on us than there was on Long Run. Everybody expected him to have his screws tightened. Kauto was like the heavyweight boxer trying to get up once more, whereas Long Run was the new kid who everybody thought would put an end to this great career. We were going there in hope. They were going in expectation.

In the end, I was wrong. I'm glad I was wrong. The race went a lot like Haydock, in that Kauto needed a good gallop and although Golan Way and Nacarat both probably set as good a gallop as they were able to, Kauto took it up himself from the time we came to the home straight the first time. He pinged the second-last fence with a circuit to go and from there we were off. When we passed the winning post the first time, I started sending him forward and he jumped his next two fences spectacularly.

His jumping was immaculate all the way around. Even when he got in close at the fourth-last and the fifth-last, he was still very quick and was making ground at the fences. Sometimes a horse will stand out a bit from the fence to make ground but it didn't matter to Kauto whether he was long or short at it. He was electric through the air. When Long Run came to challenge down the straight, Kauto put in three great jumps.

As we turned for home, I thought we'd win providing he kept jumping as well as he had been. I didn't know for sure because you're talking about thinking you're going to beat the reigning Gold Cup champion. But I was as certain as I could be that we'd have a brilliant chance of winning as long as Kauto kept jumping. I had a bit of horse left under me, we were going forward with every question I asked and I knew Long Run was going to find it very hard to get past.

You have to give Sam Waley-Cohen's horse a lot of respect, because he certainly showed a lot of guts and determination. There's something to admire about the way he keeps trying in his races. Even at Haydock when he was still a bit short on match fitness, he never stopped and never gave up. In the King George, he stuck to his task even though some of his jumping wasn't great. When we crossed the line, there was only a length and a half between us. To give an idea of how good a race Long Run ran, Captain Chris was seventeen lengths further back in third and he's an Arkle winner.

It was a brilliant feeling when we crossed the line in front. It was such a pleasure to be there and to be part of something like that. This was one day I was happy I wasn't sitting at home for. I couldn't have faced watching him win any King George on television, never mind his fifth.

We got a massive reception when we cantered back down in front of the stand. You're never aware of the crowd when you're in the middle of a race because you're concentrating on what you're doing but you could see that people were delighted to be there and to be able to say that they were there. Kempton isn't like Cheltenham, where you can have huge crowds around the winners' enclosure to give the horse a huge reception, but the people in the stands were great.

Paul and Clive were thrilled. It might have looked to be a brave call in the summer to keep Kauto in training but they knew what they wanted and they knew the horse. Paul isn't champion trainer by accident and if he thought there was another winter left in Kauto Star, people should respect that. He gets it right more often than anybody else. The call was on him, the pressure was on him and he got it right.

For me, it was a privilege to have ridden Kauto Star on that day and on every other. Trainers are closer to horses than jockeys are and stable staff are probably closest of all to them. I'll never feel the same way about a horse as I do about a person, even

Kauto Star. I couldn't say I love him. I love my wife and my kids and my family, and I couldn't ever take that and compare it to how I feel about Kauto. It's a different emotional level altogether.

But I have so much respect for him as a horse and I'm so grateful to have come across him. He's the horse of my career and I can't imagine ever being lucky enough to find another one like him. The fairytale now would be for him to stay sound and make it to Cheltenham in 2012 for another Gold Cup.

If he does, I hope I'm nowhere else in the world other than on his back.

NOTABLE CAREER FEATS

Champion jockey in Ireland eight times
Over 1,800 winners ridden, including:

Alexander Banquet
Cheltenham Bumper 1998
Royal Bond Novice Hurdle 1998
Deloitte Novice Hurdle 1999

Imperial Call
Heineken Gold Cup 1999

Moscow Express
Galway Plate 1999

Rince Ri
Powers Gold Cup 1999

Papillon
Grand National 2000

Commanche Court
Irish Grand National 2000
Heineken Gold Cup 2000

Micko's Dream
Drogheda Chase 2001
Pierse Leopardstown Chase 2001

Take Control
Scottish National 2002

Azertyuiop
Arkle 2003
Queen Mother Champion Chase 2004

Silver Birch
Welsh National 2004

Asian Maze
Sefton Novices' Hurdle 2005
World Series Hurdle 2006
Aintree Hurdle 2006

Hedgehunter
Grand National 2005

Missed That
Champion Bumper 2005

Numbersixvalverde
Irish National 2005

Kauto Star
Tingle Creek 2005, 2006
King George 2006, 2007, 2008, 2009, 2011
Betfair Chase 2006, 2007, 2009, 2011
Cheltenham Gold Cup 2007, 2009
James Nicholson Champion Chase 2008

Denman
Royal & SunAlliance Chase 2007
Lexus Chase 2007
Hennessy Gold Cup 2009

Taranis
Ryanair Chase 2007
James Nicholson Chase 2007

Neptune Collonges
Guinness Gold Cup 2007, 2008
Irish Hennessy Gold Cup 2009

Master Minded
Queen Mother Champion Chase
  2008, 2009
Tingle Creek 2008
Kerrygold Champion Chase
  2009
Melling Chase 2011

Oslot
Galway Plate 2008

Twist Magic
Kerrygold Champion Chase 2008
Tingle Creek 2009

Fiveforthree
Ballymore Properties Novice Hurdle
  2008
World Series Hurdle 2009

Big Buck's
Liverpool Hurdle 2009, 2010, 2011
Long Walk Hurdle 2009, 2010, 2011
World Hurdle 2009, 2010, 2011

Mikael D'Haguenet
Ballymore Properties Novice Hurdle
  2009
Irish Champion Novice Hurdle 2009

Cooldine
RSA Chase 2009
P.J. Moriarty Novice Chase 2009

Brave Inca
Irish Champion Hurdle 2009

Quevega
David Nicholson Mares' Hurdle
  2009, 2010, 2011
World Series Hurdle 2010, 2011

Hurricane Fly
Champion Hurdle 2011
Rabobank Champion Hurdle 2011

Al Ferof
Supreme Novices' Hurdle 2011

INDEX

Subheadings appear in alphabetical order, except for those under the author's name which are in approximate chronological order.